Abbie C. Morrow

The Bible Student's Cyclopedia

Abbie C. Morrow
The Bible Student's Cyclopedia
ISBN/EAN: 9783337225629

Printed in Europe, USA, Canada, Australia, Japan

Cover: Foto ©Lupo / pixelio.de

More available books at **www.hansebooks.com**

THE

BIBLE STUDENT'S CYCLOPÆDIA

OR

AIDS TO BIBLICAL RESEARCH

*A BOOK FOR CLERGYMEN, SABBATH SCHOOL TEACH-
ERS, AND ALL LOVERS OF THE BIBLE*

BY

A. C. MORROW

WITH AN INTRODUCTION
BY
THE REV. JAMES M. BUCKLEY, D.D.

Illustrations and Maps

NEW YORK
N. TIBBALS & SONS
37 PARK ROW

INTRODUCTION.

WHETHER the Word of God is read systematically and for devotional purposes to so great an extent as in former years may be doubted. There are many indications that it is not. But that it is studied and examined for teaching purposes much more generally, that is, by a greater number and with greater attention to details, is believed by those who have the best opportunity to form a correct opinion. The change that has taken place in the methods of Sabbath-school instruction is unquestionably very great; and it is, in some respects, a decided improvement. We do not think that every alteration is for the better. Radical changes drop something of real value because it will not incorporate with the main principle of the reformation. The present method of Bible teaching and study, is pre-eminently one of questioning. Every thing that can be known of the Bible, of its mountains, rivers and seas, its minerals and metals, its plants, beasts and fishes, as well as its tabernacle and temples, its prophets, patriarchs and apostles, its kings, judges and priests, its singers and players upon instruments, its mighty men and those who were obscure, its women, children and youth, its implements of agriculture and its weapons of war, its architecture, music, poetry and oratory, its weights and measures, its genealogy and chronology, its civil and ecclesiastical polity is searched out. Hence there is a great demand for Bible dictionaries, hand books and cyclopædias, the sale of which is constantly increasing, the demand for books of this class being the measure of their usefulness and their use. The light of cotemporaneous profane history is thrown upon the Bible as never before; and analogies drawn from other religions are employed to assist in the understanding of God's Word. Two things are now recognized; viz., that he who does not understand the Bible, does not understand human history, and that he who knows nothing but the Bible, can not fully understand that. Therefore the Bible as now taught not only requires but communicates much collateral knowledge. There is a law of the operation of the mind which has given rise to the unique compilation, herewith offered to the public, which is this; the philosophy of facts is remembered by many, much more easily than the facts themselves. When once the facts are recalled the mind classifies them, and reasoning proceeds spontaneously, or can be carried forward intentionally, with ease. It is well known that many can not recollect dates, and some find difficulty with proper names. Yet without names and dates the vision of history is nebulous. To refer to a huge work, to read an article of many pages in fine print in order to authenticate a single fact, date, or name, when its relation to history or to the unfolding of truth has long been known, is tedious and an unprofitable outlay of time. The author of the present work has attempted to supply just what the Sabbath-school teacher, ordinary reader or student of the Bible needs; an answer to every question of fact which can be asked concerning the history, contents and collateral relations of the Bible, the question with its answer isolated and complete. Vast labor has been expended and every accessible source of information explored in the preparation and arrangement of this multitude of questions and answers. It would be too much to claim for it absolute freedom from error, for the Bible itself declares, "I have seen an end of all perfection," or to assume that every answer would command the assent of all critics. But we have examined it sufficiently to see that it is far more reliable and discriminating than some widely circulated and pretentious works.

We introduce the "Bible Student's Cyclopædia," under the conviction that it will meet a known and felt want.

J. M. BUCKLEY.

CONTENTS.

CHAP.		QUESTIONS, PAGE.	ANSWERS, PAGE.
I.	The Bible	1	183
II.	Bible Curiosities	8	194
III.	Earliest Bible Facts	10	196
IV.	The Tabernacle	15	200
V.	Solomon's Temple	21	206
VI.	The Second Temple	29	214
VII.	The Patriarchs	34	219
VIII.	The Prophets	37	221
IX.	The Canonical Prophets	40	223
X.	The High Priests	42	224
XI.	The Judges of Israel	44	226
XII.	The Kings of Israel and Judah	45	227
XIII.	The Heathen Monarchs of the Bible	48	229
XIV.	The Apostles	53	233
XV.	Some of the Untitled Men of the Bible	54	234
XVI.	The Women of the Old Testament	59	238
XVII.	The Women of the New Testament	65	243
XVIII.	The Children and Youth of the Bible	67	245
XIX.	Mountains of the Bible	69	246
XX.	The Rivers of the Bible	71	247
XXI.	Seas of the Bible	73	248
XXII.	The Prominent Cities of the Bible	74	249
XXIII.	The Plants named in the Scriptures	78	251
XXIV.	The Minerals of the Bible	83	254
XXV.	Beasts, Reptiles, Birds, Insects, Fishes	86	256
XXVI.	Offices and Sects	91	260
XXVII.	The Old Testament Miracles	93	262
XXVIII.	The New Testament Miracles	100	269
XXIX.	The Parables of Christ	104	273
XXX.	The Prophecies concerning Christ	106	275

CONTENTS.

CHAP.		QUESTIONS, PAGE.	ANSWERS, PAGE.
XXXI.	Appearances of Christ after His Resurrection.	110	278
XXXII.	Chronological Itinerary of Paul's Life	111	279
XXXIII.	The Jewish Calendar	119	286
XXXIV.	Questions for Little People	121	288
XXXV.	Miscellaneous Questions	126	292
XXXVI.	Christian Eividences	135	301
XXXVII.	Prominent Countries of the Bible	138	306
XXXVIII.	Chronology	141	309
XXXIX.	Puzzles	148	314
XL.	Things Worth Knowing	171	332
XLI.	Review	175	

APPENDIX.

Tables of Bible Weights, Measures, and Moneys.................. 341
Chronological Scripture Index................................. 343
Chronological Tables.
  1. From Adam to Moses.. 349
  2. From Adam to Moses.. 350
  3. The Descendants of Adam, Shem, and Abraham............. 351
  4. The descent of David and Solomon from Judah............. 352
  5. The Genealogy of Christ.................................. 352

AIDS TO BIBLICAL RESEARCH.

CHAPTER I.

THE BIBLE.

[Answered page 183.]

1. What names are given to the book generally called the Bible?
2. What is the meaning of Bible?
3. In what language was the Old Testament written?
4. What books were written partly in Aramaic?
5. How have the Old Testament Scriptures been handed down to us?
6. On what continent was the Old Testament written?
7. How many books are there in the Bible?
8. By how many different men was the Bible written?
9. Into what two sections is the book divided?
10. What is the meaning of Testament?
11. How many books are there in the Old Testament?
12. Into what classes are the books of the Old Testament divided?
13. What are the first five books called?
14. From what Greek words is Pentateuch derived?
15. Name the books of the Pentateuch and give the meaning of each?
16. Who wrote the Pentateuch?
17. What proof have we that the books ascribed to Moses were written by him?

18. What part of the Pentateuch could Moses not have written?

19. Who wrote the last chapter of Deuteronomy?

20. Of what beside the Pentateuch was Moses the author?

21. Name the historical books of the Old Testament beside the Pentateuch?

22. Name the poetical books of the Old Testament?

23. What are the prophetical books of the Old Testament?

24. What books in the Old Testament are compilations of different authors?

25. Who wrote the book of Esther?

26. Of what book was David chiefly the author?

27. Prove from the New Testament that David wrote the Psalms?

28. To whom are twelve of the Psalms ascribed?

29. Who are believed by some to have written eleven of the Psalms?

30. What Old Testament writer was the author of two Psalms?

31. Who wrote the ninetieth Psalm?

32. What books did Solomon write?

33. Who wrote Lamentations?

34. What books were probably written by persons whose names they bear?

35. Why were the Scriptures divided into the Old Testament and New?

36. How many years intervened between the Old and New Testament?

37. What history connects the Old Testament with the New?

38. How many books are there in the Apocrypha?

39. What are the names of the Apocryphal books?

40. When were the Apocryphal books first rejected as un canonical?

41. What Church accepts the Apocrypha as canonical?

42. What Church uses the Apocrypha for example of life and instruction but does not apply it to the establishment of any doctrine?

43. Why is the Apocrypha considered of doubtful inspiration?

44. How many books are there in the New Testament?

45. Into what classes are the books of the New Testament divided?

46. What are the historical books?

47. The Pauline epistles?

48. The General epistles?

49. What is the Prophetical book?

50. Which book of the New Testament was written first?

51. Which book of the New Testament was written last?

52. What did John write?

53. What New Testament writer was a physician?

54. What did Luke write?

55. What books are named from their authors?

56. In what language was the New Testament written?

57. What New Testament book was not written originally in Greek?

58. In what language was Matthew written?

59. What names are given in the New Testament to designate the Old?

60. What is the Septuagint?

61. Why was the Septuagint version of the Old Testament so called?

62. What is the Vulgate?

63. What incident worthy of note is connected with the Vulgate?

64. What is meant by the Samaritan Version?
65. What is the Targum?
66. When were the collected books of the Old and New Testament first named The Bible?
67. When was the Bible first divided into chapters, and by whom?
68. When were verses first introduced into the Bible?
69. What Anglo Saxon poet in the seventh century paraphrased the Psalms, portions of which are still extant?
70. Who translated the Psalms and the Gospel of St. John into Anglo Saxon, completing his work on the day of his death?
71. What Saxon king translated portions of the Old Testament and was at work on the Psalms when he died?
72. What great reformer translated the Bible into English?
73. When and where was the Bible first printed in Germany?
74. What was the first Bible in Germany called, and why?
75. What price did a copy of the Mazarin Bible, printed on vellum, which was sold in 1873, bring?
76. What great reformer translated the Bible into German?
77. What Englishman, afterward martyred, translated the New Testament in the year 1526?
78. Where was William Tyndale's translation of the New Testament printed?
79. Who published the first English version of the whole Bible, where printed unknown, and dedicated it to Henry the VIIIth?
80. When and by whom was Matthew's Bible published?
81. What was the first Bible issued by royal authority?
82. Who translated Cranmer's Bible, and why was it so named?
83. What other name was given to Cranmer's Bible?

84. During whose reign was the publication of the Bible prohibited in England?

85. What two men, whose names are notably connected with the English Bible, were martyred during the reign of Bloody Mary?

86. In what country did refugees from England print the Bible during the prohibition?

87. Which was the first Bible divided into verses?

88. Who wrote the introduction to the Genevan Bible?

89. What Bible was published in Elizabeth's reign?

90. Why was the Bishop's Bible so named?

91. At what date were the Scriptures circulated throughout almost the whole of Europe in the language of each nation?

92. What was the Bible issued by order of James the First called?

93. How many men were engaged in its translation?

94. How many years were devoted to King James's translation?

95. What committee was appointed, in 1870, by both Houses of the Convocation of Canterbury to revise the authorized version of the Scriptures?

96. Who composed this committee?

97. What arrangements did these sixteen make at their first meeting?

98. What were some of the resolutions which were to control these revisers?

99. Who were invited to join the Old Testament company?

100. Who were invited to join the New Testament company?

101. Before commencing their work where did the New Testament committee meet to join in the Holy Communion?

102. Where do the Old Testament company meet for the work of revision.

103. How often do the Old Testament committee meet?

104. How often do the New Testament committee meet?

105. Who is chairman of the Old Testament committee?

106. Who is chairman of the New Testament committee?

107. How many American gentlemen were requested in 1871 to join the Old Testament company?

108. Who were they?

109. How many American gentlemen were invited to join the New Testament company?

110. Who were they?

111. Who have since been added to the American Old Testament company?

112. Who of the American New Testament company have resigned since their appointment?

113. Who were delegated to take their places?

114. When and where do the New Testament committee meet?

115. When and where do the Old Testament committee meet?

16. Who is chairman of the New Testament committee?

17. Who is chairman of the Old Testament committee?

118. Who is president of the two combined?

119. How many are engaged in this revision of the Bible?

120. Into how many different dialects is the Bible now translated?

121. What is meant by the genuineness of the Bible?

122. How do we prove the genuineness of the Scriptures?

123. What is meant by the authenticity of the Bible?

124. Can a book be genuine and not authentic, or authentic and not genuine?

125. What is meant by the credibility of the Bible?

126. What is Biblical hermeneutics?

127. What is meant by the inspiration of the Scriptures?

128. Arrange the books of the Old Testament in the order in which they were written.

129. Arrange the books of the New Testament in the order in which they were written.

130. Arrange the epistles of St. Paul in the order in which they were written?

CHAPTER II.

BIBLE CURIOSITIES.

[Answered page 194.]

1. How many letters are there in the Bible?
2. How many words?
3. How many verses?
4. How many chapters?
5. How often does the word "and" occur?
6. How often the word "Lord"?
7. How often the word "reverend"?
8. What is the middle verse of the Bible?
9. What verse contains all the letters of the alphabet except j?
10. What two chapters are alike?
11. What is the longest verse?
12. What is the shortest verse?
13. What is the longest word?
14. What is the shortest book in the Old Testament?
15. What is the shortest book in the New Testament?
16. What book has nowhere the name of God in it?
17. What are the only books in the Old Testament which are neither mentioned nor quoted in the New?
18. What sentence occurs twenty-five times in one book of the Bible and is the principal thought in the book?
19. By what four names are Christians designated in the Bible?
20. Where is the word of God compared to a looking-glass?

21. Where is the word of God called a sword?
22. Where is the word of God called a well of water?
23. Where is the word of God called a mirror?
24. When, and where, was the "Bug" Bible printed, and why was it so named?
25. Why was the "Breeches" Bible so named, and when and where was it printed?
26. When and by whom was the "Treacle" Bible printed, and what was the origin of its name?
27. When was the "Rosin" Bible printed, and why so named?
28. When, where, and by whom was the "He" Bible printed, and from what did it take its nickname?
29. Where was the "She" Bible printed, and why so named?
30. When was the "Wicked" Bible printed, and why so called?
31. When was the "Vinegar" Bible published, and from what did it derive its name?
32. By what other name was the "Vinegar" Bible called, and why?
33. What phrase is used thirty-two times in Matthew's Gospel and found in no other book?
34. What two apostles used precisely the same words with reference to humility?
35. What is the only book in the Old Testament in which "hour" is found?
36. In which book of the Bible is no reference made to the history of the Jews?
37. Where are the Chinese alluded to in the Bible?
38. Which of the books of the Bible is more a philosophical treatise than any other?

CHAPTER III.

EARLIEST BIBLE FACTS.

[Answered page 196.]

1. What was first created?
2. Of whom was the first prophecy, and what was it?
3. By whom was the first city built?
4. Who was the first tent-maker?
5. Who was the first musician?
6. Who was the first exile?
7. Who was the first giver of tithes?
8. Who was the first silversmith?
9. What is the earliest recorded answer to prayer?
10. Who made the first pilgrimage?
11. Who was the earliest judge of Irsael?
12. Who was the first historian?
13. What king is first mentioned?
14. Who was the first sinner?
15. Who told the first falsehood?
16. Who was the first agriculturist?
17. Who was the first worker in iron and brass?
18. Who was the first shepherd?
19. Who bought the first burial ground?
20. Who was the first hunter?
21. Who was the first fugitive?
22. Who wore the first bridal veil?
23. Who was the first ship-builder?

24. Who first wept?
25. Who was the first named, by the Lord, before his birth?
26. Who was the first to use a saddle?
27. Who first died a natural death?
28. Who is earliest mentioned as wearing a ring on his finger, and a gold chain on his neck?
29. What was the first wedding present?
30. Who was the first to hold the office of scribe?
31. What was the earliest thing engraved?
32. Who was the first Jewish high-priest?
33. What was the first of the ten plagues?
34. What is the first company of merchants mentioned in the Bible?
35. Who first, aside from Eve, was guilty of stealing?
36. Who was the earliest governor of Israel after the captivity?
37. What was the first present made by one brother to another?
38. Who was the first Christian martyr?
39. Who made the first confession?
40. What was the first offering recorded of woman?
41. Who was the first shepherdess?
42. Who was the first raised to life?
43. Who erected the first monument in memory of the dead?
44. What mountain is first mentioned?
45. To whom was the name Hebrew first given?
46. What were the first words spoken to man?
47. Who first commanded a navy?
48. When was the Sabbath first instituted?
49. Where have we an account of the first missionary collection?

50. Where is the first mention of printing?
51. Where is the use of money first recorded?
52. When did man first exercise the power of speech?
53. When was the first voluntary fast?
54. Who was first appointed president?
55. When was man first permitted the use of flesh as food?
56. Who was the first female ruler?
57. Which of the tribes marched first in their journeyings through the wilderness?
58. When was the first famine?
59. Where are giants earliest mentioned?
60. Who was the first slave?
61. What king first held the Israelites captive?
62. Who was the first king of Israel?
63. Who was the first king of Israel after the captivity?
64. Who was the first king of Judah?
65. Where are the wicked first mentioned as sinners?
66. Who first took an affidavit?
67. Where is a library first mentioned?
68. Where is God first referred to as King?
69. Where are beggars first mentioned?
70. Where is the first prophecy of the millennium recorded?
71. What was the first act of surveying?
72. When and by whom were the first temperance societies formed?
73. Where were mules first found, and by whom?
74. Where is the earliest account of the first Christian letter of commendation?
75. What was Christ's first miracle?
76. What was the first miracle wrought by Elijah?
77. What was the first miracle of Elisha?
78. Where is the rending of clothes first mentioned?
79. Where is a hammer first mentioned?

80. Which prophecy was first written?
81. Where is the olive first mentioned, and what was the divine law concerning it?
82. What was the first prayer for a king?
83. Where is "pen" first mentioned?
84. Who was the first prophet?
85. Who was the first disciple Jesus called?
86. Who was the first apostle to meet a violent death?
87. Where is Paul first mentioned?
88. Who was the first Gentile convert to Christianity?
89. In what city were the disciples first called Christians?
90. In what city of Europe was the Gospel first preached?
91. Who was the first convert to Christianity in Europe?
92. Where are looking-glasses first mentioned?
93. Who was first slain as a punishment for sin?
94. Where is the first mention of the appearance of an angel?
95. The first verse of what psalm did our Saviour repeat on the cross?
96. Where is chimney first mentioned?
97. Who was the first negro convert to Christianity?
98. Where is the first mention of windows?
99. What was probably the origin of the Jewish Sanhedrim?
100. What epistle did Paul first write?
101. What is the first recorded miracle?
102. In whose reign, and by whom, was Solomon's temple first plundered?
103. What month is first mentioned by name?
104. What miracle was the first sent as a punishment for sin?
105. Where is the sealing of a letter first mentioned?
106. Where is a candle first mentioned?

107. In whose funeral procession do we find the first mention of horsemen?

108. By whom is church first mentioned?

109. Where is the first division of time into hours?

110. Who made the first coats worn by the children of men?

111. Where do we first read of milk?

112. Where do we first read of bread being made?

113. Who first spoke of a race?

114. What are the first recorded words of Jesus Christ?

115. Where are the children of Judah and Benjamin first mentioned as Jews?

116. Who was the first to practice polygamy?

117. What is the first recorded prayer in the Bible?

118. Who is the first person mentioned as having crossed the river Jordan?

119. What idolatrous temple is first mentioned?

120. What was the first census mentioned in history?

121. What are the first lines of poetry in the Bible?

122. What is the first treaty mentioned in sacred history?

123. Where is the account of the first war?

124. What kind of idolatry do we first find mentioned in the Bible?

THE TABERNACLE.

CHAPTER IV.

THE TABERNACLE.

[Answered page 200.]

1. Near what mountain were the Israelites encamped when the tabernacle was ordered to be erected?
2. To whom was the order given?
3. Who were the two architects?
4. To which tribe did they belong?
5. What metals were offered for the construction of the tabernacle?
6. What ornaments of jewelry were brought?
7. What kind of cloth?
8. What precious stones?
9. What animals' skins?
10. What other articles?
11. Give the length and the width of the outer court of the tabernacle?
12. How high was the enclosing fence?
13. Of what was this fence made?
14. How were these curtains of the enclosure supported?
15. How were the open net-work curtains attached to the brazen pillars?
16. Describe the entrance to this outer court?
17. Who were allowed to enter this outer court?
18. What two articles stood in this outer court in front of the tabernacle?
19. What was the size of the altar of burnt offering?
20. Of what materials was it made?

21. What were upon the four corners?
22. Of what use were these horns?
23. Mention the articles connected with the altar of burnt offering.
24. For what were the basins used?
25. What were the flesh-hooks like?
26. What were the fire-pans?
27. How was the altar borne?
28. Of what material was the grate of network made, and how was it removed?
29. Describe the laver.
30. What was the form and size of the tabernacle?
31. Of what almost imperishable wood were the forty-eight boards used in its construction?
32. How many boards were there on the north side?
33. On the south side?
34. On the west end?
35. Give the size of each board?
36. With what were these forty-eight boards covered?
37. How were they set up?
38. How many silver sockets were there?
39. How were the boards held together?
40. How many curtains of fine twined linen were prepared for the inner covering of the frame of gilded boards?
41. Of what color were they, and how ornamented?
42. Give the size of each of these curtains?
43. How were they united or "coupled together"?
44. How many loops were there?
45. How many taches?
46. How many outer curtains of goat's hair were there?
47. Give the size of each of these eleven curtains?
48. How was the entrance at the east end of the tabernacle closed?

49. How was this veil supported?
50. Who alone were allowed to enter, or even to look into, the tabernacle?
51. With what was the whole frame of the tabernacle enclosed?
52. Which descendants of Levi carried the veil and curtains of the Sanctuary?
53. Into what two apartments was the tabernacle divided?
54. With what were the walls of the Sanctuary draped?
55. What first met the eye on entering the Sanctuary?
56. Give the size of the altar of incense?
57. Of what material was it?
58. For what was it used?
59. How was it carried?
60. What else was in the Sanctuary?
61. Describe the construction of the table of shew-bread?
62. What may have been the use of the golden crown border around the table?
63. By what other name is the table of shew-bread called?
64. To what is this generally supposed to refer?
65. How many loaves of bread were upon the table?
66. To what did the number relate?
67. How were the loaves of bread placed?
68. How often were they renewed?
69. With what were they sprinkled?
70. What must be done with the shew-bread when taken from the table?
71. Of what was the shew-bread symbolical?
72. What else adorned the shew-bread table?
73. Describe the golden candlestick or Candelabrum?
74. What was the only metal allowed to be used for the instruments of the Sanctuary?
75. What was the value of the gold in the candlestick?

76. How many lamps were placed in the candlestick?
77. What kind of oil was used?
78. With what did the priests trim the lamps every morning?
79. How was the candlestick protected when carried?
80. How was the Sanctuary separated from the Holy of Holies?
81. Who only was to pass, or even look, behind the curtain into the Holy of Holies?
82. How did the size of the Holy Place compare with that of the Sanctuary?
83. What was within the Holy Place?
84. Of what wood was the Ark made?
85. What was its length, breadth, and height?
86. What was stored in the Ark?
87. With what metal was the Ark overlaid?
88. What was its ornament round about?
89. What were at each end of the mercy-seat?
90. What was fixed in each corner?
91. What were made for carrying it?
92. Who alone even looked upon the Ark?
93. When transported how was it covered?
94. What family of the descendants of Levi bore it?
95. The descendants of what tribe were appointed the priests for the tabernacle?
96. In what part of the camp was the tabernacle placed during the wilderness journey?
97. Relate the circumstance of the children of Israel passing over Jordan with the Ark?
98. What use was made of the Ark at the taking of Jericho?
99. At what place was the tabernacle first set up?
100. How long did it remain there?

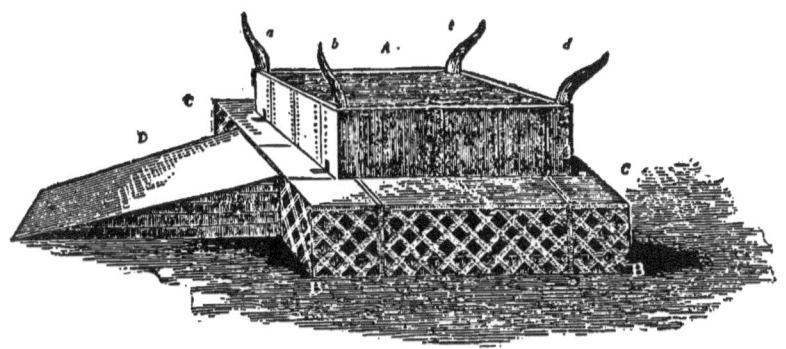

THE ALTAR OF BURNT OFFERING.

THE ALTAR OF BURNT OFFERING.

A is the open space within the boards, in which an earthen or stone fireplace was constructed.

B is the network of brass supporting the projecting ledge.

C is the projecting ledge, the carcob.—Ex. xxvii. 4, 5.

D is the incline, made of stones or earth, by which the priests reached the ledge.

a, *b*, *c*, *d* are the horns of the altar.

101. Where was it afterward erected?
102. In a battle against the Philistines who bore the Ark from the tabernacle to the camp of the Israelites?
103. What became of the Ark?
104. In what temple did the Philistines place it?
105. What happened to Dagon?
106. With what were the men of Ashdod smitten?
107. To what town did they send the Ark in consequence?
108. What happened to the men of Gath when the Ark was brought to their city?
109. To what town did they send it?
110. What did the people of this town resolve to do with it?
111. How long was the Ark in the country of the Philistines?
112. When did the Philistines return with the Ark as a trespass-offering?
113. By what animals was the Ark returned?
114. To what town of the Israelites did these animals bring the Ark?
115. Of what sinful act were the men of Bethshemesh guilty, and how were they punished?
116. To what place and to whose house was the Ark next removed?
117. How long did the Ark rest here?
118. What king removed the Ark from Kirjath-jearim?
119. Upon what was it borne?
120. Who drove the cart?
121. What befell Uzza?
122. What name was given to the place in consequence of his death?
123. Into whose house was the Ark then carried?
124. What effect had the Ark upon Obed-edom's house?

125. On hearing this what did David prepare for the Ark at Jerusalem?

126. What religious services were performed while the Ark was being set up?

127. What more stable structure than a tabernacle did David resolve to raise for the service of God?

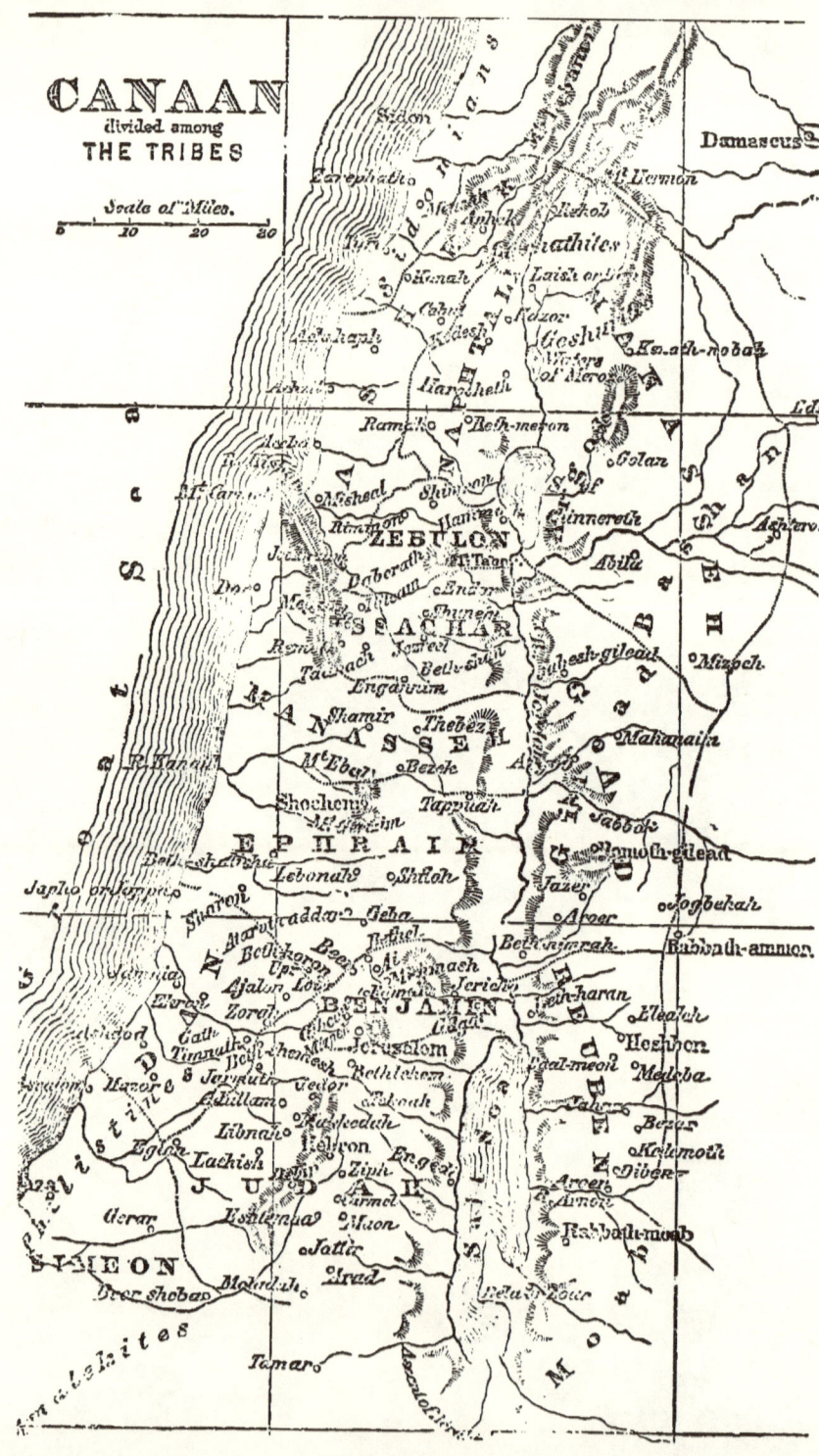

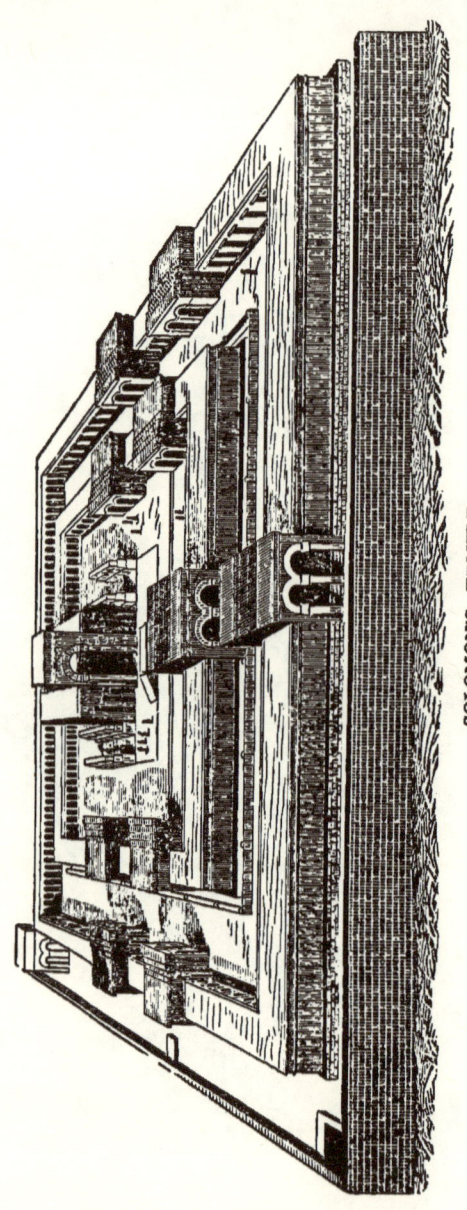

SOLOMON'S TEMPLE.

CHAPTER V.

SOLOMON'S TEMPLE.

[Answered page 206.]

1. Of what was Solomon's temple a type?
2. In what city did Solomon build the temple?
3. Upon what mountain?
4. Of whom did Solomon purchase the site of the temple?
5. For what purpose had Araunah used it?
6. How was the summit of Mt. Moriah enlarged by Solomon, that there might be space for the temple?
7. Where are portions of these ancient foundations still visible?
8. How large are some of these foundation-stones?
9. Who had collected treasure for the erection of the temple?
10. How many talents of silver did David and his princes set apart for the temple?
11. How many talents of gold?
12. How many dollars of our money do these talents of gold and silver represent?
13. Why was David not allowed to build the temple?
14. Who was commissioned to inform David that he must relinquish his desire to build the temple?
15. How do the dimensions of Solomon's temple compare with those of the tabernacle?
16. In what year of Solomon's reign was the foundation of the temple laid?

17. How many years was the temple in building?
18. What king materially assisted Solomon in building the temple?
19. What did Hiram furnish for the temple, and of what material were the articles made?
20. What was the weight of the brass used?
21. How many men were employed in building the temple?
22. How many men were bearers of burdens?
23. How many diggers and cutters of stone?
24. How many overseers?
25. How many were kept in reserve to supply the places of those who were ill?
26. What men besides these were employed in the construction of the temple?
27. Of what material were the walls of the temple?
28. By what means was all noise prevented during the building of the temple?
29. What recent discovery confirms this remarkable fact?
30. How was the top of Mt. Moriah enclosed?
31. What was just inside this enclosure?
32. How many entrances were there to this wall?
33. What was the gate for the royal family called?
34. What was the east gate called?
35. The south gate?
36. Why so called?
37. Name the gate at the north-west.
38. What were erected at every corner of this court and at the side of each gate?
39. From which of these gates was the only direct entrance to the temple itself?
40. Upon how many sides was the temple accessible?
41. How was the west side separated from Mt. Zion?

42. Which extremity looked down upon the valley of Hinnom?

43. How was the approach to the temple on the north side secured?

44. What completed the defences of the temple?

45. Who might enter the outer court of the temple?

46. What court extended on the four sides just within the outer court?

47. Where was the court of the women?

48. Where was the court of the people?

49. How high was the wall which separated the court of the people from the court of the priests?

50. Of what was this low wall built?

51. Why built so low?

52. What court was next to the temple and completely surrounded it?

53. What altar stood in this court opposite the porch?

54. How high was this altar?

55. How long?

56. How broad?

57. What was the weight of this altar?

58. For what was it used?

59. What does tradition say concerning the smoke from these sacrifices?

60. Where was the metal, of which the brazen altar was made, cast?

61. How many lavers were there in the court of the priests?

62. Where were they situated?

63. For what was the water in these used?

64. How many gallons of water did each of these lavers contain?

65. What were the "ten bases of brass"?

66. How were these ornamented?

67. What else was in the court of the priests?

68. What was the brazen sea?

69. How many gallons of water was the brazen sea capable of holding?

70. For what was the basin used?

71. What idolatrous king of Judah mutilated it by removing it from its basis of oxen and placing it on a stone base?

72. Who finally destroyed it?

73. What were the dimensions of the porch of the temple?

74. What purpose did the porch serve?

75. Name the two pillars at the entrance to the porch of the temple?

76. What was the circumference of these pillars?

77. What the height?

78. How were they adorned?

79. To what place was the porch an entrance?

80. Of what woods did the doors of the sanctuary consist?

81. How large was the sanctuary?

82. How many golden candlesticks were there?

83. Where situated?

84. How do we guess the form of the golden candlestick?

85. What other articles beside the candlestick were made of "perfect gold"?

86. How many basins of gold were there?

87. How many tables of shew-bread were on the north side, opposite the candlesticks?

88. How many loaves of bread were on each table?

89. What stood between the ten golden candlesticks and the ten tables of shew-bread, directly opposite the Holy of Holies?

90. How large was this altar?

THE BRAZEN LAVER.

THE BRAZEN SEA.

91. Of what wood was it made?
92. With what was this wood overlaid?
93. How was its top surrounded?
94. How was it portable?
95. What alone was burnt, and offered, every morning and evening, upon this altar?
96. What other things were kept in the Sanctuary of the temple?
97. What separated the Sanctuary from the Holy of Holies?
98. Of what was the veil wrought?
99. What were its colors?
100. With what was it ornamented?
101. Of what wood were the two doors made?
102. With what was this wood overlaid?
103. How were the doors ornamented?
104. What were the dimensions of the Holy of Holies?
105. How often was it entered?
106. By whom?
107. What was kept there?
108. Of what did Solomon make the Cherubims which he set up in the Holy of Holies to overshadow the two golden ones on the Ark?
109. Were there any windows in the Oracle or Holy of Holies?
110. Were there windows in the Sanctuary?
111. With what metal were the walls, roof, floor, and doors overlaid?
112. What vessel was furnished for the temple which was not found in the tabernacle?
113. What other apartments pertained to the temple besides those enumerated?
114. On how many sides of the temple were these upper chambers?

115. How many stories high?
116. How were they approached?
117. Mention the different kinds of wood used in building the temple?
118. What valuables were used to garnish the temple?
119. How long after the completion of the temple before it was dedicated?
120. Why this delay?
121. Who were appointed to minister in the temple service?
122. Into how many orders were the priests divided?
123. Just before what feast was the temple dedicated?
124. Why was this the most appropriate of all the festivals?
125. In what month was this feast held?
126. When all was ready whom did Solomon send to bring the Ark of the Covenant?
127. What else did they bring?
128. Where did they deposit the sacred vessels?
129. Where did they place the Ark?
130. What did they do to the staves of the Ark?
131. What was the object of this?
132. What was in the Ark?
133. What else was Moses commanded to put into the Ark?
134. What does the fact that only the tables of stone were in the Ark in Solomon's time imply?
135. How many priests with sounding trumpets were at the dedication of the temple?
136. What was the smallest number of trumpets ever used?
137. Where were the priests stationed?
138. What instruments of music did the Levite orchestra have?
139. Where did the singers stand?
140. What happened when the priests and Levites "lifted up their voice" and "praised the Lord"?

141. Why had the children of Israel reason to recognize this cloud as a symbol of the Divine presence?

142. Recite Solomon's address to the people.

143. Upon what did Solomon stand to address the people?

144. What were the dimensions of this brazen scaffold?

145. What was Solomon's prayer?

146. What was his benediction?

147. What happened when Solomon finished his benediction?

148. How were the priests affected?

149. How were the people influenced by the fire and glory of the Lord?

150. How many sheep and oxen were offered in sacrifice?

151. What arrangement did Solomon make for this extraordinary sacrifice?

152. How many days were occupied in the dedication?

153. What feast came immediately afterward?

154. How long did this continue?

155. For how many years did the temple retain its pristine glory?

156. What king came up against Jerusalem, in the reign of Rehoboam, and took away the treasures and the shields of the house of the Lord?

157. With what did Jeroboam replace the golden shields?

158. What king of Judah took the silver and gold from the treasury of the temple, and to whom did he send it?

159. What queen of Judah bestowed the dedicated things "of the house of the Lord upon Baalim"?

160. Who repaired the temple and restored its worship?

161. Upon whom did Joash afterward bestow money taken from the treasury of the temple?

162. What wicked king sent treasures from the Lord's house to the king of Assyria?

163. How else did he desecrate the temple?

164. What good king of Judah reopened and repaired the temple?

165. How did he afterward mutilate the temple to satisfy the demands of Sennacherib, king of Assyria?

166. Where, and how, did the Lord warn Solomon concerning the destruction of the temple?

167. What two prophets of Judah foretold the ruin of the temple?

168. By what king was this prophecy fulfilled?

169. What things did Nebuchadnezzar carry away with him?

170. What use did Beltshazzar make of the sacred vessels?

171. What did Nebuchadnezzar burn?

172. Who prophesied the restoration of the temple?

173. Under what king of Persia was it accomplished?

174. Name some of the things which formed the distinguishing glory of Solomon's temple.

CHAPTER VI.

THE SECOND TEMPLE.

[Answered page 214.]

1. What was the decree of Cyrus concerning the rebuilding of the temple?
2. Which one of the temple appointments was built before the foundation of the temple was laid?
3. What vessels did Cyrus restore?
4. How many were there?
5. Why was the interior of the temple of pure gold?
6. What arrangement was made for procuring material for building the temple?
7. Who laid the foundation of the second temple?
8. In what month and year was the foundation laid?
9. With what expressions of joy and gratitude?
10. While the young people shouted for joy how were the old men affected?
11. With what song of praise was the foundation of the spiritual temple laid?
12. How was the building of the temple interrupted?
13. For what length of time?
14. By what two prophets were the Israelites admonished to resume the work?
15. What Gentile kings have their names associated with the work?
16. Why is Artaxerxes, who reigned subsequently to the completion of the temple, named among its builders?
17. What year was the temple completed?

18. By whom was it finished?

19. Why did God finish it by the same hand which began it?

20. How many years was it from the laying of the foundation to the dedication?

21. When shall the dedication of the spiritual temple be consummated?

22. How did the second temple compare in size and magnificence with Solomon's temple?

23. What things, some of which were the distinguishing glory of the first temple, were lacking in the second?

24. In what respect was the glory of the second temple greater than that of the first?

25. Who first profaned the temple, stopped the daily sacrifice, and erected the image of Jupiter on the altar of burnt offering?

26. How many years after its dedication?

27. Who restored the Jewish worship three years later?

28. How many years was this before the birth of Christ?

29. In the year 63 B. C. what Roman Consul demolished the walls of Jerusalem, took the temple, but left untouched its golden vessels, the spices, the money, and every article pertaining to it?

30. In 64 B. C. what rapacious Roman Consul visited the city and plundered the temple, not only of the money Pompey left, but of other treasures?

31. What fact aggravated the enormity of the pillage?

32. What was the second temple called in the time of Christ?

33. Why so called?

34. What was Herod's object in rebuilding the temple?

35. In what year B. C. did he announce his intention to the Jews?

36. How did the Jews receive it?
37. How did he overcome their prejudice?
38. How many years were taken in preliminary preparations?
39. What time was occupied in building the porch, Sanctuary, and Holy of Holies?
40. In how many years did Herod finish the inner court and cloister of the temple?
41. How many years before it was altogether completed?
42. Quote a text in the New Testament in proof of this.
43. What part of Herod's temple was unknown to the other two?
44. What were the cloisters?
45. As the Brazen Sea was missing in this temple how were the priests supplied with water for the sacrifices?
46. What provision was made for disposing of the blood of the victims!
47. What was the Pastophoria?
48. What precautions were taken to prevent the birds from alighting on the temple and defiling it?
49. What three things separated the court of the Gentiles from the inner courts of the temple?
50. What was the Soreg?
51. What was the Chel?
52. How many gates were there?
53. What were the gates on the north side called?
54. What were the gates on the south side called?
55. What gate was on the east?
56. For what purpose were the apartments which alternated with these massive gates?
57. For what was the apartment Gazith used?
58. How was the court of the women situated?

59. For what were the apartments in the corners of the court of the women used?

60. Describe the treasury.

61. Give the name of the gate at which the poor and afflicted Israelites asked alms.

62. Locate and describe the Beautiful Gate.

63. What separated the court of Israel from the Sanctuary?

64. How were the people in the court of Israel enabled to see the priests offering sacrifices?

65. What was this low barrier called?

66. Which sacred room in Herod's temple was empty?

67. How often was the Holy of Holies entered?

68. By whom?

69. On what day?

70. What ceremony did he here perform?

71. What was before the entrance to the Holy Place?

72. What occurred to the veil at the moment of the crucifixion?

73. What was this designed to teach?

74. What part of the temple was the scene of Christ's early temptations?

75. What two extremes of Jewish character met at the same time to pray in the temple?

76. What great sacrament was held in the temple?

77. What did Christ afterward institute instead of this sacrament?

78. Name two apostles who regularly frequented the temple to pray?

79. What miracles did these apostles here perform?

80. With what was Paul charged while in the temple?

81. In what words of admiration did Christ's disciples speak of the temple?

82. In what prophecy did our Saviour reply?

83. When was this prediction fulfilled?

84. What nation's army was besieging Jerusalem at this time?

85. Who was the Roman general?

86. For what was the temple used during the siege of Titus?

87. How was it destroyed?

88. To confute the saying that "one stone should not be left upon another," who twice attempted to rebuild it?

89. In what year?

90. How was he twice prevented?

91. What building now stands upon its site?

92. Who is called the Great High Priest in the Heavenly Temple?

CHAPTER VII.

THE PATRIARCHS.

[Answered page 219.]

1. Who named the beasts and the fowls?
2. Who cried "My punishment is greater than I can bear"?
3. Whom did Jesus Christ mention as the first martyr?
4. What grandson of Adam is first mentioned?
5. Who is the author of the first lines of poetry the Bible contains?
6. Who was the father of such as dwell in tents?
7. Who was the inventor of the harp and organ?
8. Which of the patriarchs is believed to be the god Vulcan of the heathen?
9. What was the name of Adam's third son, and how many years did he live?
10. What great grandson of Adam lived over nine hundred years?
11. Which of the patriarchs, according to tradition, introduced idols?
12. Which of the patriarchs was the Apollo of antediluvian mythology?
13. Who was the father of Enoch?
14. To what patriarch do ancient writers ascribe the discovery of the science of astronomy?
15. Who was the grandfather of Noah?

AIDS TO BIBLICAL RESEARCH.   35

16. Who was Noah's father?

17. Of whom, beside Enoch, is it said that he "walked with God"?

18. From which of the sons of Noah were the inhabitants of Arabia and Palestine descendants?

19. Whose descendants peopled the continent of Africa?

20. From which son of Noah are we, the people of America, descended?

21. Of whom were the first inhabitants of Galatia and Phrygia, now called Poland, Hungary, Switzerland, France, Spain, Portugal, and Britain, descendants?

22. Of whom were the first people of Tartary descendants?

23. After whom was the great country Media named?

24. Of whom were the Greeks the offspring?

25. What great-grandson of Noah built the city of Babylon?

26. What son of Ham was the father of the Philistines?

27. From whom was the land of Canaan named?

28. Who was the progenitor of the Persian race?

29. From whom was Assyria named?

30. From which son of Shem is the Jewish race descended?

31. What was Abram's father's name?

32. What patriarch was first named "the Hebrew"?

33. Who was the grandfather of Rebekah?

34. What was the name of Rebekah's father?

35. Who was the father of Lot?

36. Who was the only good man in an exceedingly wicked city?

37. What Scripture character among the patriarchs is the most repulsive?

38. What patriarch was the "child of promise"?

39. What patriarch persecuted his brother?

40. To what patriarch was a famine the means of restoring his lost son?

41. What patriarch is called in the New Testament a "profane person"?

42. Who were the twelve sons of Jacob?

43. What two of Jacob's grandsons took the places of his sons, Levi and Joseph, as representatives of two of the tribes of Israel?

44. What patriarch did the Lord suffer Satan to deprive of all his possessions?

45. What are the names of the three friends of Job who essayed to comfort him in his troubles?

CHAPTER VIII.

THE PROPHETS.

[Answered page 221.]

1. Who lived as many years as there are days in our year?
2. What Old Testament prophet is designated in the New Testament as the preacher of righteousness?
3. Upon what prophet did a deep sleep fall with a vision of a burning lamp?
4. What prophet's name means "laughter"?
5. What patriarch was guilty of deception, and afterward suffered through the deceit of another?
6. To what slave was the spirit of prophecy given?
7. What prophet's life was divided into three periods of forty years each?
8. To what prophet was the command given not to drink wine under penalty of death?
9. What prophet loved the ways of unrighteousness?
10. Who that prophesied was smitten with a loathsome disease?
11. Whose name was changed as a token he should render Israel safe?
12. What prophetess was a ruler of Israel?
13. What prophet's cowardice was punished by having the honor of his victory given to a woman?
14. What judge of Israel, believed also to have been a prophet, defeated the Moabites?

15. What prophet was a good judge but an indiscreet father?

16. What prophet used to say grace before sitting down to a feast?

17. What prophetess was the mother of a prophet?

18. What prophet is described as being the Lord's priest and wearing an ephod?

19. What prophet was both priest and king?

20. Who rebuked King David for a grave sin?

21. Who was sent to inform David he should be punished for numbering the people?

22. Who tore a king's robe in twelve pieces?

23. What prophet built the temple?

24. Mention a prophet of whom we know nothing except that he wrote chronicles which are now lost?

25. What man of God warned Rehoboam, king of Judah, that he should not fight against his brethren, the children of Israel?

26. What prophet was slain by a lion for disobedience?

27. Who was the means of the release of two hundred thousand captives?

28. Who forbade the children of Israel to make slaves of their brothers?

29. What prophet reproved Asa for trusting to the king of Syria?

30. What prophet denounced Jehoshaphat, king of Judah, for his alliance with the wicked Ahab?

31. Whom did the Lord take to heaven in a chariot of fire?

32. Who was imprisoned because his prediction displeased the king?

33. Through the direction of what prophet did oil prove as efficacious as gold?

34. What man of God's prophecy animated Jehoshaphat and his army in a moment of great danger?

35. What prophet was slain in the house of the Lord, by command of a king?

36. What prophet was the counsellor of King Uzziah?

37. What prophet did a king of Judah slay with a sword?

38. What prophet heralded the coming of Christ?

CHAPTER IX.

THE CANONICAL PROPHETS.

[Answered page 223.]

1. Which author of a prophetic book was sent as a missionary to the Gentiles?

2. What writer asserts that thirsty cattle call to God?

3. Which of the prophets confirms the statement of Moses as to the length of the Israelites' march through the wilderness?

4. From whom did Christ twice quote the words "I will have mercy and not sacrifice"?

5. Who is called "The Evangelical prophet"?

6. Whose prophecies commence with the last words recorded of that prophet's namesake?

7. What writer gives a magnificent description of the siege and destruction of Nineveh?

8. Which prophet was a descendant of Hezekiah, king of Judah?

9. Who was called to be a prophet while yet a child?

10. What prophet denounces the man who makes his neighbor a drunkard?

11. What prophet, receiving a revelation from God, was sick several days?

12. What prophet was suspended between earth and heaven by a lock of his hair?

13. Whose prophecy is the shortest of all the books of the Bible?

14. Who prophesied that the glory of the second temple should exceed the glory of the first?

15. What other prophet than Haggai assisted the Jews in rebuilding the temple?

16. Who is called, "The Seal," of the prophets?

CHAPTER X.

THE HIGH PRIESTS.

[Answered page 224.]

1. Who was the first Jewish high-priest?
2. What high-priest witnessed the death of Aaron?
3. Whose bravery and zeal appeased the divine wrath, and secured to him the promise that the priesthood should remain in his family forever?
4. What son of Phinehas, of whom little is known, succeeded his father in the priesthood?
5. Who was punished for his culpable negligence in not restraining his wicked sons?
6. Who is described as the Lord's priest in Shiloh, wearing an ephod?
7. What high-priest anointed Solomon to be king?
8. Who was "thrust out from being high-priest unto the Lord," by Solomon, for his share in Adonijah's rebellion?
9. Who officiated at the consecration of Solomon's temple, and was the first high-priest that ministered in it?
10. The pontificate of what priest came in the reign of Jeroboam?
11. What son of Johanan, of whom little is known, was high-priest?
12. What high-priest seems to have seconded Jehoshaphat in his endeavor to reform Judah?
13. What high-priest hid an heir to the throne in the temple six years, and eventually replaced him on the throne of his ancestors?

THE ARK OF THE COVENANT.

14. What high-priest was stoned to death in the court of the temple, by commandment of King Joash, because he reproved his sin?

15. Who reproved King Uzziah for burning incense upon the altar in the temple?

16. Who zealously coöperated with King Hezekiah in his restoration of the temple service?

17. What priest built an altar to the Lord after the pattern of a heathen altar?

18. Who was high-priest during the reign of Manasseh and Amon?

19. What high-priest rendered his pontificate illustrious by the discovery which he made, of the book of the law of Moses, in the temple?

20. What high-priest was carried captive to Babylon and slain?

21. Who never officiated as high-priest because taken to Babylon with Seraiah his father, and a captive all his life?

22. Who, with Zerubbabel, headed the return from captivity?

23. What five high-priests are mentioned in Scripture as ruling prior to the time of Darius the Persian?

24. Who is the first high-priest mentioned in the New Testament?

25. Who was ruling high-priest during our Lord's public ministry, and at the time of his condemnation and crucifixion?

26. What high-priest, not mentioned by name in the New Testament, is probably the one who granted Saul a commission to proceed to Damascus and arrest any believers he might find there?

27. What high-priest commanded Paul to be smitten on the mouth for asserting he had lived in all good conscience before God?

CHAPTER XI.

THE JUDGES OF ISRAEL.

[Answered page 226.]

1. Who was the first judge of Israel?
2. What judge of Israel was left-handed?
3. Who slew six hundred Philistines with an ox-goad?
4. What woman was the fourth judge of Israel, and who was her associate judge?
5. Which judge refused the monarchy of Israel offered him by a grateful people?
6. Who called his armour-bearer to slay him with a sword, that it might not be said of him, "A woman slew him."
7. Who was the seventh judge of Israel?
8. Who had thirty sons, who possessed thirty cities in the land of Gilead?
9. Who, praying for a successful victory over the Ammonites, vowed a rash vow?
10. Which judge of Israel had thirty sons and thirty daughters, and obliged them to marry from abroad?
11. Of which judge is it said, he "was buried in Ajalon"?
12. Which ruler had forty sons and thirty nephews, each of whom owned a colt?
13. Who caught three hundred foxes and tied them together by the tails with firebrands between them?
14. Which judge of Israel is better known as a High Priest?
15. Who was the last judge of Israel?

THE TABLE OF SHEWBREAD.

THE GOLDEN CANDLESTICK.

CHAPTER XII.

THE KINGS OF ISRAEL AND JUDAH.

[Answered page 227.]

KINGS OF ISRAEL BEFORE THE REVOLT.

1. Who was the first king of Israel?
2. What king showed his unselfishness by declining a drink of water when suffering from thirst?
3. Under the reign of what king was silver as stones in Jerusalem?

KINGS OF ISRAEL AFTER THE REVOLT.

Ten tribes.

1. What king made two golden calves?
2. Who was slain in battle in fulfilment of Ahijah's prophecy?
3. Of whose posterity was it prophesied, "Him that dwelleth in the city the dogs shall eat"?
4. What king while intoxicated was killed by his servant?
5. What usurper of Israel's throne reigned but seven days?
6. What king bought a hill, and built thereon a city, naming it Samaria after the owner?
7. What king built an ivory house?
8. Who, when ill, sent to inquire of Baalzebub, the god of Ekron, concerning his recovery?

9. What king of Israel put away the image of Baal which Ahab made?

10. Who commanded the wicked Jezebel to be thrown from her window?

11. What king's army was reduced to ten chariots, fifty horsemen, and ten thousand footmen?

12. What ungodly king mourned Elisha's death?

13. Who was the most prosperous of the kings of Israel?

14. Who reigned but six months?

15. Whose reign lasted but two months?

16. Who exacted from the children of Israel one thousand talents of silver to buy the friendship of Pul, king of Assyria?

17. What son of Menahem reigned in his stead?

18. In whose reign did Tiglath-pileser carry many of the Israelites captive to Assyria?

19. In whose reign did Shalmanezer complete the captivity of Israel?

THE KINGS OF JUDAH.
Two tribes.

1. Who made brazen shields for the temple to supply the place of the golden ones plundered by Shishak?

2. Of what wicked prince is it said, "For David's sake did the Lord his God give him a lamp in Jerusalem"?

3. Who dethroned his mother and destroyed her idols?

4. For what king's sake was a thirsty army miraculously supplied with water?

5. To what deceased king of Judah did his subjects refuse the ordinary honors given to their dead sovereigns?

6. What wicked king of Judah reigned but one year?

7. What woman, the mother of Jezebel, destroyed the heirs to the kingdom and usurped the throne?

8. What king was but seven years of age when he commenced to reign?

9. What king was destroyed because he refused to follow a prophet's counsel?

10. What king of Judah was stricken with leprosy for burning incense in the temple?

11. What king became mighty because he prepared his ways before the Lord?

12. Whose life was prolonged fifteen years in answer to prayer?

13. What king set up a carved image in the house of the Lord?

14. What king of Judah bore the name of an Egyptian divinity?

15. Who burned the chariots and horses that Manasseh and Amon had consecrated to the sun in Jerusalem?

16. What king was carried captive to Egypt and died there?

17. Which king of Judah was the servant of Nebuchadnezzar?

18. Whom did Nebuchadnezzar carry captive to Babylon?

19. Whom did Nebuchadnezzar make king of Judah in the place of the king he carried captive to Babylon?

GOVERNORS OF JERUSALEM AFTER THE CAPTIVITY.

1. Which governor of Jerusalem laid the foundation of the second temple?

2. Who read the law to the people assembled at the water gate in Jerusalem?

3. Which governor was cup-bearer to a king?

CHAPTER XIII.

THE HEATHEN MONARCHS OF THE BIBLE.

[Answered page 229.]

1. What shepherd king was "plagued with great plagues" because of Sarai, Abram's wife?

2. Who were the four kings, and the five kings that warred together in the time of Abraham?

3. What king blessed Abraham?

4. To what monarch did God say in a dream, "Thou art but a dead man"?

5. What sovereign imprisoned two of his servants, and then on his birthday feast reinstated one and hanged the other.

6. Who was king of Egypt at the birth of Moses?

7. Who seems to have been most impious of all the heathen kings of the Bible?

8. What Egyptian monarch became the father-in-law of an Israelite about the time of the Exodus.

9. What king refused to let the Israelites cross his borders?

10. What king hired a prophet to curse Israel?

11. What heathen king were the children of Israel to exceed in greatness?

12. What king was remarkable for his great stature?

13. Mention a king whose monument was a great heap of stones?

14. What five kings were buried in a cave?

AIDS TO BIBLICAL RESEARCH.

15. What two kings, whose armies were "as the sand upon the sea-shore for multitude," fought against Joshua by the waters of Merom?

16. How many rulers were slain by Joshua on the other side of Jordan?

17. Who suffered a cruel punishment which he had inflicted upon seventy other kings?

18. What Moabite king oppressed the children of Israel eighteen years?

19. What king oppressed Israel eight years and was finally destroyed by Othniel?

20. From the hands of what king did Deborah deliver the Israelites?

21. What king did Samuel slay?

22. In the presence of what monarch did David feign madness?

23. Who sent workmen and materials to Jerusalem to build a palace for David?

24. What king did David conquer by the river Euphrates?

25. Who sent congratulations and presents to David because of his destruction of King Hadadezer?

26. What king's royal crown was placed upon David's head?

27. What heathen king was related by marriage to the royal family of Israel?

28. What monarch carried away the treasures from Solomon's temple during the reign of Rehoboam?

29. What king was the grandfather of Dido, queen of Carthage, and father of Jezebel?

30. With what foreign monarch did Ahab, king of Israel, make a covenant?

31. What king paid tribute to Israel of one hundred thousand lambs and one hundred thousand rams?

32. What heathen monarch sent to inquire of Elisha if he should recover from disease?

33. Who was sent to punish and smite Israel during the reign of Jehu?

34. Whose misfortunes in war are noticed by the prophet Amos?

35. The forbearance of what king did Menahem buy with a thousand talents of silver?

36. Who sacrificed his eldest son in a fit of despair?

37. What heathen ruler united with Pekah, king of Israel, to war against Judah?

38. To whom did King Ahaz send for assistance in his war against Israel and Damascus?

39. To what Egyptian monarch did Hoshea send presents?

40. What Assyrian sovereign besieged Samaria and carried captive a portion of the people of Israel?

41. What successful Assyrian warrior is mentioned but once in Scripture?

42. What heathen monarch is compared to a broken reed?

43. What ruler was slain in a temple at Nineveh, while worshipping his god Nisroch?

44. Who is the first King of Babylon mentioned in the Bible?

45. By whom were Zerubbabel and his companions carried into captivity?

46. By what name is Cyaxares, the conqueror of Nineveh, and king of Persia, known in the Scriptures?

47. What sovereign slew one king of Judah and carried another captive to Egypt?

48. Who was the greatest of the Babylonian kings?

49. What Egyptian monarch did Jeremiah prophesy should be destroyed by his enemies?

50. What compassionate monarch released Jehoiachin from an imprisonment which had lasted thirty-seven years?

51. Who was the last king of Babylon?

52. What king signed the decree through which Daniel was cast into the lions' den?

53. What heathen king issued an edict for the rebuilding of the temple?

54. What son of Cyrus the Great is named in the Bible?

55. Who was induced by the adversaries of Judah and Benjamin to obstruct the building of the temple?

56. What Persian monarch issued a decree threatening destruction upon those who should hinder the rebuilding of the temple?

57. What Gentile king by repentance averted the destruction of a city?

58. What great Persian monarch married a Hebrew maiden?

59. What Persian king allowed his favorite servant to spend twelve years at Jerusalem settling the affairs of that colony?

60. Of what four prominent heathen monarchs did Daniel utter a prophecy, afterwards fulfilled?

61. Who was emperor of Rome at the time of the birth of Christ?

62. Who slew all the children in Bethlehem, seeking to destroy the infant Jesus?

63. During the reign of what Roman emperor did John the Baptist commence preaching in the wilderness?

64. The fear of what ruler caused Joseph to turn aside from Judea into Galilee?

65. Who beheaded John the Baptist?

66. What was the name of the brother whose wife Herod Antipas unlawfully married?

67. Who was more ambitious for political success than for aught else in life?

68. Who built the city of Cesarea?

69. During whose reign did Agabus prophesy there should be a world-wide famine?

70. Who slew James, the disciple of our Lord, with a sword?

71. What ruler sought Paul and Barnabas and desired to hear the word of the Lord?

72. What Roman ruler refused to listen to the reports of the Jews against Paul?

73. Who kept Paul in bondage, hoping to receive money for his release?

74. By whose commandment was Paul brought before King Agrippa?

75. Who said, "Almost thou persuadest me to be a Christian"?

76. During the reign of what emperor is it believed Paul was put to death?

CHAPTER XIV.

THE APOSTLES.

[Answered page 233.]

1. To which of his apostles, upon their first meeting, did Christ give a new name?
2. On the occasion of the five thousand wanting nourishment, which apostle pointed out the lad with the barley loaves and fishes?
3. Who was the first apostolic martyr?
4. Who alone of the apostles is believed to have escaped martyrdom?
5. Who said, "Lord, show us the Father, and it sufficeth us"?
6. Whom does tradition say labored in Armenia, was there flayed, and then crucified with his head downward?
7. What loving apostle was subject to despondency?
8. What apostolic evangelist does not omit the title of infamy which belonged to him before his conversion?
9. Which apostle was bishop of the Church at Jerusalem?
10. Which apostle is mentioned only in connection with the last conversation our Lord had with his disciples?
11. Of which of the apostles do we know nothing except that he belonged to the faction of zealots?
12. Which of the apostles proved unworthy of his high calling?
13. Who was elected to take the place of the traitor Judas?
14. Who called himself the least of the apostles?

CHAPTER XV.

SOME OF THE UNTITLED MEN OF THE BIBLE.

[Answered page 234.]

1. What was his name who was steward of Abraham's house?
2. What was Moses' father's name?
3. Who was the father-in-law of Moses?
4. Who, in company with Aaron, held up the hands of Moses during the progress of the battle with Amalek at Rephidim?
5. What two sons of Aaron were struck dead for kindling the incense in their censors with strange fire?
6. What three men with their companies perished by an earthquake, and flames of fire, as a punishment for rebellion?
7. Who that joined in the rebellion of Korah probably repented and was saved, according to tradition, by following the advice of his wife?
8. What were the names of the ten spies Moses sent to search the land of Canaan?
9. Which of the ten spies sent to search the land of Canaan brought back an honest report?
10. Who was the cause of the defeat of the Israelites at Ai?
11. What enemy of Israel was slain by a woman?
12. What Israelite was driven by famine to Moab, and died there?
13. What distinguished Israelite married a beautiful woman who was renowned as a devoted daughter-in-law?
14. Who was the grandfather of David?

15. What was David's father's name?
16. What two young men are called "sons of Belial"?
17. Who was the father of the first king of Israel?
18. Who was David's most faithful friend?
19. Whom did David slay when he was but a lad?
20. Which of David's brothers chided the youth for proposing to slay the giant Goliath?
21. What servant of Saul slew eighty priests in one day?
22. Who, that had been commander-in-chief of Saul's army, was mourned, when dead, by David?
23. What drunkard was married to a woman as beautiful and wise as he was the reverse?
24. To what son of Jonathan did David show kindness after his father's death?
25. Who that had been a servant and obtained his freedom was afterward reduced to slavery?
26. Who was smitten with death for roughly and hastily handling the Ark?
27. In whose house did the Ark of God rest for three months?
28. Whom did David murder that he might have Bathsheba for his wife?
29. From whom did David purchase the site of Solomon's temple?
30. What brother of Solomon is named in the genealogy of Christ?
31. What Syrian captain came to a Hebrew prophet to be cured of a loathsome disease?
32. Who was smitten with an incurable disease for lying?
33. Who lost his eldest and his youngest son as a punishment for rebuilding the walls of Jericho?
34. Who owned a vineyard which Ahab coveted and Jezebel secured to him?

35. What false prophet prophesied in the reign of Hezekiah?

36. What four men put Jeremiah in a dry well?

37. What Egyptian eunuch rescued Jeremiah from the dungeon?

38. What general did Nebuchadnezzar send to destroy Jerusalem?

39. Who was the adopted father of Queen Esther?

40. What enemy of the Jews suffered a punishment which he had planned for another?

41. Who opposed Nehemiah in his efforts to rebuild Jerusalem?

42. Who was the father of John the Baptist?

43. What devout Jew met Joseph and Mary in the temple, took Jesus in his arms, and gave thanks?

44. Who fled by night with his wife and child to a strange country?

45. What member of the Jewish Sanhedrim came by night to learn of Jesus?

46. What Jewish tax collector, when converted, restored four times as much as he had unlawfully taken?

47. Whom did Christ raise from the grave?

48. What notorious criminal did the multitude demand that Pilate should release instead of Christ?

49. Who begged the privilege of consigning to his own new tomb, the body of his crucified Lord?

50. What two men beside Annas and Caiaphas endeavored to intimidate Peter and John?

51. Whose deception cost him his life?

52. What preceptor of St. Paul's gave prudent advice in the Sanhedrim respecting the treatment of the apostles?

53. What insurgent was slain, and his four hundred followers scattered and brought to naught?

54. What insurgent beside Theudas does Gamaliel mention in his speech before the Jewish council?

55. Which of the seven deacons, soon after he was chosen, met a violent death?

56. Which one of the seven deacons baptized a member of the royal family of Ethiopia?

57. Of which of the seven deacons is there a tradition that he was consecrated Bishop of Nicomedia by Peter?

58. Of whom does tradition say that he suffered martyrdom with Stephen?

59. Of whom is it said, he became Bishop of Bostra where he suffered martyrdom by fire?

60. Which of the seven deacons is believed to have suffered martyrdom at Philippi, in the reign of Trajan?

61. Who was a native of Antioch and a proselyte to the Jewish faith?

62. Who desired to purchase the power of the Holy Ghost that he might use it in the prosecution of magical arts?

63. Who sought Saul during the period of blindness and dejection which followed his conversion?

64. Who introduced Saul to the apostles?

65. What Roman centurion was the first Gentile convert baptized by Peter?

66. Who was struck with blindness for attempting to dissuade a proconsul from embracing Christianity?

67. What evangelist did Barnabas choose to accompany him after his separation from Paul?

68. Who was Paul's companion on his second missionary journey?

69. Whom does Paul call his beloved son in the Lord?

70. Who was attacked by a Jewish mob for entertaining Paul and Silas?

71. What eminent Athenian was converted to Christianity by the preaching of St. Paul?

72. With whom did Paul abide at Corinth, engaging in his occupation of tent-maker?

73. In the house of what godly man was Paul when the Lord appeared to him in a vision?

74. What ruler of the Jewish synagogue in Corinth was baptized by Paul?

75. What maker of silver shrines, fearful for his trade, raised a tumult against Paul?

76. What fellow-traveller of Paul's voluntarily shared his exile and captivity?

77. To whom does Luke inscribe his Gospel and the Acts of the Apostles?

78. Whom did Paul restore to life at Troas?

79. Who wrote a letter which is to us an official Roman testimony to the integrity of Paul's character?

80. Who falsely accused Paul of sedition?

81. Who received and lodged Paul and his companions when shipwrecked on the island of Melita?

82. What fellow-laborer of Paul's was distinguished for his eloquence, and knowledge of the Scriptures?

83. In behalf of what fugitive slave did Paul write his letter to Philemon?

84. Whom does Paul gratefully mention as being courageous and generous when those from whom he had expected better things deserted him?

85. Who was Paul's amanuensis when he wrote his letter to the Romans?

CHAPTER XVI.

THE WOMEN OF THE OLD TESTAMENT.

[Answered page 238.]

1. Name the four women mentioned before the flood?
2. Which four women entered the Ark?
3. Who is the only woman whose age is recorded in the Old Testament; and by what other names is she known?
4. What was the name of Nahor's wife?
5. What concubine of Nahor's is mentioned?
6. What exiled mother laid her son under a shrub and left him to die?
7. What wife had Abraham beside Hagar?
8. Who became a monument of her own folly?
9. What two women were a reproach to their father?
10. Who was "weary of life," being fearful that her son would marry an idolatrous wife?
11. Who accompanied Rebekah to her bridal home, and where was she afterward buried?
12. Name the three wives of Esau?
13. What woman was less beloved than her sister?
14. What beloved wife was a thief?
15. What two women beside Leah and Rachel were mothers of the children of Israel?
16. Who was the sister of the children of Jacob?
17. Who was the mother of the Amalekites?
18. Who was the wife of the last king of Edom, and what was her mother's name?
19. Who was the daughter-in-law of Judah?

20. What was the name of Asher's daughter?
21. What women are mentioned among the descendants of Judah?
22. Who falsely accused an innocent man?
23. Who is the only woman mentioned among the seventy members of Jacob's family who went down into Egypt?
24. What women are mentioned in the genealogy of Manasseh?
25. What daughter of Ephraim founded two cities?
26. What descendants of Benjamin are mentioned?
27. What was the name of Joseph's wife?
28. Who tempted her husband to renounce his allegiance to God?
29. What three sisters were remarkable for their beauty?
30. Who feared God rather than their king?
31. Mention the woman's name who gave her son to the care of a princess?
32. What princess adopted a Hebrew child?
33. What prophetess played on a musical instrument?
34. What was the name of Moses' wife?
35. What was the name of Aaron's wife?
36. What five orphan girls appealed to Moses to make a law in favor of women's rights?
37. What daughter of a Midianitish prince was slain by Phinehas?
38. What woman's beneficence saved her life?
39. Mention the name of Caleb's wife and those of his concubines?
40. Who was a gift to a warrior for his valor?
41. What prophetess dwelt under a palm-tree?
42. What woman's courage saved Israel from a fierce foe?
43. Who looked out of a window and cried for her son's return from battle?

44. Who slew a judge of Israel with a stone?
45. Who was sacrificed in fulfilment of a father's vow?
46. To whom did an angel announce the birth of a deliverer for Israel?
47. What woman's curiosity was a strong man's curse?
48. What woman's conduct is suggestive of one evil of polygamy?
49. Who brought her little son a coat once a year?
50. What gift came to a woman because she devoted her son to the service of the Lord?
51. What mother encouraged her son in idolatry?
52. What woman was cut in twelve pieces?
53. Who was a model mother-in-law?
54. Mention a Moabitess who married into the tribe of Judah?
55. Who was the sister-in-law of Ruth?
56. Who named her child Ichabod because she thought in her grief the glory had departed from Israel?
57. What was the name of Saul's wife?
58. What woman had a familiar spirit?
59. Name Saul's eldest daughter?
60. Which of David's wives suffered for ridiculing him?
61. Which wife of David was obtained through treachery?
62. What two wives of the Psalmist were once taken captive?
63. Who was the mother of Absalom?
64. What three other wives had David?
65. What woman will always be known in Jewish history as the mother of the three leading heroes in David's army?
66. What sister of David married a heathen Ishmaelite?
67. Who was the daughter of David and Maacah?
68. What woman restored Absalom to his father's favor?
69. Which daughter of Absalom was named for her aunt whom he loved?

70. What women did the Psalmist imprison?
71. What colored woman aided the escape of two fugitives?
72. Who saved a besieged city from the wrath of Joab?
73. Who watched in the open air day and night beside the bodies of her dead?
74. What young girl ministered to David in his extreme age?
75. Who was Solomon's first wife?
76. Who came to Solomon for the settlement of an important dispute?
77. What daughters of Solomon are mentioned by name?
78. What was the name of the wife of that Pharaoh who lived in Solomon's time?
79. Who came from afar to test the wisdom of a great king?
80. What king's wife went disguised to a prophet to inquire about her sick son?
81. Name a woman whose son was stoned to death for blasphemy?
82. What was Jeroboam's mother's name?
83. What was Rehoboam's mother's name?
84. What granddaughter of David became the wife of Rehoboam?
85. What granddaughter of Jesse became the wife of Rehoboam?
86. Mention another wife of Rehoboam who was mother to King Ahijah?
87. Which of Rehoboam's eighteen wives was his favorite?
88. What queen was removed from her high position by her son because of her idolatry?

89. What woman hid the child-heir to the throne of Judah for six years?

90. Who justly deserves the title of "the wickedest woman of Scripture"?

91. What woman's generosity saved her household from famine?

92. Who was indebted to a prophet for means to pay her debts?

93. What woman's generosity resulted in an unexpected blessing?

94. Who was instrumental in the restoration of her master to health?

95. Who was the mistress of a captive Israelite maiden?

96. What woman murdered her grandchildren and usurped the throne of Judah?

97. What was her name whose son was the fourth king who reigned forty years in Jerusalem?

98. What was her name whose royal son was a leper?

99. What was the name of Amaziah's mother?

100. What was Jotham's mother's name?

101. What was her name whose son's life was prolonged fifteen years?

102. What was the name of the prophet Hosea's wife?

103. What name did the Lord give the daughter of a prophet in token of the utterly ruined condition of Israel?

104. What was her name whose son filled Jerusalem with innocent blood?

105. What was her name whose son reigned but two years in Jerusalem?

106. Mention the queen-mother whose son was eight years of age when he began to reign?

107. What prophetess foretold the evil which should come upon Judah?

108. What was Jehoiakim's mother's name?

109. What was her name whose son was taken captive by Nebuchadnezzar?

110. What was her name whose son was appointed to be king instead of Jehoiachin?

111. What daughter of Pharaoh became the wife of the Israelite Mered?

112. What woman died whose husband the Lord commanded not to weep for her?

113. Who incurred her husband's fierce anger rather than sacrifice her honor?

114 Who jeoparded her life to save her nation?

115. What woman suggested a mode of death for her husband's enemy?

116. What woman assisted in repairing the walls of Jerusalem?

117. What false prophetess endeavored to intimidate Nehemiah when he was rebuilding the walls of Jerusalem?

118. Mention the name of the daughter of Zerubbabel?

CHAPTER XVII.

THE WOMEN OF THE NEW TESTAMENT.

[Answered page 243.]

1. What woman is said to have been righteous before God?
2. Who is the only woman whose age is recorded in the New Testament?
3. Who fled by night into a strange country to avoid persecution?
4. Who was the first person healed by Christ?
5. To what woman did Christ reveal himself at Jacob's well?
6. What young girl did Christ raise from the dead?
7. For whose sake did Herod imprison John the Baptist?
8. Upon whom did Christ have compassion as she walked by the bier of her son?
9. What sinful woman anointed Christ with alabaster ointment?
10. What young girl asked a strange gift of her uncle?
11. To whom did Christ say, "It is not meet to take the children's bread and cast it to the dogs"?
12. What member of Herod Antipas' household ministered unto our Lord?
13. What woman's name is mentioned once only, and in connection with her ministry to Christ?
14. Who requested seats of honor in the kingdom of heaven for her two sons?
15. Who complained to the Lord concerning her relative?
16. Whose piety did Christ commend?
17. Whose generosity did Christ mention with approbation?
18. Who was the only one who raised a voice against the crucifixion of Christ?

19. What sister of Jesus' mother was at His sepulchre?
20. To whom did Christ first appear, after his resurrection?
21. Who was severely punished for sin as a warning to the early Christian Church?
22. What queen of Egypt is mentioned in the New Testament?
23. Whom did Peter raise from the dead?
24. In whose home were the early Christians accustomed to meet for prayer?
25. To whom was it affirmed "Thou art mad"?
26. Who was the first Christian convert in Europe?
27. What Athenian woman was converted to Christianity through the influence of Paul?
28. What woman would willingly have sacrificed her life for Paul?
29. What four women prophesied?
30. Mention the wife of him who trembled before Paul?
31. What daughter of Herod Agrippa is mentioned in the Acts?
32. What woman in Rome labored for Paul?
33. What two Christian women does Paul say labored for the Lord?
34. To what woman did Paul give the title "beloved"?
35. Who was the bearer of Paul's Epistle to the Romans?
36. In what woman did Paul say dwelt unfeigned faith?
37. What was Timothy's mother's name?
38. What false prophetess was a curse to the Church at Thyatira?
39. What Christian woman joins St. Paul in the salutations which he sends to Timothy?
40. What Christian woman communicated to Paul an account of the dissensions at Corinth?

CHAPTER XVIII.

THE CHILDREN AND YOUTH OF THE BIBLE.

[Answered page 245.]

1. What little child was heard and answered by the Lord when crying?

2. For what little child was a great feast made?

3. What youth was hated by his brothers because of his father's favoritism?

4. What young girl watched her infant brother's cradle in the Nile?

5. What child, whose life was in danger, was adopted by a princess and named from the place whence she brought him?

6. What child, deprived of his mother's care, was the recipient of a gift from her once a year?

7. What youth, sent with bread and corn to his brethren, was the means of deciding the fate of a battle?

8. What child died as a punishment for his father's sin?

9. What child was carried into Egypt and thus escaped the massacre of Moab in which his father perished?

10. What child did Elijah raise from the dead?

11. What child was raised to life by Elisha?

12. Who was instrumental in the restoration of her master to health?

13. What child-king was on the throne of Judah at seven years of age?

14. What youth was called to the throne of Judah at twelve years of age?

15. What boy was but eight years of age when he came to the throne of Judah?

16. What child-king was carried captive to Babylon before he had reached his ninth year?

17. Who beside Samuel was endowed with the gift of prophecy while yet a youth?

18. What four youths were divinely supported in their resolve to abstain from the king's meat and wine for fear of defilement?

19. At the baptism of what babe was a miracle performed?

20. The birth of what child does Christmas commemorate?

21. What young damsel did Christ raise from the dead?

22. Who, as a child, was familiar with the Scriptures?

THE JEWS' WAILING PLACES.

CHAPTER XIX.

MOUNTAINS OF THE BIBLE.

[Answered page 246.]

1. Where did the ark of Noah rest?
2. From whence came the wood used for Solomon's temple?
3. What mountain was the source of the Abana river?
4. What summit is mentioned only as the northern landmark of the promised land?
5. What mount was probably the scene of the Transfiguration?
6. What mountainous district was allotted to half the tribe of Manasseh?
7. On what summit did Laban overtake Jacob as the latter fled from Padan Aram.
8. What was the name of the ridge and the peak from which Moses saw the promised land?
9. What mount is connected with a battle in which Lot was taken prisoner?
10. Upon what mountain did Aaron die?
11. Name a mountain mentioned only in connection with Joshua's conquest of Canaan.
12. Upon what mountain did the priests and Israel tempt the people to idolatry?
13. By what hill were the Midianites encamped when the Lord delivered them into the hand of Gideon.
14. Upon what mountain was a king of Israel, and his son, slain?

15. What place was memorable as the scene of a test between a prophet of God and false prophets?

16. Concerning what mountain did a prophet pronounce woe upon those who trusted in it?

17. Upon what mount did half the tribes of Israel stand to curse the people who sinned?

18. From what summit was a parable delivered to wicked men?

19. Where did the last ruler of the theocracy judge Israel?

20. What mountain was the scene of the massacre of the priests of Doeg, the Edomite?

21. Where was the site of Solomon's temple?

22. The remembrance of what mount caused the Israelites to weep when in captivity?

23. From what place was the Law delivered to Israel?

24. Where did the angel of the Lord appear to a prophet in a burning bush?

25. What place was the scene of the agony and betrayal of Christ?

26. What mountain is associated with the temptation of Christ?

CHAPTER XX.

THE RIVERS OF THE BIBLE.

[Answered page 247.]

1. What two rivers of Paradise are mentioned but once in the Bible?

2. By the side of what river of Paradise did a vision come to the prophet Daniel?

3. Upon the banks of what river did the prophet Jeremiah conceal a girdle?

4. What river beside the Euphrates is mentioned in connection with God's covenant with Abraham?

5. Near the ford of what stream did a patriarch wrestle with an angel?

6. What river is memorable as a meeting place of a prophet of the Midianites and a king of the Moabites?

7. What name was given to a brook because of the rich fruit in its vicinity?

8. What brook was the starting-point for Israel's conquest of Canaan?

9. What brook was the boundary line between Ephraim and Manesseh?

10. What brook did David cross with four hundred armed men?

11. Beside what brook did a king of Israel burn his mother's idol?

12. By what brook were the prophets of Baal slain?

13. By what brook was a prophet told to go and hide himself?

14. What river did a Syrian captain mention as he asked a question of a prophet of Israel?

15. What river is connected with the captivity of Israel under Pul and Tiglath-pileser?

16. By what river had the prophet Ezekiel several visions?

17. Which river occupies the most prominent place in Bible history?

CHAPTER XXI.

SEAS OF THE BIBLE.

[Answered page 248.]

1. What body of water proved a blessing to one people and a curse to another?

2. What waters were the scene of a defeat, by Joshua, of the confederate chiefs of North and East Canaan?

3. On the border of what sea were the cities of the plain?

4. What sea is mentioned only by Jeremiah?

5. What five names are given to the sea upon whose shores most of our Lord's life was passed?

6. What sea did Paul cross on his journey from Troas to Neapolis?

7. What sea did he traverse in his journey to Rome?

CHAPTER XXII.

THE PROMINENT CITIES OF THE BIBLE.

[Answered page 249.]

1. What city of Syria, now in existence, was cotemporary with Sodom and Gomorrah?
2. What was the name of the city whose walls and hanging gardens were one of the seven wonders of the world?
3. In what heathen city was Jonah reproved by the type of the gourd?
4. What prominent ancient city was destroyed with three others, because of the wickedness of its inhabitants?
5. Which city of the plain was spared to afford shelter for Lot?
6. What city, now in existence, was the scene of some of the most remarkable events in the lives of the patriarchs?
7. What place, the abode of many of the patriarchs, was the most southern landmark of Palestine?
8. In what city did the Israelites bury Joseph?
9. After crossing the Jordan, what was the first city taken by the Israelites?
10. At what place did the Israelites pass the first night after crossing the Jordan?
11. After the conquest of Canaan, where was the Ark kept for above three hundred years?
12. In the troubled times when there was no king in

Israel, to what city did the people go to ask counsel of God?

13. What city was the birth-place of David?

14. In what city was Solomon's temple?

15. What were the names of the cities of refuge?

16. What Philistine city, noted as the seat of the worship of Dagon, was never subdued by the Israelites?

17. The gates of what Philistine city did Samson carry many miles?

18. In what Philistine city did Samson slay thirty men, and take their spoil?

19. To what city of the Philistines did David flee when "he feigned himself mad"?

20. What royal city of the Philistines is notable only as being the last place where the Ark of God rested before it was returned to the Israelites?

21. The men of what city took the bodies of Saul and Jonathan and gave them honorable burial?

22. In what city was the public selection and appointment of the first king of Judah?

23. What city was founded by Omri, king of Israel?

24. What city was the extreme northern landmark of Palestine?

25. What city is meant by "Noph" in Jeremiah ii. 16?

26. What was the chief city of the Ammonites?

27. To what city did Jonah flee when sent by the Lord to warn the people of Nineveh?

28. What village is intimately associated in our minds with the scenes of the last days of Christ?

29. What city was the native place of Andrew, Peter, and Philip?

30. Upon what city beside Bethsaida did Christ pronounce woe?

31. What city did Christ say should have less tolerance in the day of judgment than Sodom?

32. In what place were Christ and His disciples when He asked them, "Whom do men say that I am"?

33. In what city did Jesus spend the first thirty years of His life?

34. In what city were the disciples of Christ first called Christians?

35. In what city were Paul and Barnabas violently persecuted by Jewish men and women?

36. In what city did Paul deliver a memorable discourse on the hill Areopagus?

37. What city was the scene of the Italian centurion's conversion?

38. In what city did Paul become acquainted with Aquila and Priscilla?

39. What city contained the temple which was one of the seven wonders of the world?

40. What celebrated city of Egypt was the birth-place of Paul's co-laborer, Apollos?

41. The inhabitants of what city were commended for their knowledge of the Scriptures?

42. To what city did Paul and Barnabas escape when persecuted at Antioch?

43. In what city was Paul stoned and left for dead?

44. In what city did Peter raise Tabitha to life?

45. Of what city was St. Paul a native?

46. Where was the home of Jason, Paul's friend, who was persecuted for showing kindness to the apostle?

47. What city was the scene of a memorable and touching farewell in the life of Paul?

48. At what city, where Paul landed on his journey to Rome, was he given liberty to visit his friends?

49. What city brings to our remembrance the scene of the most pathetic incident of St. Paul's life?

50. In what place was Paul preaching, on the occasion of the restoration of Eutychus to life?

51. In what city did Paul dwell for two years "in his own hired house"?

CHAPTER XXIII.

THE PLANTS NAMED IN THE SCRIPTURES.

[Answered page 251.]

1. From what tree was the rod which Jeremiah saw in a prophetical vision?

2. Of what material, similar to our sandal-wood, were the pillars of Solomon's temple made?

3. From what tree was the perfume obtained which Nicodemus brought to anoint the body of Jesus?

4. What plant, resembling the dill, does Christ mention in connection with the tithes of the Pharisees?

5. The fruit of what tree is compared to a fitly-spoken word?

6. What grain was gleaned by Ruth in the field of Boaz?

7. What tree does tradition say the Queen of Sheba introduced into Judea by making Solomon a present of its root?

8. What vegetable, familiar to Americans, was carried to David at the time of his flight from Absalom?

9. What other tree besides the fir and pine does Isaiah say furnished wood from Lebanon for the temple?

10. What plant, in the parable of Jotham, is represented as challenging the cedars of Lebanon?

11. What thorny shrub did Micah complain the best of men were like?

12. What plant did Jochebed render famous?

AIDS TO BIBLICAL RESEARCH. 79

13. What plant was once seen to burn, but was not consumed?

14. What plant beside cassia did Ezekiel say was in the markets of Tyre?

15. What plant, offered to God by the Israelites, was not acceptable on account of their sins?

16. What plant beside the myrrh and aloe does the Psalmist mention when prophesying of the majesty and grace of Christ's kingdom?

17. Of what wood was David's house built?

18. What odorous narcotic is mentioned in Solomon's Song, which was probably unknown to the ancients?

19. From what fruit-tree is it said Jacob made him rods?

20. What bark is enumerated in Revelation as among the merchandise of Babylon?

21. What cereal did Boaz give Ruth that she might satisfy her hunger?

22. To what seed was the manna in the wilderness compared?

23. What vegetable was mentioned as being one of the good things of Egypt for which the Israelites longed?

24. What plant, mentioned by Isaiah, does Christ class as one of the crops of which the Scribes and Pharisees paid tithe?

25. What fruit is mentioned only in the margin of our English Bible?

26. What valuable commodity besides ivory was imported into Tyre by the men of Dedan?

27. What fruit was used remedially for boils?

28. Of what wood were the musical instruments of David made?

29. What plant, used in eastern countries as a medicine and a condiment, is mentioned only by Isaiah?

30. What plant "can not grow without water"?

31. What, beside the barley of the Egyptians, was damaged by the plague of hail?

32. What Egyptian plant is mentioned among cucumbers, melons, leeks, and onions, as one, the loss of which was regretted by the mixed multitude at Taberah?

33. Of what wood was Noah's ark made?

34. What plant afforded shade to a sun-stricken prophet?

35. What fruit were the Israelites commanded not to glean, but leave for the poor and the stranger?

36. What herbage is an image of the fleeting nature of human fortunes, and the brevity of human life?

37. With what bitter and poisonous plant is judgment compared?

38. What fruit was a starving wanderer tempted to use to satisfy his hunger?

39. What plant was used to sprinkle the door-steps of the Israelites in Egypt with the blood of the Paschal Lamb?

40. Under what tree was Elijah sitting when he prayed that he might die?

41. What vegetable, mentioned but once in the Bible, was among the good things for which the Israelites longed in their journey through the wilderness?

42. Of what plant was the pottage made which Jacob sold to Esau?

43. To what flower are the gorgeous robes of Solomon compared?

44. What fruit did Reuben present to his mother?

45. What bush does Job say was cut up and used for meat in time of famine?

46. The remembrance of what fruit caused the Israelites to weep?

47. The fruit of what plant, mentioned but once, was used for bread in time of famine?

48. What fragrant herb was mentioned among those, the tithe of which the Jews were most scrupulously exact in paying?

49. To the seed of what tree did Christ compare the kingdom of heaven?

50. What tree gave a signal to a warrior when to go into battle?

51. The product of what plant was among the gifts brought by the wise men to the infant Jesus?

52. With what plant do the Jews still adorn the booths at the Feast of the Tabernacles?

53. From what plant was distilled the aromatic ointment with which Christ was anointed in Simon's house in Bethany?

54. What thorny plant does Job mention when he complains of the contempt in which he was held by the lowest people?

55. Where is the fruit of the Pistachio tree referred to in the Bible?

56. Of what material did the Tyrians make their oars?

57. To the branches of what tree are the children of the righteous man compared?

58. What favorite article of food among the Egyptians was one of the good things whose loss the Israelites regretted?

59. The branches of what tree were strewn in Christ's pathway at his triumphant entry into Jerusalem?

60. What branches beside the olive and the myrtle were the Israelites commanded to use in constructing their booths at the Feast of the Tabernacles?

61. Representations of what fruit ornamented the priest's ephod?

62. What tree is coupled with the hazel and chestnut as one of those from which Jacob cut rods?

63. Like what broken plant were the Egyptians, in their inability to aid Hezekiah against the Assyrians?

64. What flower is connected with Isaiah's prophecy of the joyful flourishing of Christ's kingdom?

65. What garden plant besides mint was tithable in the time of Christ?

66. What plant, mentioned only by Solomon, was highly esteemed as a perfume?

67. Of what wood were the boards that formed the tabernacle?

68. One of the heaviest of Egypt's calamities was the destruction of what tree?

69. To what plant did Christ compare the wicked, especially hypocrites?

70. The destruction of the wicked shall be like the burning of what plant?

71. The fruit of what tree were our first parents forbidden to eat?

72. Adam was driven from Paradise lest he should eat of the fruit of what tree?

73. What cereal is first mentioned in the account of Jacob's sojourn with Laban in Mesopotamia?

74. What tree is mentioned in the psalm which represents Israel's sorrow during the Babylonian captivity?

75. What plant is symbolical of bitter calamity and sorrow?

CHAPTER XXIV.

THE MINERALS OF THE BIBLE.

[Answered page 254.]

1. What stone occupied the first place in the first row of the high-priest's breast-plate?

2. What ancient gem, allowed to be our chrysolite, was one of the jewels that adorned the apparel of the king of Tyre?

3. What jewel is mentioned by Isaiah as embellishing the gates of the New Jerusalem?

4. To what precious stone is the rainbow around the heavenly throne compared?

5. What bright blue stone is represented as ornamenting the pavement where the Lord was seen in a vision by the Elders of Israel?

6. What stone, which was the third in the second row on the high-priest's breast-plate, is mentioned among the gems of the King of Tyre?

7. What stone, unknown in modern mineralogy, is mentioned only in connection with the high-priest's breast-plate?

8. What was the second stone in the third row of the high-priest's breast-plate?

9. What was the twelfth stone which garnished the foundations of the wall of the heavenly temple?

10. Like what gem was the man which David saw in a vision?

11. What precious stone is mentioned in connection with the spot where the garden of Eden was?

12. What precious stone was the emblematical image of the glory of the Divine Being?

13. What jewel is mentioned by Paul in his exhortation to women concerning their personal adornment?

14. What stone is mentioned only in connection with the foundation of the heavenly Jerusalem?

15. What stone garnished the fifth foundation of the heavenly Jerusalem?

16. What stone, at present found in Silesia, is only mentioned in connection with St. John's vision?

17. What stone, forming one of the foundations of the walls of the New Jerusalem, was identical with the ligure?

18. Than what gem is wisdom more precious?

19. What valuable article is enumerated among the wares which Syria brought to the markets of Tyre?

20. To what is the river of the water of life compared?

21. What mineral is used to signify the firmness with which Ezekiel should resist the sin of the rebellious house of Israel?

22. What was the earliest of known metals?

23. What precious metal is used for an emblem of purity?

24. What mineral was used in sealing?

25. Of what metal were the two vessels which Ezra sent by the priest to the temple at Jerusalem?

26. What mineral, symbolical of hospitality, were the Israelites enjoined to use in their offerings to God?

27. Of what metal was the cup Joseph caused to be placed in the sack of Benjamin?

28. What mineral is used metaphorically to signify the firmness of Isaiah in resisting his persecutors?

29. Of what material was the box, which contained the

ointment brought to our Lord while He sat at meat in Simon's house?

30. What metal was used for plummets?

31. Of what metal were Jewish weights made?

32. The burning of what substance is used to express complete destruction?

CHAPTER XXV.

BEASTS, REPTILES, BIRDS, INSECTS, AND FISHES.

[Answered page 256.]

BEASTS.

1. What animal did Solomon import every three years?
2. The head of what animal sold for eighty pieces of silver in a time of famine?
3. Of what animals' skins were coverings for the tabernacle made?
4. What animal was classed by the ancients among the birds?
5. What beast was an instrument of wrath in a miracle performed by Elijah?
6. Of what amphibious creature did Job assert "He eateth grass as an ox"?
7. What fierce and revengeful beast did David prophetically compare to those nations who should destroy the Jews?
8. What animal were the Chaldeans said to imitate?
9. What did Elijah offer as a sacrifice on Mount Carmel?
10. What animal did Abraham prepare as a feast for angels?
11. What animal carried Rebekah on her journey to meet her future husband?
12. What animal, somewhat resembling the sheep, is given in the list allowed for food?
13. What animal is connected with the prophecy of Christ's entry into Jerusalem?
14. Of what animals does Solomon say "They are but feeble folk, yet they make their houses in the rocks"?

15. What domestic animal, is it prophesied, shall feed with the bear in the millennium?

16. What animal, allowed by the Levitical law for food, was daily provided for Solomon's table?

17. What domestic animal fulfilled a prophecy concerning King Ahab?

18. What animal, beside the mare and the camel, was used to carry the king's decree in the time of Mordecai?

19. What huge animal, undoubtedly known to the ancients, is only mentioned in the margin of the English Bible?

20. What animal, seldom called in Scripture by that name, did Jacob choose two hundred of, as a present to Esau?

21. What treacherous animal is the subject of one of the feats of strength performed by Samson?

22. To what animal did Christ liken wicked men?

23. What animal is only mentioned among those not allowed for food by the Mosaic law?

24. What animal is mentioned in connection with the prophecy of Isaiah that Christ should heal the sick?

25. To what animal is Egypt likened?

26. To what did Jacob compare his son Naphtali?

27. What afforded the means of escape for Benhaded, king of Syria?

28. What animal did Joseph's brethren slay?

29. What animals were prominent in a dream which Joseph interpreted for Pharaoh?

30. To what animal is a wife likened in Scripture?

31. Of what is it said, it is easier to change its spots, than for a wicked man to change his ways?

32. What animal is mentioned in the answer to Solomon's riddle?

33. What small animals were sent as a plague to the Philistines when the Ark was in their country!

34. Upon what animal was Absalom fleeing when he met his death?

35. What animals were represented twelve times in Solomon's brazen sea?

36. To what were the kingdoms of Media and Persia likened?

37. To what was the most fleet-footed man in David's army compared?

38. What animal was typical of Christ's patience, innocence, harmlessness, usefulness, and exposure to trouble and enemies?

39. What animals are connected with a miracle performed by Christ?

40. To what fierce and dangerous beasts are wicked men compared in the Old Testament?

41. What animal is mentioned only in the list of unclean beasts?

42. To what animal did Jacob liken his son Benjamin?

REPTILES.

1. To the sting of what reptile is wine compared?

2. What venomous reptile shall be harmless during the millennium?

3. What reptile, possessing the power of changing its color, is mentioned in the Bible?

4. What other reptile beside the serpent is applied metaphorically to Satan?

5. What was the second of the ten plagues which troubled the Egyptians?

6. What was said to be "more subtle than any beast"?

7. What reptile were the Israelites to consider unclean?

8. The voice of what reptile did Solomon say proclaimed the coming of spring?

BIRDS.

1. What bird did Noah send from the ark, who returned, bearing an olive-leaf?

2. To what song-bird does the Psalmist compare himself when in trouble?

3. To prevent what bird from defiling Herod's temple was the roof thickly set with spikes of gold?

4. What brilliant birds were brought every three years to Solomon?

5. What bird is the symbol of cruelty and forgetfulness?

6. What fowl thrice reminded Peter of his denial of his Master?

7. What domestic fowl does Christ use to illustrate His tender protection?

8. What bird is likened to the covetous person who wrongfully amasses wealth?

9. What fowl was sent in great numbers to the Israelites in the wilderness?

10. Mention the birds which the children of Israel were forbidden to use for food?

11. What other bird beside the stork and the swallow, did Jeremiah say, were more observing than the Israelites?

12. What were the Israelites who could not afford to offer a lamb as a sacrifice, allowed to bring?

13. What bird, was it prophesied, should inhabit Babylon and Nineveh in their desolation?

INSECTS.

1. What insects were the Israelites permitted to use for food?

2. What did Samson find in the carcass of the lion?

3. What did the Lord send before the kings of the Amorites which drove them from the children of Israel?

4. What was the third plague sent to subdue the Egyptians?

5. What was the fourth of the Egyptian plagues?

6. The trust of the wicked is like the work of what insect?

7. What symbolized Rehoboam's promised treatment of the Israelites?

8. From what does Solomon bid us learn wisdom?

9. What worm wasted the land in the time of Joel?

10. Man's glory, beauty, and wealth, consume like what?

11. What insect does David mention in connection with the brevity of the life of the wicked?

FISHES.

1. What, beside the beasts of the earth, and the fowl of the air, did God promise Noah, should fear him?

2. What fish is memorable in connection with a miracle in the life of Jonah?

CHAPTER XXVI.

OFFICES AND SECTS.

[Answered page 260.]

1. What was the official name of the twelve disciples chosen by Jesus?
2. What spiritual overseer in the Church does Paul say should be blameless?
3. What military officer was captain of a hundred men in the Roman army?
4. Who were the officers appointed to care for the poor?
5. What were the members of the Senate and the Sanhedrim called?
6. What sect ascribed all things to chance, and considered pleasure the chief good?
7. What political party complied with heathen practices to propitiate Herod and the Romans?
8. What supreme governors of Israel were appointed by God?
9. What were the Jews or proselytes who were free citizens of Rome called?
10. What was the name of the inferior servants of the priests and Levites, who were appointed to cleave wood and draw water?
11. What idolatrous and immoral sect imputed their wickedness to God as the cause?
12. What was the name originally given to fathers of families?
13. What sect was distinguished by their pretensions to sanctity and scrupulous observance of the ceremonial law?

14. Who were appointed by God to offer up sacrifices and intercessions for the guilty?

15. What officer, as representative of the emperor, had the power of life and death over his subjects?

16. What title was given to those officers who were appointed over Roman senatorial provinces annually, by lot?

17. Who were inspired by God to declare His will and foretell future events?

18. What were those people called who were uncircumcised and kept no ceremonial law, but worshipped the true God?

19. What name was given to the Gentiles converted to Judaism?

20. Who were collectors of the Roman tribute?

21. Who celebrated marriages, declared divorce, had the highest seat in the synagogue, and was held in great respect and authority?

22. What Jewish sect denied the immortality of the soul, and pretended that the angels mentioned in the Scriptures were illusions?

23. When Shalmanezer carried the ten tribes captive he brought numbers of his own people to inhabit the Israelite cities, what were their descendants called?

24. Who were the doctors of the law and the transcribers of the sacred books?

25. Who were employed in the king's court to register the affairs of the state?

26. Who enrolled and reviewed the army?

27. What sect believed all things were ordered by fate, and that wisdom alone rendered men happy?

28. What Roman ruler had kingly power over four provinces?

29. What was the name of the governor appointed by the kings of Assyria or Persia?

CHAPTER XXVII.

THE OLD TESTAMENT MIRACLES.

[Answered page 262.]

1. What was the first miracle?
2. What was the first miracle sent as a chastisement for sin?
3. What miracle was a protection to a patriarch in a strange country?
4. What Old Testament miracle is mentioned in the Epistle to the Hebrews?
5. What nearly destroyed the human race?
6. What was the token of the covenant God made with Noah?
7. What led to the dispersion?
8. What miracle was associated with the covenant God made with the "Father of the Faithful"?
9. What was the first miracle in the life of Hagar?
10. Relate the miraculous incident connected with God's promise to Abraham and Sarah that they should have a son?
11. Mention a proof of God's care for Lot.
12. The men of what city were smitten with blindness?
13. What four cities were destroyed?
14. What woman was severely punished for disobedience?
15. What gift to an aged patriarch and his wife was a miracle?
16. Through what miracle was the life of a little child saved?

17. Through what miracle was a young man delivered from a violent death?

18. What supernatural incident occurred in the life of Rebekah?

19. What miracle is related in connection with Jehovah's promise to Jacob?

20. What miraculous incident is narrated in Jacob's life after he left Laban before his meeting with Esau?

21. What miracle occurs in Jacob's life just after his meeting with Esau?

22. What supernatural incidents are related in Joseph's early life?

23. Through what miracle did Joseph hope to escape from prison?

24. What was the means of the exaltation of a patriarch to the second position in the kingdom?

25. What was the last miracle in the life of Jacob?

26. Mention the first miracle recorded in the life of Moses?

27. What extraordinary transformation is connected with the rod of Moses?

28. What miracle in Moses' life would the word "hand" bring to your remembrance?

29. To what reptile was Aaron's rod changed?

30. What testified the power of Aaron's God over the magicians of Egypt?

31. Mention the ten plagues in their order?

32. What protected the Israelites from the burning sun by day, and gave them light at night?

33. By what miracle were the Israelites enabled to escape from the pursuit of Pharaoh?

34. What bitter waters were sweetened?

35. What animal food was miraculously sent to the Israelites?

36. What miracle confirmed the commandment concerning the Sabbath?

37. From what place were the Israelites first miraculously supplied with water?

38. What supernatural event transpired at the battle of Rephidim?

39. What miracles accompanied the giving of the Law?

40. How many of the people fell through the setting up of the golden calf?

41. What Bible author lived forty days without eating or drinking?

42. What kept Moses from entering the tabernacle directly after it was finished?

43. From whence did fire originally come which was kept perpetually burning on the golden altar?

44. Who were consumed for offering strange fire?

45. What punishment was sent to the people of Israel for complaining?

46. How was the cry of the Israelites for meat answered?

47. What affliction followed the answered prayer of the Israelites for meat?

48. What woman was smitten with, and afterward healed of, a loathsome disease?

49. What became of the ten spies who brought back an untrue report of the land of Caanan?

50. What punishment was sent to Korah, Dothan, and Abiram?

51. How many were consumed by fire for offering incense?

52. What affliction was sent to the Israelites for murmuring because many were slain for offering incense?

53. What dead branch budded, blossomed, and bore fruit in a single night?

54. What miracle was a gift to the people at the Desert of Sin?

55. What was sent to Israel as a chastisement for murmuring as they journeyed from Mt. Hor to the land of Edom?

56. What article of brass was an instrument of healing?

57. What animal spoke words of reproof to a prophet?

58. How many of the Israelites were destroyed at Shittim by a plague?

59. Relate the miracle pertaining to the clothing of the Israelites?

60. What was the first miracle in the life of Joshua?

61. The walls of what city fell at a blast of rams' horns?

62. Whose covetousness was miraculously exposed?

63. What miracle occurred at Azekah?

64. What astronomical phenomenon occurred in the life of Joshua?

65. Who slew six hundred Philistines with an ox-goad?

66. Whose sacrifice did fire from a rock consume?

67. What miracle was a proof of God's patience with Gideon's lack of faith?

68. What significance was there in three-hundred men lapping water?

69. What dream strengthened Gideon in his purpose to fight the hosts of Midian with a small band of men?

70. With what strange weapons did Gideon defeat the Midianites?

71. To what man and his wife of the tribe of Dan did an angel appear?

72. What gift to Manoah and his wife was a miracle?

73. What distinguished Samson from every other member of the human family?

74. Mention in chronological order the miracles connected with the strength of Samson?

75. State a miracle in the life of Samson which was in no way associated with his strength?

76. What was granted to Hannah in answer to her fervent prayer?

77. Mention a supernatural incident in Samuel's childhood?

78. Mention an accident connected with a heathen god?

79. In what three cities were many Philistines destroyed for having the Ark of God in their possession?

80. What disease afflicted the Philistines in consequence of their retaining the Ark of God?

81. For what were the men of Bethshemeth smitten?

82. What caused a panic in the army of the Philistines?

83. What punishment was sent to Israel because they asked a king?

84. What miracle resulted in confounding a woman and condemning a king of Israel?

85. What warned David when to attack his enemies?

86. Who was stricken dead for steadying the Ark?

87. What was the largest number ever destroyed by a plague?

88. What was the first miracle in the life of Solomon?

89. What miracle is associated with the dedication of Solomon's temple?

90. The hand of what king of Israel withered as he tried to injure a man of God?

91. How was a lion an instrument of God's wrath?

92. What affliction came to Jehoram, king of Judah?

93. What king of Israel was stricken with leprosy?

94. For how long a time was rain withheld from Israel during the reign of Ahab?

95. How was Elijah fed morning and evening by the brook Cherith?

96. What was the first instance of the multiplication of food?

97. Whom did Elijah raise from the dead?

98. When did fire from heaven prove God's omnipotence?

99. Who brought water from the clouds?

100. How was Elijah provided with food in the wilderness?

101. For how many days was Elijah sustained by food miraculously supplied?

102. Relate the miracles before the presence of the Lord when he reproved Elijah.

103. Who were consumed by fire from heaven at the command of Elijah?

104. What miracle in the life of Elijah is connected with the river Jordan?

105. What was the last miracle in the life of Elijah?

106. What is the first miracle recorded in the life of Elisha?

107. With what were the waters of Jericho healed?

108. Of what miracle of wrath would forty-two remind you?

109. How was Jehoshaphat's army supplied with water?

110. How was a woman furnished with means to pay her debts?

111. What was given to a woman for her kindness to a prophet?

112. Who was raised from the dead in answer to Elisha's prayer?

113. By what means was poisoned food changed to healthful?

114. How many men were fed with twenty loaves?

115. On what occasion was the river Jordan used to restore to health?

116. Who was stricken with leprosy for theft and lying?

117. At whose command did iron swim?

118. How was the king of Israel saved from the wrath of the Syrian king?

119. To whom was spiritual perception supernaturally imparted?

120. What army was smitten with blindness?

121. What miracle occurred at the sepulchre of Elisha?

122. How was Jonah saved when thrown into the sea?

123. By what type did the Lord reprove Jonah?

124. How was Sennacherib's army destroyed?

125. Whose life was prolonged fifteen years?

126. What sign was given to a king of Judah that his prayer for lengthened life was answered?

127. What two men did the Lord hide from their enemies?

128. Who were delivered from the burning fiery furnace?

129. What king was smitten with insanity?

130. Whose feast was interrupted by the handwriting on the wall?

131. Who was saved from the lions?

CHAPTER XXVIII.

THE NEW TESTAMENT MIRACLES.

[Answered page 269.]

1. What is the first miracle recorded in the New Testament?
2. What token was granted to Zacharias that his prayer was heard?
3. What miracle was a preparation for Christ's coming?
4. What miracle in the life of a woman was God's best gift to the human race?
5. By what were the wise men guided to the infant Saviour?
6. How were the wise men prevented from returning to Herod?
7. What miracle would shepherds bring to your remembrance?
8. What warning had Joseph to flee into Egypt?
9. Who informed Joseph of Herod's death?
10. As Christ commenced His ministry by what miracle did God publicly acknowledge Him?
11. For how many days and nights did Jesus fast?
12. What was the first miracle performed by Christ?
13. Which of Christ's miracles was wrought in righteous anger?
14. Who was healed of disease in Cana of Galilee?
15. Of what disease was one at Capernaum healed who was let down through a roof?

16. What was the first miracle performed by Christ, apparently solely for His own benefit?

17. What relative of Peter's did Christ heal?

18. What followed?

19. What miracle is connected with the call of Peter, James, and John?

20. To whom did Christ say, "Go show thyself to the priest"?

21. Whose sins did Christ forgive before healing his body?

22. At what pool did Christ heal a man who had an infirmity for thirty-eight years?

23. What was the first miracle wrought on the Sabbath day?

24. Of what miracle would centurion remind you?

25. What miracle was wrought in Nain?

26. What miracle led the Pharisees to assert that Christ cast out devils by Beelzebub?

27. What miracle occurred on the sea of Galilee?

28. What miracle was partly one of mercy and partly one of wrath?

29. What resulted from a woman's touching Christ's garment?

30. Who was the first restored to life by Jesus?

31. What happened to two blind men who followed Jesus?

32. What miracle immediately followed the healing of the blind men?

33. What objective miracle do the four Evangelists record?

34. What miracle did Peter endeavor to imitate?

35. In what land were many healed by just touching the hem of Christ's garment?

36. Whose daughter was healed of an unclean spirit?

37. Which miracle was wrought by the utterance of a single word?

38. Which passage fulfils Isaiah's prophecy?

39. How many did Christ miraculously feed the second time?

40. What was the only miracle wrought at Bethsaida?

41. What miracle was witnessed by Peter, James, and John only?

42. What did Christ do which His disciples had failed to do?

43. What miracle proved Christ's allegiance to the Roman government?

44. How did Jesus prevent the angry Jews from injuring Him, when blaspheming they sought to stone Him?

45. Whom did Christ send to wash in the pool of Siloam?

46. How did Jesus prevent His premature arrest?

47. Relate a miracle which corroborates the doctrine of the Resurrection?

48. How did Christ relieve a blind man from other misery than blindness?

49. Of what miracle would eighteen remind you?

50. Whom did Christ heal in a Pharisee's house on the Sabbath day?

51. Of what disease were ten men healed?

52. Give the name of the beggar Christ healed.

53. What miracle occurred near Jericho?

54. What was Christ's one miracle of wrath?

55. By what miracle did Jesus teach a lesson of forgiveness?

56. What miracle was wrought in the temple at Christ's death?

57. What attended the earthquake sent at Christ's death?

58. What miracle does Easter Sunday commemorate?

59. What miracle caused Christ's disciples to fear?

60. What miracle occurred near the sea of Galilee after Christ's resurrection?

61. To how many of His disciples did Christ, on the day of

His ascension, offer ocular and tangible demonstration of the reality of His resurrection?

62. What is the last miracle in the life of Christ?

63. What gift did Christ send after His resurrection to the disciples and the world?

64. What miracle was wrought at the Beautiful Gate of the temple?

65. Who were punished with death for falsehood?

66. In what city did the shadow of Peter heal the sick?

67. By whom were Peter and John rescued from prison?

68. By which of the deacons were miracles wrought?

69. What miracle is associated with Philip?

70. What was the first miracle in the life of Paul?

71. Whom did Peter heal of the palsy, and in what place?

72. Who was restored to life by Peter?

73. What miracle was an answer to petitions offered at a prayer meeting?

74. What tetrarch was smitten with disease and death?

75. What sorcerer was smitten with blindness?

76. What led the people of Lystra to worship Paul and Barnabas as heathen gods?

77. For what were Paul and Silas imprisoned?

78. How were Paul and Silas liberated from prison?

79. In what city did Paul communicate the Holy Ghost to twelve?

80. How was healing power transmitted?

81. Whom did Paul restore to life?

82. What led the people of Melita to believe Paul to be a god?

83. Whose father did Paul heal of a long standing disease?

84. How did Paul requite the kindness of the people on the island where he was shipwrecked?

CHAPTER XXIX.

THE PARABLES OF CHRIST.

[Answered page 273.]

1. In what parable did our Saviour describe the different classes of hearers of the gospel?

2. Which parable teaches that ministers should not rashly expel offenders from the Christian Church?

3. What parable illustrates the growth of religion in the soul?

4. Which parable is a representation of the progress of the gospel in the world?

5. What parable was prophetic of the spread of the gospel among all the nations of the world?

6. Which parables illustrate the preciousness of the gospel?

7. Which one teaches the salvation of the just and the punishment of the wicked?

8. By what parable did Christ reprove Simon, the Pharisee?

9. By what parable did He teach that masters should be compassionate to servants?

10. What parable instructs us to be kind to our neighbors?

11. Which parable shows the vanity of earthly treasures?

12. Which parable contrasts the faithful and unfaithful minister of the Gospel?

13. What one probably refers to the Jewish church and its destruction?

14. What parable was a justification of Christ's conduct in receiving sinners?

15. Which one is typical of a sinner enslaved to habits of iniquity?

16. What parable most strongly teaches Christ's love for the sinner?

17. What parable exhibits the foresight of the men of the world in contrast with that of the children of light?

18. In what parable are the rich in this world's goods, and the rich in faith, contrasted?

19. What parables inculcate importunity in prayer?

20. In what are the self-righteous and the humble man contrasted?

21. What parable taught that the Gentiles as well as the Jews were to be partakers of the kingdom of God?

22. What parable was uttered in the house of the rich man, the chief of the Publicans?

23. By what parable did Christ rebuke the chief priests and elders in the temple?

24. In which of His parables did He quote a verse from the Psalms referring to Himself?

25. Which parable illustrates the privileges and honors men neglect by their over-weening attention to this world's affairs?

26. By what parables did Christ show the necessity of watchfulness?

27. Which parable teaches our individual responsibility?

28. Which parables show that kindness to our fellow-men is kindness to Christ?

29. Which parable teaches humility?

30. Which parable illustrates the frivolous excuses made for rejecting the gospel?

31. Which parable warns us against taking credit to ourselves for doing our duty?

CHAPTER XXX.

THE PROPHECIES CONCERNING CHRIST.

[Answered page 275.]

1. What prophecy was made to Adam when driven from Paradise?
2. To what faithful patriarch was the promise of Christ's coming given?
3. To what son of Abraham was the prediction renewed?
4. Who unlawfully obtained a blessing already promised him?
5. Which of the twelve tribes was the favored one?
6. What grandson of Boaz inherited the promise?
7. To which of the kings of Israel was the promise of the Messiah given?
8. What prophecy refers to the mother of our Lord?
9. What did Daniel prophecy concerning Christ?
10. In what city was it predicted Christ should be born?
11. What is the prophecy referring to John the Baptist?
12. To what does the passage, "The Gentiles shall come to thy light" refer?
13. Where is the prophecy ascribing five different names to Christ?
14. What is implied in the words of Isaiah, "the Lord our righteousness"?
15. What was prophesied concerning Christ's temporal adversity?

16. What attribute belonging to Christ was foretold by Moses?

17. Where is the prophecy concerning His piety?

18. Where the prediction referring to His integrity?

19. What cruel act of Herod's was the subject of prophecy?

20. What prophecy is there concerning the flight into Egypt?

21. What prediction refers to an event that occurred at Christ's baptism?

22. Where is the prophecy that Jesus was to foretell future events?

23. What sacerdotal office was prophesied should belong to Christ?

24. What is the prophecy concerning a single personal triumph of Christ?

25. Where is the prediction referring to His meekness and patience?

26. What miracles was it foretold He should perform?

27. What greater work than miracles was predicted of Christ?

28. What prophecy familiar to the Jews can not be found in the Old Testament?

29. What was David's prediction concerning a daring and summary proceeding of Christ?

30. Of what nations was it predicted that they should conspire to destroy Him?

31. Where is the prophecy that kings should be subject to Him?

32. What prophecy refers to the unfavorable reception of Christ and His acquaintance with sorrow?

33. Where was it prophesied that the ministry of Christ should commence?

34. Of what people beside the Jews was it predicted that they should be converted?

35. What was the prediction relating to the price of Christ's betrayal?

36. What was prophesied should be done with the betrayal money?

37. What prophecy relates to the treachery of Judas?

38. What was foretold concerning the death of Christ's betrayer?

39. What prediction refers to the action of Jesus' disciples toward Him in His trial?

40. By what witnesses was it prophesied that He should be accused?

41. What is the prophecy pertaining to Christ and His accusers?

42. What prophecy of Isaiah's concerning Christ was a punishment inflicted by Pilate?

43. Where is the prophecy that He should be insulted, buffeted, and spit upon?

44. What was foretold concerning the manner of Christ's death?

45. What indignity beside physical suffering was it prophesied Christ should be forced to endure on the cross?

46. What was insultingly offered Him to drink?

47. Relate the prediction concerning the garments of Christ?

48. What was foretold which was fulfilled by the soldiers?

49. What indignity did Micah prophecy our Lord should bear?

50. For whom should Christ suffer?

51. What should be His condnct under suffering?

52. What was it predicted Christ should do for His enemies?

53. Where was His innocence predicted?

54. With whom was it foretold that He should be crucified?

55. What prophecy, fulfilled, preserved the body of Jesus from an injury which was inflicted upon the malefactors?

56. What is the prophecy of Christ's early death?

57. What public calamity was predicted which happened at Christ's death?

58. What astronomical phenomenon was predicted?

59. What was the prophecy concerning Christ's burial?

60. What was the fulfilment of the prophecy that Christ's human body being without sin, should not suffer corruption?

61. What was the prophecy relating to the ascension of Christ?

62. What promise made by Christ to His disciples was a subject of prophecy?

63. What was the prediction pertaining to the extent of Christ's kingdom?

64. What was prophesied concerning the duration of Christ's kingdom?

CHAPTER XXXI.

THE APPEARANCES OF CHRIST AFTER HIS RESURRECTION.

[Answered page 278.]

1. Who was the first to welcome Christ from the grave?
2. To whom did Christ after His resurrection address the words, "All hail"?
3. To which of His disciples did Christ appear first after His resurrection?
4. Who entertained a stranger and found they had "entertained an angel unawares"?
5. To what company did Christ appear first?
6. To whom did Christ utter the words, "Blessed are they that have not seen and have believed"?
7. Who spent the whole night at their accustomed occupation and were unsuccessful?
8. To whom did Christ speak the comforting words, "Lo, I am with you alway unto the end of the world"?
9. What was the largest number to whom Christ appeared after His resurrection?
10. What other disciple beside Peter saw Christ alone after His resurrection?
11. Who were with Christ the last time He appeared upon earth?

CHAPTER XXXII.

CHRONOLOGICAL ITINERARY OF PAUL'S LIFE.

[Answered page 279.]

1. Of what tribe was Paul a descendant?
2. In what city was Paul born?
3. What trade was Saul taught in accordance with Jewish custom?
4. Where and by whom was Saul educated?
5. To what city did Saul start as a persecutor?
6. What strange incident occurred on the way?
7. To what country did Saul first journey after his conversion?
8. How many years did Saul remain in Arabia?
9. To what city did he return from Arabia?
10. Which one of the twelve disciples did Saul meet at Jerusalem?
11. To what city was Saul driven by persecution?
12. From Cæsarea where did he journey?
13. Who accompanied him to Antioch?
14. How long did he remain in Antioch?
15. Where did Saul go with Barnabas, bearing contributions to the Jewish churches?
16. Who accompanied Saul and Barnabas to Antioch?

FIRST MISSIONARY JOURNEY.

17. From what city did Paul start on all his missionary journeys?

18. Who accompanied Paul on his first missionary journey?

19. To what seaport did they come and embark?

20. At what city on what island did they land?

21. After crossing the island, at what place did they stop?

22. Who was converted at Paphos?

23. What change in Paul's history is noticeable on his becoming an apostle to the Gentiles?

24. Who was smitten for his wickedness at Paphos?

25. Sailing from Cyprus where did they land?

26. Which one of the three apostles grew weary at Perga and returned?

27. To what place did Paul and Barnabas continue their journey?

28. Who accepted the Gospel at Antioch?

29. To what city did they journey next?

30. In what city was Paul first worshipped and then stoned?

31. To what city did he journey the following day?

32. Through what cities did Paul and Barnabas pass on their return to the Church in Antioch?

33. To what city were Paul and Barnabas sent by the Church at Antioch?

34. What did they bring back from Jerusalem to Antioch?

SECOND MISSIONARY JOURNEY.

35. With whom did Paul depart from Antioch on his second missionary tour?

36. What city did Paul and Silas visit first and how did they reach it?

37. Where did Paul first meet Timothy?

38. What two provinces did Paul and Silas pass through?

39. In what city were Paul and Silas joined by Luke?

40. To what country were Paul and Silas summoned by a vision?

41. At what island in the Ægean sea did Paul and Silas touch?

42. At what city did they land in Macedonia?

43. Where was Lydia converted?

44. What miracle was first wrought at Philippi?

45. What was the result of Paul's restoration of the damsel at Philippi?

46. What answer was sent to the prayers of Paul and Silas?

47. What was the result of the opening of the prison doors?

48. When the magistrate sent orders for the departure of Paul and Silas, what did Paul demand?

49. Through what towns did Paul and Silas pass before reaching Thessalonica?

50. What experience befell Paul after preaching at Thessalonica?

51. While Silas and Timotheus remained at Berea, to what city did Paul proceed?

52. What sects did Paul encounter at Athens?

53. What historical place was made memorable by Paul's preaching?

54. What two persons are mentioned as becoming converts in Athens?

55. Where was Paul when he wrote his letters to the Thessalonians?

56. How long did Paul remain in Corinth?

57. With whom did Paul abide in Corinth?

58. What was Paul's occupation at Corinth, and what epistles did he write there?

59. How did the apostle employ his Sabbaths at Corinth?

60. When opposed and blasphemed by the Jews, where did Paul resort to preach?

61. Who, in Corinth, was baptized by Paul?

62. How was Paul encouraged while at Corinth?

63. Leaving Corinth with Aquila and Priscilla, at what place did Paul stop to perform a vow?

64. At what city did he embark, taking leave of Aquila and Priscilla?

65. At what port in Palestine did the apostle land?

66. What feast did Paul journey from Cæsarea to attend?

67. In what city did Paul rebuke Peter for conduct into which he had been betrayed through the influence of emissaries from Jerusalem?

THIRD MISSIONARY JOURNEY.

68. After spending some time in Antioch, through what countries did Paul start on his third missionary journey?

69. Where was the temple of Diana, one of the seven wonders of the world?

70. How long did Paul remain at Ephesus?

71. What extraordinary miracles were wrought in Ephesus?

72. What epistle did Paul write during this visit to Ephesus?

73. What did Paul do at Ephesus, under compulsion, which brought him into imminent danger?

74. Driven from Ephesus what countries did Paul next visit?

75. What epistles did Paul write during this journey?

76. Returning to Asia, how long did Paul abide at Troas, and in the company of what fellow-workers?

77. What miracle was wrought at Troas?

78. To what city did Paul travel from Troas on foot?

79. At what towns did the apostle stop before coming to Miletus?

AIDS TO BIBLICAL RESEARCH. 115

80. For whom did Paul send while at Miletus?

81. In what did Paul quote the words of Christ, "It is more blessed to give than to receive"?

82. What affecting incident in Paul's life occurred at Miletus?

83. What city did Paul and Luke pass before coming to the Isle of Rhodes?

84. At what place did they change their ship?

85. At what seaport did they stop in Palestine?

86. How long did they remain in Tyre?

87. At what port did they land?

88. What disciple who lived at Cæsarea did Paul visit?

89. What remonstrance grieved Paul at Cæsarea?

90. Where did Paul go, contrary to the expressed wishes of his friends?

91. What apostle did Paul meet at Jerusalem?

92. What befell Paul at Jerusalem?

93. What address did Paul commence, "Men, brethren, and fathers"?

94. In what address did Paul unwittingly call a high priest a hypocrite?

95. How many men bound themselves under a curse that they would neither eat nor drink until they had slain Paul?

96. Who informed the Roman captain of the conspiracy?

97. Where did the Roman captain send Paul, and how?

98. Before whom did Paul reason of "righteousness, temperance, and judgment to come"?

99. Who, disposed to befriend Paul, refused a favor to the heads of the Jewish nation?

100. To what monarch did Paul pay a true compliment that he might obtain a favorable hearing?

101. How long did Paul remain at Cæsarea?

102. What did Paul do in hope of obtaining liberty?

VOYAGE TO ROME.

103. From what city did Paul sail as a prisoner to Rome?
104. In whose charge was he placed?
105. Who were his companions?
106. At what city did they stop the next day after they set sail?
107. What liberty was allowed Paul at Sidon?
108. At what stopping-place were Paul and his companions transferred to a ship of Alexandria?
109. What places did they pass before reaching Lasea?
110. What distress and peril, predicted by Paul, befell the ship in which they sailed?
111. To what island did the shipwrecked company escape?
112. What miracles were wrought on the island of Melita?
113. How long was Paul on the island of Melita?
114. At what famous city of antiquity did they tarry three days?
115. At what place did they wait for a southerly wind to carry the ship through the straits of Rhegium?
116. At what place did Paul and Luke land in the Alexandrian ship which brought them from Malta?
117. At what places was Paul met by friends?
118. In what place was Paul, though a prisoner, allowed to dwell in his own hired house?
119. How was Paul occupied during his first imprisonment in Rome?
120. What epistles was he engaged in writing?
121. After Paul's liberation from his imprisonment in Rome, what country is he believed to have visited?
122. What epistle did he write in Macedonia?
123. In what city is the Epistle to Titus believed to have been written?

124. What epistle was written during Paul's second captivity in Rome?

125. In what city did Paul suffer martyrdom?

126. What date has tradition fixed as that of Paul's martyrdom?

127. Under what Roman emperor?

128. Where does tradition say he was buried?

PAUL'S JOURNEYS.

1. Mention in order, and point out on the map, the places Paul visited on his first missionary journey?

2. Mention in order, and point out on the map, the places Paul visited on his second missionary journey?

3. Mention the places which Paul visited on his third missionary journey?

4. Mention the places visited by Paul on his journey to Rome?

THE EPISTLES OF PAUL IN CHRONOLOGICAL ORDER.

1. What was the first epistle written by St. Paul?

2. Which was the shortest of all St. Paul's epistles to the churches?

3. What epistle was written by St. Paul at the close of his nearly three years' stay at Ephesus?

4. What was the first epistle written by Paul in Macedonia?

5. In which epistle does Paul vindicate his own apostleship and show that even Peter was not his superior?

6. Which one of Paul's epistles was sent by a woman?

7. What letter did Paul send by a slave to his master?

8. What epistle was called forth by the information St. Paul received from Epaphras and Onesimus?

9. What epistle was written by Paul to a church which he himself founded, and to whose elders he was warmly attached?

10. What letter was written as a reward for kindness shown to the apostle?

11. In what epistle does Paul mention Hymeneus and Alexander, who made shipwreck of their faith?

12. What pastoral epistle was written from Ephesus?

13. In what epistle does Paul mourn the desertion of his friends, even the disciples of Asia?

CHAPTER XXXIII.

THE JEWISH CALENDAR.

[Answered page 286.]

1. In what month was the Passover kept?
2. In what month did Solomon begin to build the temple?
3. On the 23d day of what month was an important decree written?
4. What was the name of the fourth Jewish month?
5. On the first day of what month did Ezra arrive at Jerusalem?
6. In what month was the wall of a great city finished?
7. In what month was the Feast of Tabernacles held?
8. In what month was Solomon's temple finished?
9. In what month did word come to Nehemiah of the misery of the Jews and Jerusalem?
10. In what month did Esther enter Ahasuerus' house?
11. Which month is referred to in the Bible only in connection with the numbering of Israel by David?
12. In what month was the feast of Purim held?
13. When the Jewish year consisted of thirteen months, what was this intercalary month called?
14. What was the length of the Natural Day in the Jewish Calendar?
15. The Natural Night?
16. The Civil Day?

17. At what hour did King Joash command that those who would defend the worship of Baal should be put to death?

18. At what hour was Abraham sitting in his tent door, when the Lord appeared to him, in the plains of Mamre?

19. At what hour is it said Adam and Eve heard the voice of God in the garden?

20. At what hour does Jeremiah, in his prophecy lamenting the destruction of Jerusalem, warn the Jews to cry out?

21. What hour did Gideon choose to defeat the Midianites?

22. At what hour was the Egyptian host destroyed?

23. At what hour was the crucifixion of Christ?

24. At what time of day did the vision of Peter, which taught him not to despise the Gentiles, occur?

25. At what hour is it said Cornelius saw a vision?

26. What hour is not mentioned in the Bible?

27. At what hour on the day of His resurrection did Christ meet His assembled disciples?

28. How late is it said Paul preached at Troas?

29. Before the coming of what hour did Christ say Peter should deny Him?

30. At what hour did Jesus, walking on the sea, come to the relief of His disciples?

CHAPTER XXXIV.

QUESTIONS FOR LITTLE PEOPLE.

[Answered page 288.]

1. Who was the oldest man?
2. Who was the wisest man?
3. Who was the meekest man?
4. Who was the strongest man?
5. Who was the largest man?
6. Who was the most patient man?
7. Who was the most faithful man?
8. Who was the most beautiful man?
9. Who went to heaven in a chariot of fire?
10. Who was cast into a lion's den?
11. Who were cast into the fiery furnace?
12. Whom did God bury?
13. Who became a pillar of salt?
14. Who were struck dead for lying?
15. Who was born in a manger?
16. Who was swallowed by a whale for disobedience?
17. Who killed his brother?
18. Who built the temple?
19. Who was sold as a slave by his own brothers?
20. Who was the beloved disciple of Jesus?
21. Who denied Christ?
22. Who betrayed Christ?
23. Who killed the giant Goliath?

24. Whom did Jesus raise from the grave?
25. Who tried to walk on the water?
26. Who was the first Christian martyr?
27. Who led the children of Israel through the wilderness?
28. Who built the ark?
29. What city is the type of heaven?
30. Who made an iron axe float on the water?
31. Who offered to sacrifice his only son to God?
32. What three persons lived forty days and forty nights without eating or drinking?
33. Who was the first of Christ's disciples to suffer death by violence?
34. Who anointed the Saviour's feet with costly ointment?
35. Who was smitten with blindness for persecuting the Christians?
36. What was Saul's name after his conversion?
37. Who is called the "Sweet Singer of Israel"?
38. What woman came to learn of the wisdom of Solomon?
39. Who was the leader of the children of Israel after the death of Moses?
40. Who wrestled all night with an angel?
41. Whose life was lengthened fifteen years in answer to prayer?
42. Who wished to die the death of the righteous?
43. Who concealed one hundred prophets of the Lord in a cave?
44. What woman was buried under an oak?
45. What prophet prayed in his chamber by an open window?
46. Who had six fingers and six toes on each of his hands and feet?
47. What prophet's bones restored a dead man to life?
48. What king had an iron bedstead?

49. What righteous man's house was smitten with the wind and destroyed?

50. What patriarch did God command to be perfect?

51. What tree did Zaccheus climb?

52. Who rested under a vine which grew up in a single night?

53. Who that had been a prisoner was afterward clad in scarlet and gold with a chain about his neck?

54. Who were the four persons whose birth was announced by angels?

55. Who was borne to heaven by angels after his death?

56. Who was told by an angel to put on his sandals?

57. What two men were told by an angel to take off their sandals?

58. Who was told by an angel to flee into Egypt?

59. When did Jesus and His disciples sing a hymn?

60. Who from his childhood never drank wine nor strong drink?

61. What good man knew the Holy Scriptures from a child?

62. Unto whom did an angel appear with a drawn sword?

63. What two angels' names are mentioned in the Bible?

64. Whom were angels sent to deliver from the destruction of a city?

65. What present did Jacob give to Joseph his favorite son?

66. Who had a coat without a seam?

67. What was Elijah's last gift to Elisha?

68. What desolate mother was comforted by an angel?

69. What brute beast saw an angel?

70. Who offered broth to an angel?

71. Who once stole money from his mother?

72. Who went up to the house-top to pray?
73. How many times a day did David and Daniel pray?
74. How old was Joseph when he was sold by his brethren?
75. Who by prayer brought water from the clouds?
76. What is the smallest gift of money ever recorded?
77. What is the first mountain mentioned in the Bible?
78. What beautiful Jewish girl became a queen?
79. What was Saul's first transgression after he became king of Israel?
80. What gift did a king choose from the Lord?
81. What man's hair was the means of his death?
82. Who put goats' hair on his arms with intent to deceive?
83. Who was clothed in camels' hair?
84. What man in a vision was suspended by a hair?
85. How did the wisest man show his respect for his mother?
86. What king and his queen appropriated the vineyard of a poor man?
87. Who was the most distinguished military leader?
88. Who was the next captain of eminence after Joshua?
89. Who was the chief musician of the Levites?
90. What is the only place in the Scriptures where hats are mentioned?
91. Who made the first coats worn by the children of men?
92. Which of Paul's relations embraced Christianity before the apostle himself?
93. What king and what patriarch planted trees?
94. What is the only place in the Bible where wardrobe is mentioned?
95. What is the name of the only person mentioned in the Bible whose name commences with a Q?

AIDS TO BIBLICAL RESEARCH.

96. Who has recorded a list of a lady's wardrobe?

97. Who are the only three Bible characters whose names commence with F?

98. Who are the only four Bible personages whose names begin with V?

99. How many days for repentance were granted to a city doomed to destruction?

100. Who was translated?

101. What man's hair when cut weighed over four pounds?

CHAPTER XXXV.

MISCELLANEOUS QUESTIONS.

[Answered page 292.]

1. When was Noah's prediction that Canaan should be under servitude to Shem fulfilled?

2. Who, attended only by his armor-bearer, attacked the garrison of the Philistines?

3. Of what two kings was it prophesied that they should die in battle?

4. To whom was it prophesied that he should die within a year?

5. What unusual circumstance occurred in connection with that battle of the Israelites and the Midianites in which Balaam was slain?

6. What promise is there to those who keep the Sabbath day holy?

7. Who hid and fed one hundred prophets of the Lord in a cave?

8. What did a pious king of Judah destroy which had been an instrument of healing, and was made by the command of God?

9. What was written on the rolls which Jehoiakim commanded to be burned?

10. What king of Judah worshipped the gods of that heathen people whom the Lord delivered into his hand?

11. Mention three instances recorded in the Old Testament of the deliverance of Israel wrought by a woman?

12. Who prophesied the name of the king that should deliver the Jews from the Babylonian captivity?

13. How often was Jerusalem taken and plundered after its possession by the Israelites before its destruction by Nebuchadnezzar?

14. What heathen nation offered human sacrifices in cases of extreme danger?

15. Which tribe of the Israelites owned no land?

16. What transgression is not recorded against the Jews after the captivity?

17. What three godly men does Ezekiel mention in his book of prophecy?

18. How many of the sons of the prophets sought vainly for Elijah?

19. What were the only trees allowed to be felled during a siege?

20. Who is believed to have slain the prophet Isaiah?

21. What was Gideon's other name, and by whom was it given him?

22. Who beside aged men and youths were exempt from military duty?

23. What woman endeavored to utterly destroy the prophets?

24. What relation was Mordecai to Esther?

25. To what tribe did Daniel belong?

26. Who was obliged to break a rash oath which he had taken?

27. While Paul was a prisoner at Rome, whom did the Philippians send to him?

28. What did the apostle Paul request might be done with his letters to the churches?

29. What street, mentioned in the life of St. Paul, is still in existence?

30. Upon what two important occasions, after the time of Moses, was Israel called to choose between God and another master?

31. Who, in high position, distrusted the Lord's provision for the morrow, and suffered death in consequence of that provision?

32. What judge, on retiring, challenged the people to show an instance of his unjust judgment?

33. What Old Testament passage contains the golden rule?

34. What impossibility did God assent which is now a constant occurrence?

35. What familiar constellations are mentioned in the Bible?

36. How many of the seven wonders of the world are mentioned in the Bible?

37. Mention three rebellions which occurred during David's reign.

38. To which one of the high priests was given the honor of burial in the sepulchres of the kings?

39. What island is mentioned in the Bible upon which one of the seven wonders of the world was situated?

40. Was the Colossus of Rhodes standing when Luke wrote the Acts?

41. What phrases, used in our own day, go to prove that because Joshua said, "Sun, stand thou still," it is no evidence that he did not understand the revolution of the earth around the sun?

42. What covenant did God make with Noah?

43. To whom did He afterward use this covenant as an illustration of His faithfulness to His people?

44. What daily astronomical occurrence established the perfect fulfilment of this covenant?

45. How did the Jews ascertain the time of the new moon?

46. Why was it important that the fact of the new moon should be communicated to the people?

47. What is remarkable in the history of the judges?

48. In which book of the Old Testament are the future state and resurrection of the dead distinctly mentioned?

49. What verse in the Bible proves that Moses was utterly free from jealousy?

50. What evidence have we in the Bible that there were thirty days in a month in antediluvian times, as at present?

51. What proof have we that the years at the time of the deluge were of the same length as the years at present?

52. Who was called "the king's friend," during the time of David?

53. Who showed kindness to David when he fled beyond the Jordan on account of Absalom's rebellion?

54. What feast was instituted to commemorate an event before the event occurred?

55. What particular mark of respect was required toward the aged by the Mosaic law?

56. From whence did David obtain the pattern of the temple which he gave to Solomon?

57. Where is the last recorded instance of the Lord being consulted by Urim and Thummim?

58. Give an instance both in the Old and New Testament where one was betrayed by a kiss?

59. From what four insignificant things should man learn wisdom?

60. Who, at eighty-five, claimed that he was as vigorous as at forty?

61. Who were buried in the cave in which they hid themselves?

62. Which of the prophets was a gatherer of sycamore fruit?

63. What king gave twenty cities to another king who was not pleased with the gift?

64. Which was the largest tribe when they were numbered in the desert?

65. Which of the tribes went first in their journeying through the desert?

66. In what year did the land of Israel bring forth fruit for three years?

67. The Bible tells of three persons who were gathering sticks, the first was punished with death, the second was rewarded for generosity, the third was preserved from harm, who were they?

68. What captive, who had been kindly treated by a fellow-prisoner, forgot him in the hour of his prosperity?

69. What king went to meet an invading army with a band of singers in advance of his force, singing hymns of praise to God?

70. What unhallowed feast caused the death of a good man?

71. Where are the Chinese referred to in the Scriptures?

72. What was the value of the gold presented to Solomon by the queen of Sheba?

73. Where were the Israelites commanded to erect pillars and inscribe upon them the Law?

74. What was Elisha doing when Elijah called him?

75. Of which of the kings of Judah is no sin recorded in the Bible?

76. Where do we find the fact of the Israelites laying aside ornaments in time of trouble mentioned?

77. Who, under pretext of performing a vow, wrought great mischief?

78. What was the greatest number of stripes permitted by the Jewish law as a punishment for an offence?

79. Of whom was it said that when he was frightened his hair stood on end?

80. What prophet stood between the dead and the living and averted a plague which had slain fourteen thousand seven hundred people?

81. What laborers were so honest in their dealings that no account was kept?

82. Whose descendants alone of all Bible characters are named dukes?

83. How many evangelists record the incident of the ear of the high priest's servant being cut off?

84. Who alone mentions the name of Peter and the name of the servant?

85. Who alone narrates the fact that Jesus healed the high-priest's servant's ear?

86. Who refused to seek refuge in the temple in time of danger?

87. Who put out King Zedekiah's eyes?

88. What king had eighty-eight children?

89. Whose raiment was forbidden to be taken in pledge?

90. To what artificer was a prophet sent to learn an important and spiritual truth?

91. What prophet likens the wicked to ashes under the soles of his feet?

92. Who wrapped his face in a mantle, as a token of humility?

93. What two persons saved their lives by hiding in a well?

94. Who said "Give me neither poverty nor riches"?

95. Name two good men who employed deceit for their own preservation?

96. What two Scripture passages teach that bad roads are an evidence of want of peace and prosperity in a nation?

97. What presents were given by a monarch's son to his friend?

98. What angry king endeavored to slay his son?

99. What tax-gatherer was stoned to death by the people?

100. Who became a terror to himself and his friends, as a punishment for smiting the prophet Jeremiah?

101. Give the names of the eight women who were prominent prophetesses?

102. What three righteous men under severe trial wished they might die?

103. What king fell on his face before a captive?

104. What three sad events occurred in a garden?

105. What three remarkable prophecies occur in the last chapter of the Old Testament?

106. How were dogs anciently employed?

107. Who slew a giant in self-defence?

108. Who once used a monument as a table for eating?

109. Who erected a pillar to commemorate his name because he had no son?

110. Name six persons mentioned in the Bible who committed suicide?

111. What three things does the Bible say God can not do?

112. What was the value of the books which the converted exorcists burned?

113. What persons did God cause to sleep?

114. What three men, mighty in strength, each slew a lion?

115. What successful general demanded of a conquered tribe their golden earrings as a trophy of the victory?

116. Who was punished for vanity, but allowed his choice of three punishments?

117. What punishment did he choose?

118. Upon what day of the week were the two greatest acts of divine power which affect man accomplished?

AIDS TO BIBLICAL RESEARCH. 133

119. To what is an unfaithful friend compared?

120. Why were the children of Israel during their forty years' wandering in the wilderness, each a perpetual miracle?

121. How many Egyptian chariots of war were lost in the Red Sea?

122. On what occasion did man first exercise judgment and the power of speech?

123. What man's capture was considered so important that an army was sent to take him?

124. What two incidents is it said happened by chance —one an act of destruction and the other resulting in neglect?

125. How many men and women perished with Samson?

126. How many stalls had Solomon for his horses?

127. On what three occasions is it recorded Jesus wept?

128. What three incidents are recorded of Nicodemus?

129. On what two occasions did angels minister to our Lord?

130. Who were the Hittites?

131. Who were the Persians?

132. Who were the Amalekites?

133. Who were the Ammonites?

134. Who were the Zebuzites?

135. Who were the Canaanites?

136. Who were the Perizites?

137. Who were the Midianites?

138. Who were the Edomites?

139. Who were the Philistines?

140. Who were the Egyptians?

141. Who were the Arabians? (Ishmaelites.)

142. Who were the Syrians?

143. Who were the Israelites?

144. Who were the Hivites or Horites?

145. Name eleven men mentioned in the Bible eminent for youthful piety.
146. What heathen gods are mentioned in the Bible?
147. What heathen goddesses?
148. Mention two heathen writers whom Paul quoted.
149. What heathen temples are mentioned in the Bible?

CHAPTER XXXVI.

CHRISTIAN EVIDENCES.

[Answered page 301.]

1. What are Christian evidences?

2. Into what three classes are the evidences of Christianity usually divided?

3. What are external evidences?

4. What is the difference between the authenticity and the genuineness of any book?

5. Can a book be authentic and not genuine or genuine and not authentic?

6. Give some of the reasons why we are safe in concluding that our Bible has been preserved to us in its integrity.

7. How many manuscripts of the Old Testament are in existence?

8. What great historian who lived in the first century gives the numbers and names of the Old Testament books precisely like ours?

9. How many quotations from the Old Testament are contained in the New?

10. If all the Bibles in the world were destroyed how might the New Testament be again compiled?

11. What was one of the canons of the celebrated council of forty-four bishops, held at Carthage in 397?

12. Did any number of persons in the earliest ages regard the Old Testament as an accurate record of divine authority?

13. Did any large number of people in New Testament times accept the gospel as authentic and genuine?

14. How did millions prove that their belief in the Bible was a positive faith?

15. Mention some of the prominent authors of the fourth century who furnished catalogues of the books of the Bible exactly to correspond with ours.

16. Mention some of the great men in the third century who quoted from or alluded to our Scriptures as authentic.

17. Who in the second century bore abundant testimony to the truth of the Gospels?

18. Mention three men called apostolic fathers, who were contemporary with the apostles, and are named in the New Testament, whose authentic testimony to the Bible we have.

19. Mention a disciple of St. John and a friend of the apostles, whose names are not given in the New Testament, but whose writings confirm the authenticity of the New Testament.

20. What is perhaps a stronger proof of the authenticity of the Bible than the testimony of its friends?

21. Mention the names of several learned controversialists, who persecuted the Christians, who wrote bitterly against the Scriptures, but never once questioned their authenticity

22. Mention some incidents which show how rigidly careful were the Jews in transcribing their sacred books.

23. What is perhaps the best proof of the genuineness of the Gospel history?

24. Which is the only religion that has appealed to miracles for evidence of the divine authority of its teaching?

25. Name some of the distinctive characteristics of the miracles of the Bible which prove their genuineness.

26. What coin confirms the Mosaic narrative of the deluge?

27. What rock, discovered in the present century, bears testimony to the truth of an Old Testament miracle?

28. What external evidence of Christianity do we of the present age pre-eminently enjoy?

29. How many predictions concerning Christ did He literally fulfil?

30. What prophecy concerning the Jews uttered by Moses is strangely fulfilled at the present day?

31. Mention several cities now in ruins whose utter destruction was prophesied in the Old Testament.

32. Jeremiah foretold that Zedekiah king of Judah should go to Babylon, and Ezekiel prophesied that Zedekiah should not see Babylon, though he should die there. How could Zedekiah be taken to Babylon and behold her king and die there, and yet never see the city?

33. Of what four great empires did Daniel predict a history which has been fulfilled?

34. What seemingly improbable prophecy uttered by Christ was wholly realized less than forty years afterward?

35. What prediction was uttered by Christ concerning the temple and literally fulfilled?

36. What prophecy uttered by Christ is being realized at the present day?

37. What prediction uttered by Agabus was afterward fulfilled?

38. What are internal evidences?

39. What internal evidence of Christianity should commend it to all lovers of law and order?

40. Mention some of the other internal evidences of the truth of the Gospel religion.

41. What is meant by collateral evidence?

42. Mention some of the collateral evidences of the truth of Christianity?

CHAPTER XXXVII.

PROMINENT COUNTRIES OF THE BIBLE.

[Answered page 306.]

1. Of what country was Gallio the proconsul when Paul was brought before him?
2. In what country is Mount Sinai?
3. From what country was Balaam brought to curse Israel?
4. To what land did the sons of Sennacherib flee after they had slain their father?
5. What country mentioned in Scripture was a Roman province of which Ephesus was the capital?
6. To what country did Tiglath-pileser carry the Israelites captive?
7. What country is famed as the dwelling place of a giant king?
8. What country was Paul prevented from visiting by a vision?
9. In what land is it said Abram dwelt ten years?
10. From what country were the Jewish people who heard Peter's first sermon, and the Christian people who were among the readers of Peter's first epistle?
11. Of what country was Abram a native?
12. What was the native country of St. Paul?
13. To what country, mentioned twice only, did Paul send Timothy?
14. What country was named after Esau?

15. Over all of what country was Joseph made lord?

16. Of what country was Candace the queen?

17. To what country did Paul send his fellow-worker Crescens?

18. What was the most northern of the three provinces into which Palestine was divided in the time of Christ?

19. Of what country was Elijah an inhabitant?

20. In what country of Egypt were the children of Israel enslaved?

21. Of what country is it said that the inhabitants bartered their brazen vessels for slaves?

22. What country is mentioned but once and that in Paul's letter to the Romans?

23. What country which must have been well known to the Jews is only named in connection with the reign of Ahasuerus?

24. From what country were Aquila and Priscilla exiled by command of Claudius?

25. What was the most southern of the three provinces into which Palestine was divided in the time of Christ?

26. What country did Paul traverse from west to east on his first missionary journey?

27. To what country was Paul summoned by a vision?

28. In what plain did three angels visit Abraham?

29. Over what country was Darius ruler by right of birth?

30. Of what country was Cushan-rishathaim king?

31. In what country was Jethro the father-in-law of Moses a priest?

32. What country was named after Lot's eldest daughter's son?

33. In what land did Abraham offer up Isaac?

34. What country did Paul and Luke and Timothy pass through before reaching Troas?

35. To what country did Jacob go in search of a wife?

36. Mention all the different names by which Palestine is known in the Bible?

37. The inhabitants of what country mentioned but once, are prominent in the list of those present at Pentecost?

38. What country of Egypt did Ezekiel prophesy should be desolate?

39. What country did Daniel prophesy should be overthrown by Greece?

40. In what country were the cities of Tyre and Sidon situated?

41. In what Roman province was Iconium situated?

42. In what wild country is it believed Paul suffered "perils of robbers" and "perils of rivers"?

43. What was the native country of Aquila?

44. In what land of Egypt did Pharaoh give Joseph's father and brethren a possession?

45. In the time of Christ if one would journey from Galilee to Judea, what country must they "needs go" through?

46. From what country did a wealthy woman come to visit a wise king?

47. In what plain was the tower of Babel built?

48. Under what name is China once referred to in the Bible?

49. What distant country did Paul hope to visit which it is doubtful whether he ever saw?

50. What was the New Testament name for the Old Testament Aram?

CHAPTER XXXVIII.

CHRONOLOGY.

[Answered page 309.]

1. How many days did Job's friends spend with him before they essayed by a single word to comfort him?
2. How long did Job live after his great affliction?
3. How many years was it from the fall of Adam to the birth of Christ?
4. How many years does the book of Genesis embrace?
5. How many years was it from the fall of Adam to the Deluge?
6. How many years was it from the Deluge to the call of Abram?
7. How many years from the call of Abram to the birth of Christ?
8. How long was it from the call of Abram to the removal into Egypt?
9. How many years were the Israelites in Egypt?
10. How many years did the Israelites wander in the wilderness?
11. What was the length of the period of the judges?
12. For how many years was the kingdom of Israel in existence before the division?
13. For how many years were the kingdoms of Israel and Judah divided?
14. How long was the Babylonish captivity?

15. How many years intervened between the return from captivity and the birth of Christ?

16. Name the seven men, and their ages, who lived over nine hundred years.

17. What man lived above eight hundred years?

18. How old was Lamech?

19. Who lived the shortest number of years of any whose ages are given before the flood?

20. How many years was Methuselah cotemporary with Adam?

21. How many years was Methuselah cotemporary with Noah?

22. How many years was Methuselah cotemporary with Shem?

23. How many years did Shem live while Isaac was living?

24. How many years was Isaac cotemporary with Levi?

25. How many years was Levi cotemporary with Amram?

26. How many years was Amram cotemporary with Moses?

27. In what year was the Deluge?

28. How many years of warning did God give the antediluvians before sending the flood?

29. How old was Noah when he entered the ark?

30. How long were Noah and his family in the ark?

31. How many years did Noah live after the flood?

32. What man born after the flood lived to the greatest age?

33. How many years was it from the fall of Adam to the call of Abram?

34. What three important events between Abram's call and Christ's birth divide that time into four nearly equal parts?

35. How long was it from the flood to the dispersion?

36. In what year were the cities of the plain destroyed?

AIDS TO BIBLICAL RESEARCH. 143

37. How old was Jacob at Abraham's death?

38. How long did Abraham reside in Canaan?

39. How old was Joseph when sold into slavery by his brethren?

40. How many years had Joseph been in Egypt when made second ruler in the kingdom?

41. For how many years did the famine last which occurred in Joseph's time?

42. For how many years did Joseph rule over Egypt?

43. How old was Joseph when he died?

44. Which of Jacob's son's survived all his brothers and how old was he when he died?

45. How many years after Joseph died in Egypt was he buried in Canaan?

46. How long was Moses hidden by his mother to escape the edict of Pharaoh?

47. How long did the children of Israel journey in the wilderness before they found water?

48. How long did the first Egyptian plague last?

49. How many days after the exodus from Egypt was the giving of the law on Mt. Sinai?

50. How many days and nights was Moses on Mt. Sinai?

51. How long did the children of Israel remain encamped at the foot of Mt. Sinai?

52. How long were the spies in searching the land of Canaan?

53. Into how many periods of how many years each was Moses' life divided?

54. How long did the people mourn for Moses and Aaron?

55. How old was Aaron at his death?

56. How many years from the death of Joseph to the erection of the tabernacle?

57. What length of time was occupied in the construction of the tabernacle?

58. How long did the famine last which occurred in David's time?

59. How long did the Ark rest at Shiloh?

60. How many years did Gideon judge Israel?

61. How long did the Ark remain with the Philistines after they captured it?

62. How long was the Ark hid in the house of Obed-edom?

63. How many years were the children of Israel oppressed by the Midianites?

64. How many years were the children of Israel oppressed by the Ammonites?

65. How long was Israel oppressed by the Moabites?

66. In what year before Christ was Saul anointed king?

67. How many years did David reign in Hebron?

68. How many years did Saul, and David, and Solomon, each reign?

69. What was David's age?

70. How many years were the children of Israel in Palestine before the erection of the temple?

71. How many years was Solomon in building his house?

72. How many years were occupied in the construction of the first temple?

73. How many days were spent in dedicating Solomon's temple?

74. How long did Solomon's temple stand?

75. In what year was Solomon's temple destroyed?

76. How long after the destruction of the first temple was the foundation of the second temple laid?

77. What length of time was occupied in building Zerubbabel's temple?

78. In what year did the children of Israel commence the erection of Zerubbabel's temple?

79. How many years was Herod in rebuilding the second temple?

80. In what year was Herod's temple destroyed?

81. What king of Israel reigned the longest?

82. What king of Judah reigned the longest?

83. What king of Israel reigned the shortest?

84. How long did Jehoahas, king of Judah, reign?

85. How many years was Jehoiakim subject to Nebuchadnezzar?

86. How many years before Christ was the kingdom of Israel divided?

87. How long a time was required to elapse before the Israelites could gather the fruit of a young tree?

88. On what day was the Passover appointed to be kept?

89. How old was Eli when he died?

90. At what age were the Levites bound to enter on their respective duties?

91. How many years had the Levites to perform actual service?

92. How old was Abraham when Isaac was born?

93. How many years did Jacob serve Laban, for his wives and cattle?

94. How many years did Jacob live after he went down into Egypt?

95. How many years did Israel serve Cushan-rishathaim?

96. How long had the children of Israel rest from war after Othniel conquered Cushan-rishathaim?

97. How many years were the Israelites oppressed by the Philistines?

98. How often did the year of jubilee occur?

99. What was the length of the drought in the time of Ahab?

100. How many days for repentance were granted to the Ninevites?

101. How many years was Ezekiel in captivity before he had the vision of the temple?

102. How often did Solomon's ships return with merchandise?

103. How long after the time of Moses did David write?

104. How long after David's death did Isaiah write his prophecy?

105. How often did the land of Israel bring forth fruit for three years?

106. How long did the Assyrians besiege Samaria?

107. How long must a man who had slain another unwittingly remain in a city of refuge?

108. How long did prophecy continue in the time of the second temple?

109. When was Nehemiah sent as governor?

110. In what year did Alexander establish the Macedonian empire?

111. In what year was the Septuagint version of the Bible made by order of Ptolemæus Philadelphus?

112. In what year was Jerusalem taken by Antiochus?

113. In what year did Judea become a Roman province?

114. In what year did Herod begin to rebuild the temple?

115. In what year was John the Baptist born?

116. In what year was Christ born?

117. How many years between the Old Testament canon and the New?

118. What year was Pilate sent from Rome as governor of Judea?

119. How many years was Christ upon earth?

120. How long was His public ministry?

121. How long did He fast in the wilderness

122. In what year was Christ crucified?

123. How many days intervened between the resurrection and the ascension?

124. How long did the apostles wait at Jerusalem for the descent of the Holy Ghost?

125. In what year was Saul converted?

126. For how many days was Saul blind after his conversion?

127. In what year was the apostle James beheaded?

128. In what year was Paul sent a prisoner to Rome?

129. For how many years did Paul dwell in his own hired house while a prisoner at Rome?

130. In what year did Paul write his first epistle?

131. In what year did Paul write his last epistle?

132. In what year did Paul suffer martyrdom?

133. When was Jerusalem besieged by Titus?

134. In what year was John banished to Patmos?

135. In what year was Revelation written?

136. In what year of our Lord was the New Testament completed?

137. In what year did John, the last surviving apostle, die?

138. How many years intervened between the time the first book of the Bible was written and the last book was written?

CHAPTER XXXIX.

PUZZLES.

[Answered page 314.]

1.

BIBLICAL ENIGMA.

91 Letters.

9, 32, 62, 90, 4; 15, 41, 50, 5, 10, 77, one of Paul's companions in travel.

67, 83, 36, 26, 72, 3, 6, 10, 7, a man zealous in the worship of Diana.

14, 20, 43, 85, 47, 91, carried a gift to her absent child once a year.

Rebekah brought 61, 24, 56, 64, 3, from the 73, 70, 88, 49, at Padan-aram.

28, 44, 82, 12, 23, 48, one of the twelve sons of Ishmael.

76, 33, 39, 77, 30, 37, 76, the grandfather of Boaz.

77, 58, 75, 17, 57, 46, a name given to Christ in prophecy.

27, 51, 53, 19, 83, tormented a rich man.

42, 74, 3, 57, 76, one of the prophets.

68, 78, 75, 32, 29, 89, 86, 21, the number of years Solomon was building his house.

60, 38, 79, 25, 55, 11, used in transporting a sacred article.

87, 65, 54, 84, 10, 41, Solomon says is deceitful.

12, 10, 56, 71, 8, 69, 10, 45, was restored to life after he had 63, 74, 16, 81, 31, 66.

1, 59, 35, 52, 17, 75, 72, 71, a marked trait in the character of Jonathan.

13, 18, 19, 10, 23, 22, anointed the first king of Israel.
40, 80, 2, 34, one of the judges of Israel.
The whole is a saying of Christ's relating to marriage.

2.
ACROSTIC.

1. A family noted for their temperance principles.
2. A priest.
3. A word signifying "light or fire."
4. A daughter of Herod Agrippa.
5. A word meaning to reverberate.
6. One healed of a loathsome disease.

The *initials* and the *finals* give the names of two patriarchs.

3.
ACROSTIC.

1. A man of Judah of the family of Pharez.
2. A prophet.
3. A country.
4. A mountain.
5. One of the sons of Ham.
6. A musical instrument.
7. A river.
8. An adjective which describes the nationality of a prominent apostle.

The *initials down* and the *finals up* give the names of two brothers.

4.
ENIGMA.
22 *Letters*.

8, 18, 19, 11, 21, 22, 13, 10, 15, 14, 20, 12, we all should render to God.

4, 19, 2, 1, 17, 7, a favorite word with Solomon.
16, 6, a patriarch's son.
9, 3, 19, 15, 5, 11, we all desire to reach.
The whole is an injunction of St Paul's.

5.

A Double Acrostic.

1. A woman's name which is also a name given to Egypt.
2. A fruit.
3. The occupation of Dedan.
4. One of the books of the Bible.
5. A word miraculously written.
6. A chamberlain.
7. One who made intercession to the king not to destroy the prophecy of Jeremiah.
8. A word found but once in the Bible.
9. A grandson of Ham.
10. A just man but an indulgent father.
11. A mountain.
12. A city visited by Paul.

The *initials* give the name of a city in Palestine and the *finals* a descriptive name applied to Jesse.

6.

An Acrostic.

1. A king of Assyria who distressed a king of Israel.
2. One punished with death for sin.
3. A place where the Israelites encamped.
4. A surname of one of Christ's disciples.
5. One of the Gospels.
6. A son of Jonathan.
7. One at whose grave David wept.

8. A Persian king.
9. One who was made king at sixteen years of age.
10. An aquatic animal.
11. A mountain in the land of Moab.
12. A title.
13. A godly woman.
14. A friend of Christ's mentioned but once.
15. A younger brother of Caleb.
16. A Jewish month.
17. A murderer.
18. A New Testament name for an Old Testament prophet.
19. A Jewish feast.
20. The father of Abraham.
21. The son of Phinehas.
22. A Levite in whose house the Ark of God rested.
23. A city intimately connected with the life of Christ.

The *initials* designate a miracle.

7.

An Acrostic.

1. One of the princes who condemned Vashti.
2. Slew the giant brother of Goliath.
3. A prophet distinguished for moral courage.
4. A prophet believed to have been slain by Manasseh.
5. One of the apostles.
6. One of Jacob's grandsons.
7. The wife of a patriarch.
8. One of Jacob's sons.
9. A wife of David.
10. A prophet who reproved David.
11. The father of the oldest man.
12. One of the cities of the plain.

13. Captain of the tribe of Judah.
14. To whom Peter said, "Thy money perish with thee."
15. One of the grandchildren of Jacob.
16. One of the kings of Judah.

The name formed by the *initials* is familiarly associated with St. Paul's Journey to Rome.

8.

Hidden Bible Characters.

1. "And the priest shall bring her near and set her before the Lord."
2. "Pilate said unto him, What is truth?"
3. "Mark well, O Job; hearken unto me."
4. "There was neither hammer nor axe nor any tool of iron heard in the house."

9.

Hidden Acrostic.

In Lemuel, but not in Cain.
In Bethlehem, but not in Nain.
In Vashti, but not in Jezebel.
In Israel, but not in Jubal.
In Antioch, but not in Tyre.
In trumpet, but not in eyre.
In Meshach, but not in fire.
In Perga, but not in Endor.
In Nathan, but *not* in Achor.
An aquatic animal here lies hidden,
And to find it you are bidden.

10.

RHOMBOID.

```
  .  .  .  .
   .  .  .  .
    .  .  .  .
     .  .  .  .
```

Across: A plague; an image; invocations; a country.

Down: A consonant; a city; a mountain in Crete; an attribute of God; conducted; a king; a consonant.

11.

BIBLICAL ARITHMETICAL PUZZLE.

Add the number of months the Ark of God was with the Philistines to the years Noah was building the ark; from that subtract the time David reigned over Israel; multiply the remainder by the days Lazarus remained in the grave; divide the product by the number of years Jacob served Laban for his cattle; and take therefrom the number of years between the jubilee; and you will have the number of cubits in the length of Og's bed-stead.

12.

BIBLE ANIMALS HIDDEN IN BIBLE TEXTS.

1. "Therefore he made the rampart and the wall to lament."
2. "And Elam bare the quiver with chariots of men and horsemen."
3. "The words of a man's mouth are as the well spring of wisdom."

13.

ENIGMA.

62 *Letters*.

48, 33, 42, 18, 7, 47, 62, 57, a plant mentioned in Scripture.

46, 5, 2, 61, 56, 40, 48, the place where Joseph was buried.

32, 6, 23, 4, 37, 59, 15, 37, 19, an orator.

8, 24, 47, 14, a king.

49, 41, 27, 34, 47, 28, a mountain.

58, 25, 17, 38, 37, 13, 47, 55, 37, 9, one of whose coming Paul was glad.

30, 60, 44, is an animal.

1, 20, 39, a city.

21, 8, 52, 28, 53, 31, a queen.

11, 45, 43, 22, 26, 3, a place familiar to David.

"Hiel the 10, 35, 4, 5, 29, 50, 12, 32, 51, did build Jericho."

36, 59, 54, 16, 26, one of the ten plagues.

An exhortation of St. Peter's.

14.

KINGS HIDDEN IN SCRIPTURE TEXTS.

"And then shall they see the Son of man coming."

"And whosoever shall compel thee to go a mile, go with him twain."

"And he rode upon a cherub and did fly."

"Like as a father pitieth his children, so the Lord pitieth them that fear Him."

"Let me pull out the mote out of thine eye."

15.

Perspective Cross.

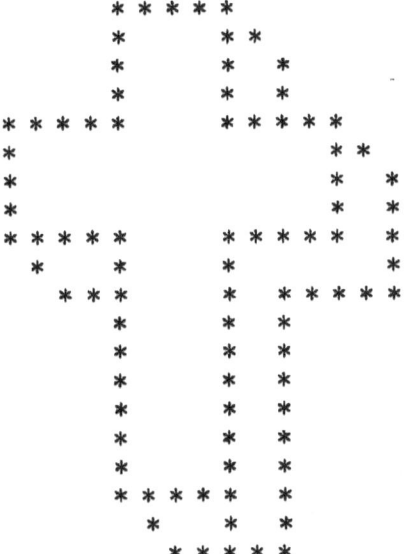

Across: A patriarch; a king of Bashan; a personal pronoun transposed; a son of Judah; a king; is prefixed to Paul's name; a verb; a goddess; a city; an interjection; a prophet; the brother of a prophet; a fruit; a king of Hamath; a daughter of Job.

Down: The father of Moses; a Hebrew writer; the father of one who built the tabernacle; a wicked king; one to whom Paul wrote; was put to death for sin; committed suicide; a friend of Luke; a city mentioned in Acts.

16.

Perspective Cube.

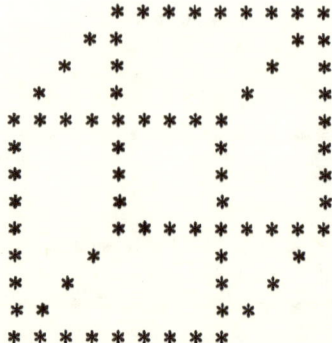

Across: An Israelite whom Christ commended; a city of Judea; an animal; a Scripture proper name.

Down: A son of Herod the Great; a son of Jesse; a New Testament city; the nationality of Nympha.

Diagonals: A priest; a city where David dwelt; the land to which a company of Philistine spoilers went; a judge of Israel.

17.

Puzzle.

The ancient name of a gum; a coin equal to three cents of American money; a recluse; a period of time; a Hebrew word for grace, will reveal five important Scriptural personages whose names read forward and backward, alike.

18.

Word Square.

A seer; what a servant was to his master; a fruit; a prince.

19.

Star Diamond.

A vowel; a reptile; one of Jacob's sons; the father of twelve princes; God gives his followers; a small Portuguese coin; a consonant.

20.

An Acrostic.

A king of Egypt; a valley; a judge of Israel; one who penned a letter; the father of Samson; a son of Shem; a city visited by Luke; a father-in-law of David; a city built seven years after Hebron; the name of a stone; the name of a god.

The initials name a heathen king.

21.

Scripture Anagram.

My twenty-three letters will a text unfold
To Christians dearer than untold gold.

1. One, eight, twenty, thirteen, eighteen, and twenty-one,
   The cause of many an evil under the sun.
2. Two, twenty-one, and six, seventeen, and seven,
   A king who forfeited his right to heaven.
3. Sixteen, four, and twelve, you'll see
   A mighty man of God to be.
4. Four, five, twelve, nineteen—a woman there
   Endowed with godly virtues rare.

5. Seventeen, eleven, twelve, five, and twenty, will show
   A group of heavenly bodies that nightly glow.
6. Twenty-one, six, and nine proclaim
   An unrenowned patriarch's name.
7. Seven, twenty-one, twenty, will show
   Where a prophet was forced to go.
8. Seventeen and thirteen well may bring
   The name of a wicked heathen king.
9. Nine, eleven, and twelve—these I claim
   Will give a porter's Biblical name.
10. Six, eight, and sixteen, an animal show
    Brought often to sorrow by arrow and bow.
11. Ten, eighteen, fifteen, and two, you apprehend
    A woman who deserved the name of friend.
12. Twelve, six, eight, twenty, twenty-two, 'tis claimed
    Only once in Scripture you will find named.
13. Thirteen, twelve, fourteen, five, twenty, recall
    A river mentioned before the fall.
14. Fourteen, three, and twenty will spell
    A man's name and a fowl as well.
15. Number one, fourteen, ten, sixteen, and three,
    A Biblical number as you may see.
16. Sixteen, thirteen, four, five, and twenty—the name
    Of "a very fat man," of Biblical fame.
17. Seventeen and twenty find and then
    Have one from the tribe of Reuben.
18. Find numbers nine and eleven, they,
    A land from which Abraham went away.
19. Twenty-three and seventeen will bring
    The name of an Egyptian king.
20. Twenty and seventeen though numbers few,
    Are both a negative and city, too.

21. Twenty-one and seven if you ne'er falter
Will reveal the name of Israel's altar.
22. Twenty-three, three, fifteen, and two, well done,
Bring to your mind the name of Adam's son.
23. Twenty-two, sixteen, twelve, and ten,
Will reveal a prominent mountain.

22.

Reversals.

1. Reverse the name of an unjust man and have the name of a churlish man.

2. Reverse the name of one mentioned in the genealogy of Judah and have a wicked ruler.

3. Reverse loyal and have a prince of the Gershomites?

4. Reverse manner and have a patriarch.

5. Reverse anger and have a grandson of Israel.

6. Reverse a companion and have a village in the tribe of Simeon.

7. Reverse part of a horse and have a Bible city.

8. Reverse a certain kind of animals and have a granddaughter of Jacob.

23.

Transpositions.

1. Transpose an injury and have an affectionate woman.

2. Transpose a garment and have a rock upon which a chieftain was slain.

3. Transpose a city and have the name of a holy woman.

4. Transpose a falsehood and have a priest.

5. Transpose net-work and have one who helped build the ark.

6. Transpose a part and have one mentioned in the genealogy of Christ?

7. Transpose calamity and have one of the patriarchs.

8. Transpose sparse and have a king of Midian.

9. Transpose animal and have a Jewish month.

10. Transpose single and have a city in the tribe of Dan.

24.

Hollow Square.

Across: a city; the father of the Virgin Mary.

Down: a faithful woman; one mentioned in the genealogy of Christ.

25.

Star Diamond.

A consonant; a Bible name; a celebrated town; a prophetess; a wicked king; one who did a service for Christ; a consonant.

26.

Hollow Squares.

Across: a country; one sent to spy the land.
Down: a friend of Paul's; a king.

27.

Star Diamond.

A consonant; grandfather of King Saul; a disciple; a body of water; a consonant.

28.
NUMERICAL CITIES.

1, 2, 3, 4, 5, 2, 4, 2, 6, 7, 8, 9, 10, 4.
1, 2, 3, 4, 2, 5.
1, 2, 3, 4, 5, 2, 4, 2, 6.
6, 11, 12, 13, 10.
7, 2, 14, 8, 12, 10, 5, 2, 6.
3, 13, 6, 15, 10, 3, 4.

The same figures denote the same letters. The first town gives the key to the whole, with the exception of additional letters.

29.
A DROP LETTER PUZZLE.

T e, o d, s, m, h e h d, s a l, n t, a t.

30.
WORD SQUARE.

A son of Ishmael; a judge of Israel; to lament; a godly woman.

31.
DOUBLE ACROSTIC.

The *primals* down and the *finals* up give the names of two apostles.

        A scribe.
        A king's refuge.
        Traders.
        An altar Moses named.
        A king's counsellor.
        An officer of Queen Esther.

32.

Scripture Enigma.

1. Find but the numbers eight and two,
   A town they will disclose to you.
2. The numbers seven, one, and nine will show,
   A mountain where a prophet used to go.
3. Numbers six, three, and eight, and nine are meant,
   To reveal a place where two prophets went.
4. Eleven and five and two disclose,
   What surely brings unnumbered woes.
5. Numbers four and ten and two tell you,
   That under which there is nothing new.
6. When you my whole have found 'twill tell,
   One whom Timothy loved full well.

33.

Double Diagonals.

Across: One who boasted; a city given the tribe of Joshua; a faithful servant; a friend of Paul; according to Timothy should be modest; a son of Aaron; a king of Judah.

Diagonals: The right diagonal is a New Testament name for an Old Testament city. The left diagonal is a place where the Israelites provoked the Lord to wrath.

34.

Mesostich.

The centrals name a patriarch.
A heathen god.
A female deity of the Phœnicians.
One of the twelve tribes.
A city visited by Paul and Barnabas.

A king of Moab.
It is said Jacob was.
The husband of a distinguished woman.
A letter of the Greek alphabet.
A place of retreat for two fugitives.
A landmark of the boundary of Ashur.

35.

An Acrostic.

1. A queen.
2. The angel of the bottomless pit.
3. A country.
4. A mighty man.
5. A well.
6. A Jewish month.
7. One guilty of parricide.

The *initials* give the name of a high priest.

36.

Numerical Cities.

1, 2, 3, 4, 5, 6, 1, 1, 5, 7, 7, 8, 9, 10, 11.
7, 2, 3, 7, 5, 1.
12, 10, 12, 2, 13, 2, 1.
5, 7, 2, 4, 5, 1.
5, 15, 1, 4, 2, 3, 14, 12.
1, 5, 11, 5, 6, 1.

37.

Numerical Enigma.

Omit 1, 3, 4, 6, 7, 8, 9, 10, 12, 13, 14, 15, 17, 18, 19, and have one punished with death for disobedience.

Omit 1, 2, 3, 4, 5, 6, 7, 8, 9, 10, 11, 12, 16, 17, and leave what every true Christian has.

Omit 2, 5, 7, 8, 9, 10, 11, 12, 13, 14, 15, 16, 17, 18, 19, and have a vehicle used in the time of David.

Omit 1, 2, 3, 4, 5, 6, 7, 8, 11, 12, 13, 14, 15, 16, 18, 19, and have one chastened for sin.

Omit 1, 2, 3, 4, 5, 6, 8, 9, 10, 12, 13, 15, 16, 17, 18, 19, and have an affirmative used by Christ.

Omit 1, 2, 3, 4, 5, 6, 7, 9, 10, 11, 12, 13, 17, 18, 19, and have an instrument once used by a murderer.

Omit all my numbers and have an assertion of St. Paul.

38.

SCRIPTURE ENIGMA.

26, 16, 33, 43, a port of Syria.

36, 41, 7, 39, 40, 3, 11, 14, 52, Christ mentioned in connection with the adjective good.

56, 2, 57, 60, 58, 15, a Levitical city.

22, 54, 55, 50, 42, a Hebrew measure.

17, 8, 18, 27, 28, 34, 21, 55, a Roman coin.

35, 6, 10, 24, 3, 5, a Jewish month.

13, 3, 15, 44, 33, 8, 9, 20, 23, a fruit mentioned in Genesis.

3, 12, 8, 51, 59, 53, 46, 25, 36, a heathen king.

48, 29, 4, 31, 52, a fruit for which the Israelites longed in the wilderness.

38, 47, 30, 4, 41, 60, a tree mentioned in connection with Jacob.

45, 37, 1, our words should be.

32, 26, 49, 15, 19, 20, 4, a judge.

The whole is a proverb.

39.

RIDDLES.

1. Out of the eater came forth meat, out of the strong came forth sweetness.
2. Who was the first person that broke all the commandments?
3. Who was the smallest man mentioned in the Bible?
4. Who was the next smallest?
5. How could Methuselah be the oldest man, yet die before his father?
6. What were the only sweetmeats known to have been in the ark?
7. Where are greenbacks first mentioned?
8. Who is the first man mentioned in the Bible?
9. Who is the first woman mentioned in the Bible?
10. What man beside Adam had no father?
11. Who was the last man to leave the ark?

40.

ACROSTICAL CENTRAL DELETIONS.

A woman of Jericho.
A city allotted to the tribe of Benjamin.
A place from which some Jewish exiles returned who could not prove their pedigree.
One active in repairing the walls of Jerusalem.
The eldest son of Asher.

The *centrals* give the name of a person remarkable for his wisdom?

41.

A Scripture Alphabet.

A is a name God gave the first pair.
B is a tower built in the air.
C is a mount overlooking the sea.
D is a city as old as can be.
E is a prophet both true and brave.
F a coward as well as a knave.
G is a beast in sacrifice slain.
H is a virtue lacking in Cain.
I is a traitor deserving death.
J is a prophet the Bible saith.
K is a patriarch's daughter fair.
L is a mountain high in the air.
M is a gate of the Holy City.
N is a captain deserving pity.
O is a true son of Boaz and Ruth.
P is a man unmindful of truth.
Q is a Christian, friend to St. Paul.
R is a wife beloved best of all.
S is a Danite wonderfully strong.
T a disciple whose doubting was wrong.
U is a careless man punished for sin.
V to a spy was the nearest of kin.
W should never be trifling and bold.
X is a monarch of Grecia old.
Y is a color the Bible named.
Z is a Jew, of short stature, famed.

42.

Hour Glass Puzzle.

1. The place where the battle was fought which decided the fate of Absalom.
2. Is what Amon the king did "more and more."
3. One of the canonical prophets.
4. John saw in a vision.
5. One of the tribes of Israel.
6. The father of a noted architect.
7. An animal whom Asahel resembled in swiftness.
8. A country mentioned in the Bible.
9. A Bible bird.
10. An inhabitant of Ramah.
11. A Roman God.
12. They who practiced divination.

The *centrals* name one sent from Philippi to Paul, while at Rome.

43.

Scripture Enigma.

1. A Christian woman firm and true and bold.
2. A place to which they used to send for gold.
3. A queen who loved her honor most of all.
4. Mother of him the Lord did early call.
5. That which 'tis good in youth to bear.
6. A man who feared not to do or dare.
7. A name which many startled eyes did see.
8. Is given where the many mansions be.
9. His birthright for a mess of pottage sold.
10. One of the mighty patriarchs of old.
11. A place where David rested in a cave.

12. A prophet faithful, true, and brave.
13. One who prophesied the Lord would save.
14. A dutiful son of a faithful priest.
15. A prominent country in the East.

The *initials* form a command Christ gave His disciples.

44.

ARITHMOREMS.
Bible Cities.

1600 + ssaau =
150 + uab =
1500 + oraai =
1100 + uiino =
1050 + eeyint =
1050 + ase=

45.

BIBLE CITIES HIDDEN IN BIBLE VERSES.

1. "A gracious woman retaineth honour."
2. "All the saints salute you."
3. "I will turn their mourning into joy."
4. "Even from everlasting to everlasting thou art God.'
5. "Thou shalt not steal."
6. "I was a gatherer of sycamore fruit."
7. "These were more noble than those."
8. "Shall be in danger of the judgment."
9. "Can any good come out of Nazareth?"

46.

ACROSTICAL CENTRAL DELETION.

1. Died in Egypt, but was buried in Canaan.
2. One punished for covetousness.

3. One Peter healed.
4. A tree chosen for making graven images.
5. A city of Nimrod's kingdom.
6. A grandson of Esau.
7. A Hebrew measure.
8. A city Paul visited.
9. A place where Jeremiah was thrown.
10. A Christian woman.
11. A friend of St. Paul's

The *centrals* name a body-guard of David.

47.

ARITHMOREMS.

Bible Islands.

505 + raa =
650 + aau =
100 + eert =
600 + tail =
500 + shore =
100 + sohi =
100 + s =

48.

BIBLE CHARACTER HIDDEN IN BIBLE TEXTS.

1. "That thy days may be long in the land."
2. "The floods have lifted up their voice."
3. "Abraham took the knife to slay his son."
4. "Thou has killed Urijah the Hittite."
5. "Yet man is born to labor."
6. "The merchandise of gold and silver."
7. "The whole country of the Gadarenes."
8. "My servant Caleb had another spirit in him."

49.

LETTER RIDDLE.

The Seven Churches of Asia.

One eighth of the last church of Asia.
One twelfth of the sixth church of Asia.
One eighth of the fourth church of Asia.
One eighth of the third church of Asia.
One sixth of the fifth church of Asia.
One seventh of the first church of Asia.
One sixth of the second church of Asia.

These *initials* form one of the seven churches of Asia.

50.

ANAGRAMS.

Bible Countries.

1. Hciaaa.
2. Briaaa.
3. Hinibtay.
4. Nermaai.
5. Delcaah.
6. Yraassi.
7. Iiialcc.
8. Pmmtoosaaie.

51.

BIBLICAL ARITHMETICAL PUZZLE.

Add the number of feet in the length, breadth, and height of Noah's ark; divide the sum by the number of years Absalom dwelt at Jerusalem and saw not his father; subtract from this the number of years of the life of Terah; add the number of years Isaiah walked barefoot, and the number of years the famine was in Egypt in Joseph's time, and you will have the years of Amram's life.

CHAPTER XL.

THINGS WORTH KNOWING.

[Answered page 332.]

1. Mention the Seven Wonders of the world.
2. Mention the fifteen decisive battles of the world.
3. Mention the eight leading events from the creation to the close of Bible history.
4. Mention the seven leading events from the close of the New Testament canon to the present time.
5. Mention the seven greatest Bible authors in chronological order.
6. Mention seven great rulers who have fulfilled the prophecy of Isaiah, "And Gentiles shall come to thy light, and kings to the brightness of thy rising."
7. Name the Seven Wise Men of Greece.
8. Name the Nine Worthies.
9. Name the Nine Muses.
10. Name the Three Furies.
11. Name the Three Gorgons.
12. Name the Three Fates.
13. Name the Three Graces.
14. Who was the greatest hero of antiquity?
15. What were the Twelve Labors of Hercules?
16. Who is the God of the Winds?
17. Of the Light?
18. Of Wine?
19. Of Revelry?

20. Of Love?
21. Of Medicine?
22. Of Heaven?
23. Of War?
24. Of Eloquence?
25. Of Folly?
26. Of Water?
27. Of Hunting?
28. Of the Lower Regions?
29. Of Riches?
30. Of Chronology?
31. Of Sleep?
32. Of Groves?
33. Of Boundaries?
34. Of Fire?
35. Who is the Goddess of Justice?
36. Of the Morning?
37. Of Tillage?
38. Of Chronology?
39. Of Hunting?
40. Of Flowers?
41. Of Woods?
42. Of Youth?
43. Of Health?
44. Of the Rainbow?
45. Of Heaven?
46. Of Corn?
47. Of Wisdom?
48. Of Honey?
49. Of Vengeance?
50. Of Night?
51. Of Fruit?

52. Of the Lower Regions?
53. Of Law?
54. Of Discord?
55. Of Beauty?
56. Of the Hearth?
57. Who were the Centaurs?
58. Who were the Sirens?
59. Who were the Hesperides?
60. Who were the Dryads?
61. Who were the Naiads?
62. Who were the Nereids?
63. Who were the Tritons?
64. Who were the Lares and Penates?
65. Who were the Titans?
66. Who were the Gorgons?
67. Who were the Cyclops?
68. Who were the Harpies?
69. Who were the Manes?
70. Who were the three judges of the infernal regions?
71. Name the mythological abode of the blessed, and the mythological place of punishment.
72. What three criminals abode in Tartarus?
73. Name the six great Grecian heroes.
74. Mention the four great Greek festivals.
75. Mention the four great Grecian Philosophers in the order of their birth.
76. Mention five distinguished Grecian generals.
77. Who was the greatest poet of antiquity?
78. Who was the great Grecian lawgiver?
79. Who was the greatest Greek orator?
80. Who was the greatest Roman orator?
81. Who was the greatest Persian general?

82. Who was the greatest modern dramatist?
83. Who was the originator of cyclopedias?
84. Who was the first Christian martyr of Great Britain?

CHAPTER XLI.

REVIEW.

1. What are the ten names of the Bible?
2. Mention the first five books of the Bible and the meaning of each.
3. Mention the canonical prophets in chronological order.
4. Mention five Old Testament authors other than the canonical prophets.
5. Mention nine New Testament authors.
6. Name the Apocryphal books.
7. Give some of the reasons why the Apochryphal books are not considered canonical.
8. Name the books of the Old Testament in the order in which they were written.
9. Name the epistles of Paul in the order in which they were written.
10. Name the other books of the New Testament in the order in which they were written.
11. Give some of the evidences of the authenticity of the Scriptures.
12. Give some of the evidences of the genuineness of the Bible.
13. Mention the historical books of the Old Testament.
14. Mention the poetical books of the Old Testament.
15. Mention the prophetical books of the Old Testament.
16. Mention the historical books of the New Testament.

17. Mention the Pauline epistles.
18. Mention the General epistles.
19. Which of the prophetical books of the Old Testament was written first?
20. Which of the prophetical books of the Old Testament was written last?
21. Name five prominent patriarchs between Adam and Enoch.
22. Mention three patriarchs between Enoch and Shem.
23. Name seven prominent patriarchs between Noah and Jacob.
24. Give the names of Noah's three sons.
25. Give the names of Jacob's sons.
26. State three prominent events in the life of Noah.
27. State seven prominent events in the life of Abraham.
28. Mention three of the principal events in the life of Isaac.
29. Mention four prominent incidents in Jacob's life.
30. Mention the two sons of Joseph.
31. Mention the twelve tribes of Israel.
32. State the names of fifteen prophets who were not writers.
33. Mention seven distinguished high priests of Old Testament history.
34. Mention two high priests of New Testament history.
35. Who was the first judge of Israel?
36. Who was the last judge of Israel?
37. How many judges of Israel were there?
38. Name the judges of Israel in chronological order.
39. What was the length of the reign of each of the three kings of United Israel?
40. Who was the first king of Israel after the division?
41. Who was the last king of Israel after the division?

42. Name the kings of Israel.
43. Name the kings of Judah.
44. Mention three good kings of Israel.
45. Mention four wicked kings of Israel.
46. Mention two good kings of Judah.
47. Mention five wicked kings of Judah.
48. Mention ten prominent heathen monarchs of the Bible.
49. Mention the names of Christ's twelve apostles.
50. Mention the ten most prominent women of the Old Testament.
51. Mention the ten most prominent women of the New Testament.
52. Give the names of three wicked women of the Bible.
53. Mention five children of Bible history.
54. Name ten Bible mountains.
55. Name seven Bible rivers.
56. Mention all the seas named in the Bible.
57. Mention twenty prominent countries of the Bible.
58. Give the names of thirty principal cities of the Bible.
59. Give the names of three shrubs mentioned in Scripture.
60. Give the names of two flowers.
61. Mention five fruits.
62. Name ten trees.
63. Name the precious stones in the high priest's breastplate.
64. Mention four minerals of the Bible.
65. Mention seven precious stones referred to in the New Testament.
66. Name the seven churches in Asia.
67. Give the principal islands in Bible history.
68. Give the divisions of Asia Minor in the time of Paul.

69. Mention twenty distinguished persons connected with the translation of the English Bible.

70. Name the principal authors of the book of Psalms.

71. Mention ten miracles which occurred between Adam and Moses.

72. Mention nine miracles in the life of Moses after he left Egypt.

73. Name five miracles in the life of Elijah.

74. Name six miracles in the life of Elisha.

75. Mention two miracles in the life of Hezekiah.

76. Name three miracles in the life of Daniel.

77. Mention twelve miracles of healing in the life of Christ.

78. How many persons did Christ restore to life?

79. Mention six miracles of Christ having no reference to disease or death.

80. Mention two miracles which Peter wrought.

81. Mention six miracles wrought by the apostle Paul.

82. Mention ten of the parables of Christ.

83. State twelve of the Old Testament prophecies which refer directly to Christ's coming.

84. Name the different appearances of Christ after His resurrection in the order in which they occurred.

85. Mention twenty incidents in the life of Paul.

86. Name seven cities which Paul visited.

87. Mention two islands which are connected with the life of Paul.

88. Mention a hill familiar to Paul.

89. Mention seven towns connected with Christ's ministry.

90. Name two mountains mentioned in the life of Christ.

91. Mention a sea and a river familiar to Christ.

92. Give the dimensions of Noah's ark.

93. Name the three Jewish feasts.

94. Mention three battles in the subjugation of Canaan.

95. Name three Hebrews who were preserved by a miracle.

96. Mention ten names of the Holy Land.

97. Give the name of Moses' father, mother, sister, brother, and wife.

98. Give the name of Abram's father, brother, and beloved wife, and the names of two of his sons.

96. Mention the name of Isaac's father, mother, wife, and two sons.

100. Mention five kings who fought against Israel.

101. Name the spies sent to search the land of Canaan.

102. Which of the spies brought a good report of the land?

103. Mention the names of David's wives.

104. Mention the names of three sons of David.

105. Mention four cities connected with the history of the Ark of God.

106. Name ten cities mentioned in the lives of the patriarchs.

107. Name five cities connected with the life of Moses.

108. Mention six cities connected with David's life.

109. Mention the divisions of Palestine in the time of Jesus Christ.

110. Mention eight events in the life of Samson.

111. Mention four sects in the time of Christ.

112. Name five metals mentioned in the Bible.

113. Name the months in the Jewish calendar.

114. What cities did Paul visit on his first missionary tour?

115. Mention and point out on the map the places Paul visited on his second missionary journey.

116. What cities were visited by Paul on his third missionary journey?

117. What places did Paul visit on his journey to Rome?

118. Mention fifteen of the prominent men of the Bible who held no office.

119. Name five Bible measures.

120. Mention four Bible weights.

121. Mention ten of the best women of the Bible.

122. Mention ten of the best men of the Bible.

123. Mention thirty of the worst men of the Bible.

124. Give the names of the coins of the Bible.

125. Mention three Bible martyrs.

126. Mention five heathen tribes who inhabited the land of Canaan, and tell from whom they were descended.

127. Give the names of Ishmael's twelve sons.

128. How many Bible kings reigned over half a century?

129. How many kings of Israel and Judah reigned forty years?

130. How many kings of Israel reigned more than forty years?

131. How many judges of Israel reigned forty years and over?

132. How many patriarchs lived to be over nine hundred years old?

133. Mention all the animals used in sacrifice.

134. Mention five animals not used in sacrifice.

135. Name four reptiles mentioned in Scripture.

136. Name the birds allowed to be offered as a Jewish sacrifice.

137. Mention fifteen birds not used in sacrifice.

138. Name five birds by the Jewish law unclean.

139. Mention four insects of the Bible.

140. Give the names of the five gates which were entrances to Solomon's temple.

ANSWERS.

CHAPTER I.

THE BIBLE.

1. The Bible; Oracles; Scriptures; The Word; The Law; Law, Prophets, and Psalms; Testaments or Covenants; The Holy Bible; The Canonical Scriptures.
2. The Book.
3. Hebrew.
4. Ezra and Daniel.
5. The sacred books were preserved in the ark. The law was among the spoils of Titus after his destruction of Jerusalem. Copies of the original Hebrew text written upon animals' skins have descended to our times.
6. Asia.
7. Sixty-six.
8. About thirty-six.
9. Old Testament and New Testament.
10. Covenant.
11. Thirty-nine.
12. Pentateuch; The Historical Books; The Poetical Books; The Prophetical Books (Greater and Lesser.)
13. The Pentateuch.
14. *Pente* (five) and *teuchos* (volume).
15. Genesis—Generation.
    Exodus—Departure.
    Leviticus—The Law.
    Numbers—Numbering.
    Deuteronomy—The Second Law.
16. Moses.

17. Christ and the apostles refer to him as the author of the Pentateuch.

18. The last chapter of Deuteronomy.

19. Joshua or Ezra.

20. The Ninetieth Psalm.

21. Ruth, Samuel, Kings, Chronicles, Esther, Nehemiah, Ezra.

22. Job, Psalms, Proverbs, Ecclesiastes, Song of Solomon.

23. *Greater:* Isaiah, Jeremiah (Lamentations), Ezekiel, Daniel. *Lesser:* Hosea, Joel, Amos, Obadiah, Jonah, Micah, Nahum, Habakkuk, Zephaniah, Haggai, Zechariah, Malachi.

24. Judges, Ruth, Samuel, Ezekiel, Kings, Chronicles.

25. Probably Mordecai.

26. Psalms.

27. See Luke xx. 42.

28. Asaph.

29. Sons of Korah.

30. Solomon.

31. Moses.

32. Proverbs, Ecclesiastes, Song of Solomon.

33. Jeremiah.

34. Joshua, Ezra, Nehemiah, all the prophetical books, possibly Job.

35. One is a record of the Old Dispensation and one of the New. To distinguish between those books held sacred by the Jews, and those received by Christians only.

36. Four hundred and fifty years.

37. The Apocrypha.

38. Fourteen.

39. I Esdras, II Esdras, Tobit, Judith, the rest of Esther, the Wisdom of Solomon, the Wisdom of Jesus, Baruch, the

Song of the Three Holy Children, Susanna, Bel and the Dragon, the prayer of Manasseh, I Maccabees, II Maccabees.

40. In the time of Jerome, fifth century.

41. The Roman Catholic Church.

42. The Church of England.

43. None of the New Testament writers mention the books of the Apocrypha. Neither Philo nor Josephus speak of them. They were written after the days of Malachi, in whom, according to the universal testimony of the Jews, the spirit of prophecy ceased. Origen, Athanasius, Cyril, and all orthodox writers who have given catalogues of the canonical books unanimously reject these.

44. Twenty-seven.

45. Historical, Epistolary (Pauline Epistles, General Epistles), and Prophetical.

46. Matthew, Mark, Luke, John, Acts.

47. Romans, Corinthians, Galatians, Ephesians, Philippians, Colossians, Thessalonians, Timothy, Titus, Philemon.

48. James, Peter, John, Jude.

49. Revelation.

50. James.

51. Revelation.

52. John, John, Revelation.

53. Luke.

54. Luke and Acts.

55. Matthew, Mark, Luke, John, John, Peter, James, Jude.

56. Greek.

57. Matthew.

58. Hebrew.

59. Scriptures, Law, Prophets.

60. The most ancient Greek translation of the Old Testament which has come down to us. Translated in Alexandria

during the reign of Ptolemy Philadelphus (died, B. C. 247), and used in the time of Christ.

61. So called because it was believed to have been the work of seventy translators.

62. A Latin translation of the Scriptures by Jerome in the 4th century. It is used by Roman Catholics.

63. A copy of this Latin version was the first book ever printed.

64. The Bible translated from the original Hebrew into the Samaritan dialect, it is believed, by Ezra.

65. A translation of the sacred Scriptures into the Chaldaic language.

66. The 5th century.

67. Middle of the 13th century; some assign it to Cardinal Hugo, some to Stephen Langton.

68. In the Vulgate by Pagninus in 1528, in the English Bible in 1560, into the Hebrew Bible, by Athias of Amsterdam, in 1661.

69. Cædmon, a monk of Whitby (670).

70. Venerable Bede (735).

71. King Alfred (901).

72. John D. Wycliffe (b. 1323—d. 1384).

73. 1455, in Mentz, by Gutenberg and Faust.

74. Mazarin Bible, because a copy was found in the library of Cardinal Mazarin.

75. $70.000.

76. Luther.

77. William Tyndale. Martyred 1536.

78. At Worms, for fear of persecution in England.

79. Miles Coverdale (1535).

80. In 1537 by John Rogers and Thomas Matthew, un der the supervision of Cranmer, with the permission of Henry the VIIIth.

81. Cranmer's.
82. Cromwell, Coverdale, and others. Because Cranmer revised it and wrote the preface.
83. The Great Bible.
84. Bloody Mary's.
85. John Rogers, Thomas Cranmer.
86. In Switzerland.
87. The Genevan Bible.
88. John Calvin.
89. The Bishops' Bible.
90. Eight of the scholars engaged on it were bishops.
91. By the middle of the 16th century.
92. "The authorized version."
93. Forty-seven. Fifty-four were appointed.
94. Seven. 1604–1611.
95. A committee of eight from the Upper House and eight from the Lower House. Liberty was given them to invite the co-operation of any men eminent for scholarship to whatever nation or religious body they belonged.
96. Dr. S. Wilberforce, Bishop of Winchester.
   Dr. C. Thirlwall, Bishop of St. David's.
   Dr. A. Ollivant, Bishop of Llandaff.
   Dr. C. J. Ellicott, Bishop of Gloucester and Bristol.
   Dr. G. Moberly, Bishop of Salisbury.
   Dr. E. H. Browne, Bishop of Ely (now of Winchester).
   Dr. C. Wordsworth, Bishop of Lincoln.
   Dr. A. C. Hervey, Bishop of Bath and Wells.
   Dr. E. H. Bickersteth, now Dean of Lichfield.
   Dr. H. Alford, Dean of Canterbury.
   Dr. A. P. Stanley, Dean of Westminster.
   Dr. H. J. Rose, Archdeacon of Bedford.
   Dr. W. Selwyn, Canon of Ely.

Dr. J. W. Blasesley, Canon of Canterbury, now Dean of Lincoln.

Dr. J. Jebb, Canon of Hereford.

Dr. W. Kay, late Principal of Bishop's College Calcutta.

97. That two companies should be formed, one for the revision of the Old Testament and one for the New Testament. That eighteen scholars and divines should be invited to join the eight engaged on the Old Testament, and nineteen scholars and divines the eight engaged on the New Testament.

98. To introduce as few alterations as possible consistent with faithfulness.

Each company to go twice over the work revised. To make no change in the final revision except two thirds of those present agreed to it.

99. Dr. W. L. Alexander, Professor of Theology, Congregational Church Hall, Edinburgh.

Mr. T. Chenery, Lord Almoner's Professor of Arabic, Oxford.

Rev. F. C. Cook, Canon of Exeter.

Dr. A. B. Davidson, Professor of Hebrew, Free Church College, Edinburgh.

Dr. B. Davies, Professor of Hebrew in the Baptist College, Regent's Park.

Dr. P. Fairbairn, Principal of the Free Church College, Glasgow.

Dr. F. Field, Editor of the Septuagint, Origen's Hexapla, etc.

Dr. Ginsburg, Editor of Canticles, Ecclesiastes, etc.

Dr. F. W. Gotch, Principal of the Baptist College, Bristol.

Rev. B. Harrison, Archdeacon of Maidstone.

Rev. S. Leathes, Professor of Hebrew, King's College, London.
Rev. J. McGill, Professor of Oriental Languages, St. Andrew's.
Dr. R. Payne Smith, now Dean of Canterbury.
Dr. J. J. S. Perowne, Canon of Llandaff.
Dr. E. H. Plumptre, a Professor at King's College, London.
Dr. E. B. Pusey, Professor of Hebrew, Oxford.
Dr. W. Wright, Professor of Arabic, Cambridge.
Mr. W. A. Wright, Librarian (now Bursar) of Trinity College, Cambridge.

100. Dr. R. C. Trench, Archbishop of Dublin.
Dr. J. Angus, Pres. of the Bapt. Coll., Regent's Park.
Dr. J. Eadie, Professor of Biblical Literature and Exegesis to the U. P. Church, Scotland.
Dr. F. J. A. Hort, Fellow of Emmanuel College, Cambridge.
Rev. W. G. Humphry, Prebendary of St. Paul's.
Dr. B. H. Kennedy, Canon of Ely.
Dr. W. Lee, Archdeacon of Dublin.
Dr. J. B. Lightfoot, Canon of St. Paul's.
Dr. W. Milligan, Professor of Divinity, Aberdeen.
Dr. W. F. Moulton, Professor of Classics, Wesleyan, Richmond.
Dr. J. H. Newman.
Dr. S. Newth, Principal, New College, London.
Dr. A. Roberts, Prof. of Humanity, St. Andrew's.
Dr. G. Vance Smith, joint author of a revised translation of the Scriptures.
Dr. R. Scott, Dean of Rochester.
Dr. F. H. Scrivener, Editor of the Cambridge Paragraph Bible.

Dr. S. P. Tregelles, Editor of the Greek Testament.
Dr. C. J. Vaughan, Master of the Temple.
Dr. B. F. Westcott, Canon of Peterborough.

101. Henry the VIIIth's Chapel in Westminster Abbey.
102. In the Jerusalem Chamber.
103. For a session of ten days five times a year.
104. For a session of four days every month except August and September.
105. Dr. S. Wilberforce, Bishop of Winchester.
106. Dr. J. C. Ellicott, Bishop of Gloucester and Bristol.
107. Eleven.
108. Dr. T. J. Conant (Baptist), Brooklyn, N. Y.
Dr. E. Day (Cong.), New Haven, Conn.
Dr. J. DeWitt (Ref'm'd), New Brunswick, N. J.
Dr. W. H. Green (Pres.), Princeton, N. J.
Dr. G. E. Hare (Epis.), Philadelphia, Penn.
Dr. C. P. Krauth (Lutheran), Philadelphia, Penn.
Dr. J. Packard (Epis.), Fairfax, Vir.
Dr. C. E. Stowe (Cong.), Cambridge, Mass.
Dr. Strong (Meth.), Madison, N. J.
Dr. C. V. A. Van Dyck (Missionary), Beyrout, Syria.
Dr. T. Lewis (Ref'm'd), Schenectady, N. Y.
109. Fifteen.
110. Bishop Lee (Epis.), Wilmington, Delaware.
Dr. E. Abbott (Unitarian), Cambridge, Mass.
Dr. G. R. Crooks (Meth.), New York.
Dr. H. B. Hacket (Bap.), Rochester, N. Y.
Dr. J. Hadley (Cong.), New Haven, Conn.
Dr. C. Hodge (Pres.), Princeton, N. J.
Dr. M. B. Riddle (Ref'm'd), Hartford, Conn.
Dr. C. Short (Epis.), New York.
Dr. H. B. Smith (Presbyterian), New York.
Dr. J. H. Thayer (Cong.), Andover, Mass.

Dr. W. F. Warren (Meth.), Boston, Mass.
Dr. E. A. Washburn (Epis.), New York.
Dr. T. D. Woolsey (Cong.), New Haven, Conn.
Dr. P. Schaff (Pres.), New York.
Dr. A. C. Kendrick (Bap.), Rochester, New York.

111. Dr. C. A. Aiken, Princeton, New Jersey.
Dr. C. M. Mead, Andover, Mass.
Dr. H. Osgood, Flushing, L. I.

112. Dr. Crooks, Dr. Hadley, Dr. Smith, and Dr. Warren.

113. Dr. J. K. Burr, Madison, New Jersey.
Prof. T. Chase, Haverford College, Penn.
Dr. H. Crosby, New York.
Dr. T. Dwight, New Haven, Conn.

114. On the last Friday and Saturday of each month, at the Bible House, and for a five days' session in the summer at New Haven or Andover.

115. On the last Friday of each month at the Bible House, and during the summer at Rochester and other places.

116. Dr. Woolsey.

117. Dr. Green.

118. Dr. Schaff.

119. About eighty.

120. Two hundred and forty-three.

121. That the books of the Bible were written by the men whose names are given as the authors.

122. As we would prove the genuineness of Milton's "Paradise Lost," or Augustine's "City of God," or any other book.

123. That it is true and reliable, and the events related in it really happened.

124. Either. "The History of the Island of Formosa" is a *genuine* book, because written by Psalmanazar, but not

an *authentic* book, for the author late in life confessed it was not a history but a romance. "Anson's Voyage" is an *authentic* book, it being a true narrative, but is not *genuine*, because it was not written by Waller (to whom it is ascribed) but by Robbins.

125. Having just claim to credit. Worthy of being believed.

126. The science of interpretation which strives to find out the true meaning of Scripture.

127. A divine influence on the sacred writers by which they were qualified to communicate religious truth with authority.

128. Job, Genesis, Exodus, Leviticus, Numbers, Deuteronomy, Joshua, Judges, Ruth, Samuel, Psalms, Proverbs, Song of Solomon, Ecclesiastes, Jonah, Amos, Hosea, Isaiah, Joel, Micah, Nahum, Zephaniah, Jeremiah, Lamentations, Habakkuk, Obadiah, Kings, Ezekiel, Daniel, Chronicles, Ezra, Esther, Nehemiah, Haggai, Zechariah, Malachi.

129.

	A. D.		A. D.
James	45	Acts	63
I Thessalonians	52	I Peter	63–67
II Thessalonians	53	I Timothy	67
I Corinthians	57	Titus	67
II Corinthians	57	Jude	67
Galatians	57	II Timothy	68
Romans	57	II Peter	68
Matthew	58–60	Hebrews	68–70
Philemon	62	I John	70–85
Colossians	62	II John	70–85
Ephesians	62	III John	70–85
Philippians	62	John	70–85
Luke	63	Revelation	70–85
Mark	63		

130.

	A. D.		A. D.
I Thessalonians	52	Colossians	62
II Thessalonians	53	Ephesians	62
I Corinthians	57	Philippians	62
II Corinthians	57	I Timothy	67
Galatians	57	Titus	67
Romans	58	II Timothy	68
Philemon	62		

CHAPTER II.

CURIOSITIES OF THE BIBLE.

1. 3,586,489 letters in the Bible.
2. 773,692 words in the Bible.
3. 31,173 verses in the Bible.
4. 1,189 chapters in the Bible.
5. 46,277 times the word "and" occurs.
6. 1,855 times the word "Lord" occurs.
7. Once. Psa. cxi. 9.
8. See Psa. cxviii. 8.
9. See Ezra. vii. 21.
10. II Kings xix., Isaiah xxxvii.
11. See Esther viii. 9.
12. See John xi. 35.
13. Mahershalalhashbaz. Isa. viii. 1.
14. Obadiah.
15. The Second Epistle of John.
16. Esther.
17. Judges, Ecclesiastes, Song of Solomon, Esther, Ezra, and Nehemiah.
18. "All is vanity." Ecclesiastes.
19. Saints, believers, disciples, brethren.
20. See James i. 23.
21. See Heb. iv. 12.
22. See John iv. 14, Isa. xii. 3.
23. See II Cor. iii. 18.
24. In 1551, in London, by Nicholas Hyll. From the following, "So that thou shalt not nede to be afraid for any Bugges by nights," Psa. xci. 5.

25. From the following, "And made themselves breeches." Geneva, 1560. Gen. iii. 7.

26. In 1568, by Richard Jugge. From, "Is there no tryacle in Gilead?" Jer. viii. 22.

27. In 1609. "Is there no rosin in Gilead?" Jer. viii. 22.

28. In 1611, in London, by Robert Baker. From a curious error in Ruth iii. 17, "And he said" in the first clause, instead of "And she said."

29. In 1611. A separate edition correcting the mistake made in the "He" Bible.

30. 1631. So called from the mistake of omitting the negative from the seventh commandment, making it read, "Thou shalt commit adultery."

31. In 1737, and derived its name from the heading of the twentieth chapter of Luke which read, "The Parable of the Vinegar."

32. "Basket full of errors," because of its numerous typographical faults.

33. Kingdom of heaven.

34. James and Peter. James iv. 6, I Peter v. 5.

35. Daniel. Dan. iii. 6; iv. 19, 33; v. 5.

36. Job.

37. Sinim. Isa. xlix. 12.

38. Ecclesiastes.

CHAPTER III.
"IN THE BEGINNING."

1. Light ....Gen. i. 3.
2. Of Christ: concerning His coming..Gen. iii. 15.
3. Cain ....Gen. iv. 17.
4. Jabal ....Gen. iv. 20.
5. Jubal ....Gen. iv. 21.
6. Adam............................Gen. iii. 24.
7. Abraham ....Gen. xiv. 20.
8. Bezaleel ....Ex. xxxi. 2–4.
9. See..............................Gen. vi. 4.
10. Abram ....Gen. xii. 1–6.
11. Moses ....Ex. xviii. 13.
12. Moses ....Ex. xviii. 13.
13. Pharaoh ....Gen. xii. 15.
14. Eve ....Gen. iii. 6.
15. Cain ....Gen. iv. 9.
16. Adam............................Gen. iii. 23.
17. Tubal-cain......................Gen. iv. 22.
18. Abel ....Gen. iv. 4.
19. Abraham ....Gen. xxiii. 4.
20. Nimrod ....Gen. x. 9.
21. Cain ....Gen. iv. 12.
22. Rebekah ....Gen. xxiv. 65.
23. Noah ....Gen. vi. 14.
24. Hagar ....Gen. xxi. 16.
25. Ishmael ....Gen. xvi. 11.
26. Abraham ....Gen. xxii. 3.

AIDS TO BIBLICAL RESEARCH. 197

27. Adam......................Gen. v. 5.
28. Pharaoh....................Gen. xli. 42.
29. Jewelry....................Gen. xxiv. 22.
30. Moses ....Ex. xxiv. 4.
31. Aaron's mitre ....Ex. xxviii. 36.
32. Aaron ....Ex. xxviii. 1.
33. Water turned to blood ....Ex. vii. 17.
34. See........................Gen. xxxvii. 28.
35. Rachel.....................Gen. xxxi. 19.
36. Zerubbabel ....Haggai i. 1.
37. Jacob's to Esau ....Gen. xxxii. 13-15
38. Stephen ....Acts vii. 58.
39. Jacob ....Gen. xxxii. 9, 10.
40. Jewelry ....Ex. xxxii. 2.
41. Rachel ....Gen. xxix. 9.
42. The widow's son............I Kings xvii. 21, 22
43. Jacob's at Rachel's grave ....Gen. xxxv. 20.
44. Ararat ....Gen. viii. 4.
45. Abram ....Gen. xiv. 13.
46. See........................Gen. i. 28.
47. Solomon ....I Kings ix. 26.
48. By God, after the creation ...Gen. ii. 2, 3.
49. At Antioch ....Acts xi. 29, 30.
50. See........................Job xix. 23.
51. See ....Gen. xxiii. 9.
52. On naming the animals .....Gen. ii. 19.
53. See........................Judges xx. 26.
54. Daniel ....Dan. vi. 2.
55. To Noah, after the flood ....Gen. ix. 3.
56. Deborah ....Judges iv. 4.
57. The tribe of Judah ....Num. x. 14.
58. In Abram's time ....Gen. xii. 10.
59. Comp. Gen. xiv. 5, Deut. ii. 10, 11.

60. Joseph ....Gen. xxxvii. 28.
61. Pharaoh......................Ex. i. 13, 14.
62. Saul ....I Sam. xi. 15.
63. Jeroboam....................I Kings xii. 20.
64. Rehoboam ....I Kings xii. 17.
65. In Sodom ....Gen. xiii. 13.
66. Abraham ....Gen. xxi. 24.
67. See..........................Ezra vi. 1.
68. The Lord shall reign forever and ever. Ex. xv. 18.
69. See..........................Psalm cix. 10.
70. See..........................Isa. ii. 4.
71. The division of Canaan..........Josh. xviii. 8.
72. 607 B. C. By Rachel's children...Jer. xxxv. 1-11.
73. In the wilderness, by Anah.......Gen. xxxvi. 24.
74. See..........................Acts xv. 23.
75. Water changed into wine.........John ii. 1-10.
76. Widow of Zarephath's meal increased. I Kings xvii. 14.
77. Dividing the river Jordan.........II Kings ii. 14.
78. When Reuben missed Joseph.....Gen. xxxvii. 29.
79. See..........................Judges iv. 21.
80. Jonah........................
81. See..............Gen. viii. 2; Deut. xxiv. 20.
82. See..........................I Sam. x. 24.
83. See..........................Job xix. 24.
84. Enoch ....
85. Simon Peter..................Matt. iv. 18.
86. James........................Acts xii. 1, 2.
87. At the stoning of Stephen.........Acts vii. 58.
88. Cornelius....................Acts x. 1-4.
89. Antioch ....Acts xi. 26.
90. Philippi ....Acts xvi. 12.
91. Lydia........................Acts xvi. 14, 15.
92. See..........................Ex. xxxviii. 8.

93. Lot's wife.....................Gen. xix. 26.
94. See..........................Gen. xvi. 7.
95. The twenty-second.............
96. See..........................Hosea xiii. 3.
97. See..........................Acts viii. 27–37.
98. See..........................Gen. vii. 2.
99. See..........................Ex. xxiv. 1.
100. I Thessalonians...............
101. The creation..................
102. Rehoboam. Shishak, king of Egypt. I Kings xiv. 26.
103. Abib ....Ex. xiii. 4.
104. The flaming sword.............Gen. iii. 24.
105. See..........................I Kings xxi. 8.
106. See..........................Job xviii. 6.
107. See..........................Gen. l. 9.
108. See..........................Matt. xvi. 18.
109. See..........................Dan. iii. 6.
110. The Lord......................Gen. iii. 21.
111. See..........................Gen. xviii. 8.
112. See..........................Gen. xiv. 18.
113. See..........................Psalm xix. 5.
114. See..........................Luke ii. 49.
115. See..........................II Kings xvi. 6.
116. Lamech ....Gen. iv. 23.
117. See..........................Gen. xxxii. 9–12.
118. Jacob ....Gen. xxxii. 10.
119. Temple of Dagon...............I Sam. v. 2.
120. Moses numbering the people....Num. i.
121. See..........................Gen. iv. 23, 24.
122. Between Abraham and Abimelech..Gen. xxi. 27–32.
123. See..........................Gen. xiv. 2.
124. Sabeanism, worship of the heavenly bodies ....Job xxxi. 26.

CHAPTER IV.

THE TABERNACLE.

1. Mt. Sinai.
2. Moses. Ex. xxv. 9-40.
3. Bezaleel and Aholiab. Ex. xxxi. 1, 6.
4. The tribe of Judah and the tribe of Dan. Ex. xxxi. 1, 6.
5. Gold, silver, and brass. Ex. xxxv. 22-24.
6. See Ex. xxxv. 22.
7. Linen. Ex. xxxv. 23.
8. See Ex. xxxv. 27.
9. See Ex. xxxv. 23; last clause of 24.
10. See Ex. xxxv. 28.
11. Fifty yards long and twenty-five yards wide.
12. About nine feet.
13. Of a connected series of curtains made of fine twined linen yarn, woven into a kind of net-work so that the people could see through.
14. By sixty brazen pillars—twenty on each side and ten on each end, five cubits apart, which stood upon pedestals of the same metal fixed in sockets of silver. The circular net-work held down to the ground by pins so that the wind should not waft them aside.
15. By hooks and fillets of silver.
16. The four centre pillars at the east end sustained a large curtain embroidered and dyed with gorgeous colors, and furnished with cords for pulling it up or drawing it aside.

17. Every clean Hebrew or proselyte of the covenant.
18. The altar of burnt-offering. The Laver.
19. Nine feet square aud five feet high.
20. Shittim wood (acacia) covered with brass.
21. Angular projections in the form of horns.
22. The animals sacrificed were bound to them, and part of the blood was applied to them.
23. See Ex. xxxvii. 3–7.
24. For receiving the blood of the sacrifice to be sprinkled upon the people.
25. Curved, three-pronged forks.
26. Large vessels, wherein the sacred fire which came from heaven was kept burning while they cleaned the altar and the grate, and while the altar was carried in the wilderness.
27. See Ex. xxvii. 6–7.
28. Made of brass and removed by means of four brazen rings.
29. A large basin of brass standing upon a brass pedestal. It was kept very bright, and here the priests washed their hands and feet before entering the tabernacle.
30. It was of an oblong, rectangular form, fifty-five feet long, eighteen feet wide, and eighteen feet high.
31. Shittim (acacia) wood.
32. Twenty.
33. Twenty.
34. Eight.
35. Length, ten cubits (eighteen feet), width, one and a half cubits (two and three-quarter feet).
36. Gold.
37. Each board had two tenons at its lower extremity which fitted into sockets of solid silver placed on the ground.
38. Ninety-six.
39. Each board had a ring of gold fixed to its front out-

wards, into which were inserted gilded bars five cubits long, and these bound together the boards, the head of one bar running into another after the manner of one tenon inserted in another. For the wall behind there was only one bar which went through all the boards, into which one of the ends of the bars on both sides was inserted.

40. Ten.

41. Blue, purple and scarlet, embroidered with figures of cherubim of cunning work.

42. Twenty-eight cubits long, four cubits broad.

43. By loops of blue and taches of gold.

44. Fifty.

45. Fifty.

46. Eleven.

47. Thirty cubits long and four cubits broad.

48. By a veil of blue, purple, and scarlet fine twined linen.

49. By five pillars of acacia wood, overlaid with gold and set in sockets of brass.

50. The priests only.

51. By a tent of goats' hair with two coverings or ornamentations, one of rams' skins dyed red, and the other of fine furs supposed to be seal-skin.

52. The Gershonites. Num. iv. 25.

53. The Sanctuary, or Holy Place, and the Holy of Holies.

54. With rich hangings of fine linen, wrought with cherubim and branches of plants, in gold, purple, crimson, and blue.

55. The Altar of Incense.

56. Three feet high, and one foot three inches square.

57. Shittim wood, covered with gold.

58. For the people's offering of perpetual incense.

59. By means of rings of gold and staves of wood overlaid with gold.

AIDS TO BIBLICAL RESEARCH. 203

60. The table of shew-bread and branched golden candlesticks.

61. See Ex. xxv. 23-28.

62. To hinder that which was placed upon the table from falling off accidentally.

63. The table of the Faces.

64. To the unalloyed gold with which it was covered.

65. Twelve.

66. To the twelve tribes. Rev. xxii. 2.

67. In two rows; six in each.

68. Once a week; on the Sabbath.

69. With incense.

70. It might not be removed from the Sanctuary, but must be eaten by the priests.

71. The heavenly life.

72. Dishes, spoons, and bowls, of pure gold.

73. From a base or stand rose an upright central shaft, bearing a central lamp; from two opposite sides of it proceeded other shafts, three on a side, making six branches upon the main shaft, all being in the same plane with it, and each bearing a lamp. Each of the six side branches had three flower-cups shaped like the calyx of an almond blossom, and terminated in a crown or capital with its ornamental flower, as a receptacle for the lamp. The central shaft was composed of four such combinations of calyx, capital and flower, each pair of side-branches resting on the capital of one of the three lower, the fourth and uppermost bearing the central lamp. Whether all the lamps were on the same level, as represented in the lamp of Zerubbabel's temple, or whether the central lamp was highest, is a matter of speculation. Ex. xxv. 31-37.

74. Gold.

75. $24,567.84.

76. Seven.

77. Olive oil.

78. With golden snuffers and carried away the snuff in golden vessels.

79. It was covered with a cloth of blue, and put with its appendages in badgers' skins, which were supported on a bar. Num. iv. 9, 10.

80. By a screen of four pillars of shittim overlaid with gold hung with embroidered curtains.

81. The High Priest, one day in the year.

82. It was just half the size.

83. The Ark.

84. Shittim (acacia) wood.

85. Two and a half cubits in length, one and a half in breadth, one and a half in height.

86. The tables of stone, the pot of manna, and Aaron's rod. Heb. ix. 4.

87. Gold.

88. A crown of gold.

89. Cherubims.

90. A gold ring.

91. Staves of shittim-wood covered with gold.

92. The High Priest.

93. It was enveloped in the veil of the dismantled tabernacle, in the curtain of badgers' skins, with a blue cloth over all.

94. The family of Kohath.

95. Levi.

96. In the centre surrounded by the twelve tribes.

97. See Josh. iv. 5–12.

98. See Josh. vi. 67.

99. Gilgal.

100. Forty years.

101. At Shiloh.
102. Eli's two sons, Hophni and Phinehas.
103. The Philistines captured it.
104. Temple of Dagon, in Ashdod. I Sam. v. 2.
105. See I Sam. v. 3.
106. See I Sam. v. 6.
107. Gath.
108. See I Sam. v. 9.
109. Ekron. I Sam. v. 10.
110. Return it to the Israelites.
111. Seven months. I Sam. vi. 1.
112. See I Sam vi. 17, 18.
113. See I Sam. vi. 10.
114. Beth-shemesh. I Sam. vi. 12.
115. See I Sam. vi. 19.
116. See I Sam. vii. 20.
117. Twenty years. I Sam. vii. 2.
118. David. I Chron. xiii. 6.
119. A new cart. I Chron. xiii. 7.
120. Uzza and Ahio. I Chron. xiii. 7.
121. "He died before the Lord." I Chron. xiii. 10.
122. Perez-uzza. I Chron. xiii. 11.
123. Obed-edom.
124. See I Chron xiii. 14.
125. See I Chron. xv. 1.
126. See I Chron. xv. 25–28.
127. A temple.

CHAPTER V.

SOLOMON'S TEMPLE.

1. See John ii. 19-21.
2. Jerusalem. II Chron. iii. 1.
3. Mt. Moriah. II Chron. iii. 1.
4. Of Araunah or Ornan, a Jebusite.
5. As a threshing floor.
6. He constructed massive walls on the eastern, southern, and western sides, and filled the enclosed space nearly to the level of the mount.
7. At the north-eastern corner and on the western side, at the Jews' wailing place.
8. Thirty feet long, and six feet in breadth and height.
9. David.
10. 1,017,000.
11. 108,000.
12. $9,108,975,075.08.
13. See II Sam. vii. 5.
14. Nathan.
15. The dimensions of every part of the temple were exactly double those of the tabernacle.
16. Fourth year. I Chron. iii. 2.
17. Seven years. I Kings vi. 38.
18. Hiram, king of Tyre. I Kings v.
19. Pots, shovels, basins, lavers, etc., etc., all of "bright brass." II Chron. iv. 11-16; I Kings vii. 45.
20. See II Chron. iv. 18.

21. 153,600. I Kings v.
22. 70,000. I Kings v. 15.
23. 80,000. I Kings v. 15.
24. 3,300. I Kings v. 16.
25. Three hundred.
26. Servants of Hiram.
27. Of a beautiful white stone, neatly polished, the stone of Lebanon; and a row of cedar beams.
28. See I Kings vi. 6, 7.
29. A subterranean quarry has been discovered near Jerusalem, which bears unequivocal evidence that the stones of the temple were dressed there. In this quarry are blocks exactly similar in size and substance to the ancient remains of the temple.
30. By a wall.
31. A single row of pillars.
32. Five. One on each side, and one towards the southwest for the entrance of the royal family.
33. Gate of Shallecheth.
34. Sur.
35. Asuppim.
36. Because the Levites convened there to receive their directions.
37. Parbar.
38. Houses.
39. The eastern gate.
40. Three.
41. By a deep ravine.
42. The southern extremity.
43. The platform of rock adjoined the rest of the city by a narrow neck, the approach to which was secured by a tower of immense strength.
44. Its walls.

45. Every clean Hebrew, or proselyte.
46. A court with a double row of pillars.
47. On the eastern side extending north and south.
48. It extended around the four sides of the temple and was just without the court of the priests.
49. Four feet.
50. Of three courses of stones and a row of cedar beams highly ornamented.
51. That the people might witness the sacrifices of the priests.
52. The court of the priests.
53. The brazen altar.
54. Twenty cubits or thirty-five feet.
55. Twenty cubits or thirty-five feet.
56. Ten cubits or seventeen and a half feet.
57. Two hundred tons.
58. On it were offered the morning and evening sacrifices, and a multitude of other oblations.
59. Let the wind be which way it might, the smoke always ascended directly upwards to heaven.
60. Near Succoth and Zaretan.
61. Ten.
62. Five on the north and five on the south side.
63. For washing the animal sacrificed.
64. Three hundred gallons.
65. Trucks, or four-wheeled carriages, for the support and conveyance of the lavers, from the brazen sea to the different parts of the temple where water was needed.
66. See I Kings vii. 27-37.
67. The brazen sea.
68. A circular basin supported by twelve brazen oxen, three on each side, all looking outward.
69. From sixteen to twenty thousand gallons.

70. It provided water for washing the victims, the parts of the sacrifices, the floor of the pavement, the feet and hands of the priests.

71. Ahaz.

72. The Assyrians.

73. Thirty-five feet from east to west, thirty-five feet from north to south, and two hundred and ten feet high.

74. As a steeple to adorn the temple, and as a place of shelter and prayer for the serving priests.

75. Jachin, stability—Boaz, strength.

76. Twelve cubits or twenty-one feet.

77. Eighteen cubits or thirty-one and a half feet.

78. With chapiters and four hundred pomegranates of brass.

79. The Sanctuary.

80. Olive, cedar, and cypress.

81. Forty cubits or seventy-five feet long, twenty cubits or thirty-five feet broad, and thirty cubits or fifty-two and a half feet high.

82. Ten.

83. On the west end, south side of the sanctuary.

84. On the triumphal arch of Titus at Rome is still to be seen the golden candlestick.

85. See II Chron. iv. 20–22.

86. One hundred.

87. Ten.

88. Twelve.

89. The altar of incense.

90. Twenty-two inches broad and fourty-four inches high.

91. Shittim (acacia) wood.

92. Gold.

93. By a cornice of gold.

94. By means of staves of shittim wood overlaid with gold.

95. Incense.

96. The silver trumpets, standards of weight and measure, and the sacred treasures.

97. A rail and two doors.

98. Linen.

99. Blue and scarlet and purple.

100. Cherubims.

101. Olive-tree.

102. Gold.

103. See I Kings vi. 32.

104. It was square. Twenty cubits or thirty-five feet every way.

105. Once a year on the day of atonement.

106. The high priest only.

107. The Ark.

108. Of olive wood, overlaid with gold.

109. No. It was perpetually dark.

110. See I Kings vi. 4.

111. Gold.

112. The brazen sea.

113. The upper chambers. I Kings vi. 5, 6.

114. Three.

115. Three.

116. On the right hand side in the interior of the under story, by a winding staircase of stone. They were connected with the temple without interfering with the Sanctuary.

117. Cedar, olive, fir, palm, shittim, and cypress.

118. Precious stones. II Chron. iii. 6.

119. Eleven months.

120. To choose a fitting opportunity when there should

be a general rendezvous of the people, which was not till the next or jubilee year.

121. Sons of Aaron.

122. See I Chron. xxiv. 1–4.

123. Feast of Tabernacles.

124. It had been instituted in commemoration of the Israelites dwelling in booths in the wilderness, and of the erection of the tabernacle. As the temple was to supersede the tabernacle there was admirable propriety in choosing the time for the feast of tabernacles in which to dedicate the new place of worship.

125. The seventh month, Tisri, corresponding to our September and October.

126. See I Kings viii. 1

127. All the holy vessels that were in the tabernacle.

128. In the Sanctuary.

129. In the Holy of Holies under the cherubims.

130. See II Chron. v. 9.

131. That the projecting staves might serve as a guide to the high priest; otherwise he might miss his way in the dark, the Ark being over under the cherubims.

132. The tables of stone.

133. Aaron's rod and the pot of manna.

134. That the other relics had disappeared.

135. One hundred and twenty.

136. Two.

137. In the sanctuary, on the south-west of the altar of incense.

138. See II Chron. v. 12.

139. At the east end of the altar.

140. The house was filled with a cloud.

141. See Ex. xvi. 10, Num. ix. 15.

142. See II Chron. vi. 1–11.

143. See II Chron. vi. 13.

144. Eight and three-quarters feet long, eight and three-quarters feet broad, and five and one-sixth feet high.

145. See II Chron. vi. 14–42.

146. See I Kings viii. 56–61.

147. Fire came from heaven and consumed the sacrifices, and the glory of the Lord filled the house.

148. They were filled with terror, and for a time unable to perform their usual functions.

149. See II Chron. vii. 3.

150. Twenty-two thousand oxen, one hundred and twenty thousand sheep.

151. See II Chron. vii. 7.

152. Seven.

153. Feast of Tabernacles.

154. Seven days.

155. Only thirty-three years.

156. Shishak, king of Egypt.

157. With brazen shields.

158. Asa. To Ben-hadad, king of Syria, who dwelt in Damascus. I Kings xv. 8.

159. Athaliah. II Chron. xxiv. 7.

160. Joash.

161. Hazael, king of Syria.

162. Ahaz.

163. See II Kings xvi. 8–17.

164. Hezekiah.

165. He cut off the gold from the doors and pillars of the temple.

166. See I Kings ix. 2, 6, 7.

167. See Jer. vii. 13, 14, Eze. xxiv. 21.

168. Nebuchadnezzar, king of Babylon.

169. See II Kings xxvi. 13.

170. See Dan. v. 2, 3.
171. See Jer. lii. 13.
172. See Zech. vi. 15, Isa. xliv. 28.
173. Cyrus.
174. The Ark, the Shechinah, the Urim and Thummim, the holy fire, and the spirit of prophecy.

CHAPTER VI.

THE SECOND TEMPLE.

1. See Ezra i. 2-4.
2. The Altar. Ezra iii. 2.
3. See Ezra i. 7.
4. Five thousand, four hundred. Ezra i. 11.
5. See I Cor. iii. 16, 17, II Cor. vi. 16, 17.
6. See Ezra iii. 1-10.
7. Zerubbabel.
8. Abib or Nisan, corresponding to our March and April, 536 B. C.
9. See Ezra iii. 10, 11.
10. See Ezra iii. 12, 13.
11. See Luke ii. 13, 14.
12. See Ezra iv. 4, 5.
13. Sixteen years.
14. Haggai, Zechariah. Ezra v. 1, 2.
15. Cyrus, Darius, Artaxerxes. Ezra vi. 14.
16. See Ezra vii. 12, 13, 23, 27.
17. 515 B. C.
18. Zerubbabel. Zech. iv. 9.
19. See Heb. xii. 2 (first clause).
20. Twenty.
21. See Rev. xxi. 1-3, 26, 27.
22. It was one third larger in size, but did not compare in magnificence.
23. The Brazen Sea, the Shechinah, or cloud of Divine

presence, the Ark and its furniture, the Urim and Thummim, the holy fire, and the spirit of prophecy.

24. See Hag. ii. 9, John i. 14.
25. Antiochus.
26. About three hundred and forty-seven.
27. Judas Maccabeus.
28. About one hundred and sixty-four.
29. Pompey. Jos. Ant. xiv. 4; Tacitus, Hist. v. 9.
30. Crassus.
31. Crassus had received from the priest a costly beam of solid gold on condition that every thing else should be spared.
32. Herod's temple.
33. Because Herod rebuilt it.
34. To humor his pride and gain the affection of the Jews.
35. 19 B. C.
36. They opposed it, fearing that Herod would tear down the old temple and not rebuild it.
37. By engaging to make all the necessary preparations before pulling down any of the existing buildings.
38. Two years.
39. One year and a half.
40. Eight years.
41. Forty-six years.
42. See John ii. 20.
43. Court of the Gentiles and cloisters or porches.
44. The cloisters (in an architectural point of view the most magnificent part of the temple) were double rows of Corinthian columns covered with flat roofs, resting against the outer wall of the temple.
45. To the south an inclined plane led down to the water-gate, so called because immediately in front of it was a great cistern excavated in the rock, from which water was supplied to the altar and to the temple.

46. At the south-west angle of the altar was an opening through which the blood of the victims flowed westward and southward to the king's garden at Siloam.

47. A lofty watch-tower, from which a priest with a trumpet announced the exact time when the Sabbath commenced and ended.

48. The roof was thickly set with golden spikes.

49. The Soreg, the Chel, and the walls, apartments, and gates surrounding the inner court.

50. The stone balustrade four and a half feet high surmounted at intervals by the pillars of the cloisters bearing inscriptions in Greek and Latin, forbidding all foreigners to pass that boundary on pain of death, and was called by Paul, "the middle wall of partition."

51. A platform fifteen feet wide, to which was an ascent by a flight of fourteen steps on all sides except the eastern, which had but five steps.

52. Nine—four on the northern, four on the southern, and one on the eastern side.

53. The "Gate of Song," the "Gate of Nitzouts," the "Gate of Corban," and the "Women's Gate," opening to the court of the women.

54. "Gate of Kindlings," through which wood was brought, "Gate of Firstlings" through which came the animals, "Water Gate," which led to the cistern, and the "Women's Gate."

55. The "Beautiful Gate."

56. They were devoted to the storing of wood, salt, culinary utensils, musical instruments, etc.

57. As a session room of the Sanhedrim.

58. It did not surround the temple, but was situated on the eastern side.

59. For the cure of lepers, for the use of persons under a vow, and for storing wood and oil.

60. It was fourteen trumpet-shaped boxes, situated seven on each side of the "Beautiful Gate," in the court of the women, and here the Jews deposited their gifts.

61. The "Beautiful Gate."

62. It was the entrance from the court of the women to the court of Israel, and so named from the magnificence of its ornaments, and from its two gates of brass each seventy-five feet wide, and thirty feet high, and so heavy that it required twenty men to move them on their hinges. It was covered with carvings richly gilded and had apartments over it.

63. The court of the priests.

64. The wall which separated the courts was so low they might easily look over.

65. The Thrigeos.

66. Holy of Holies.

67. Once a year.

68. By the high priest.

69. On the day of atonement.

70. See Ex. xxviii. 29.

71. A beautiful, ornamented silken vail.

72. See Mark xv. 38.

73. That the Priesthood of Christ superseded the priesthood of the law.

74. See Matt. iv. 5.

75. See Luke xviii. 10.

76. The Passover.

77. The Lord's Supper.

78. Peter and John. Acts iii. 1.

79. See Acts iii. 2–8.

80. See Acts xxi. 28.

81. See Mark xiii. 1.

82. See Mark xiii. 2.

83. At the destruction of Jerusalem.

84. Rome's.

85. Titus.

86. As a fort.

87. After it had been polluted with murder and every other wickedness, it was, to the extreme grief of Titus, brought to the ground.

88. Julian, the Roman emperor.

89. 390, A. D.

90. Earthquakes, and flames of fire dispersed his material and killed his workmen.

91. A Mahometan mosque.

92. Jesus Christ.

CHAPTER VII.

THE PATRIARCHS.

1. Adam.   930 years.............Gen. ii. 19.
2. Cain......................Gen. iv. 13.
3. Abel......................Matt. xxiii. 35.
4. Enoch....................Gen. iv. 17.
5. Lamech...................Gen. iv. 23, 24.
6. Jabal.....................Gen. iv. 20.
7. Jubal.....................Gen. iv. 21.
8. Tubal-cain................Gen. iv. 22.
9. Seth.   912 years..............Gen. v. 8.
10. Enos.   905 years.............Gen. v. 11.
11. Cainan.   910 years...........Gen. v. 14.
12. Mahalaleel.   895 years........Gen. v. 17.
13. Jared.   962 years.............Gen. v. 18–20.
14. Enoch.   365 years............Gen. v. 23.
15. Methuselah.   969 years........Gen. v. 26.
16. Lamech.   777 years...........Gen. v. 30.
17. Noah.   950 years.............Gen. vi. 9.
18. Shem.   600 years.............Gen. xi. 10, 11.
19. Ham......................Gen. x. 1.
20. Japheth...................Gen. x. 1.
21. Gomer (son of Japheth)........Gen. x. 2.
22. Magog....................Gen. x. 2.
23. Madai....................Gen. x. 2.
24. Javan....................Gen. x. 2.
25. Nimrod...................Gen. x. 10.
26. Mizraim..................Gen. x. 13.

27. Canaan ....Gen. x. 15–20.
28. Elam ....Gen. x. 22.
29. Asshur.....................Gen. x. 22.
30. Arphaxad. 438 years........Gen. xi. 13.
31. Terah. 205 years............Gen. xi. 27.
32. Abram. 175 years...........Gen. xiv. 13.
33. Nahor ....Gen. xxiv. 47.
34. Bethuel ....Gen. xxiv. 47.
35. Haran ....Gen. xi. 27.
36. Lot ....Gen. xix. 15.
37. Laban ....
38. Isaac ....Gal. iv. 28.
39. Ishmael....................Gal. iv. 29.
40. Jacob. 147 years........Gen. xliii. 1; xlvi. 29, 30.
41. Esau ....Heb. xii. 16.
42. Reuben ....Gen. xxix. 32.
    Simeon ....Gen. xxix. 23.
    Levi. 137 years..............Ex. vi. 16.
    Judah ....Gen. xxix. 35.
    Zebulun....................Gen. xxx. 20.
    Issachar...................Gen. xxx. 18.
    Gad ....Gen. xxx. 11.
    Dan ....Gen. xxx. 6.
    Asher......................Gen. xxx. 13.
    Naphtali ....Gen. xxx. 8.
    Joseph. 110 years............Gen. l. 26.
    Benjamin.... ....Gen. xxxv. 18.
43. Ephraim ....Num. ii. 18.
    Manasseh ....Num. ii. 20.
44. Job ....Job i.
45. Eliphaz, the Temanite.. ......Job iv. 1.
    Bildad, the Shuhite............Job viii. 1.
    Zophar, the Naamathite.........Job xi. 1.

CHAPTER VIII.

THE PROPHETS.

1. Enoch ....Gen. v. 23.
2. Noah ....II Peter ii. 5.
3. Abraham ....Gen. xv. 17.
4. Isaac ....Gen. xxi. 6.
5. Jacob ....Gen. xxvii. 24; Gen. xxix. 25.
6. Joseph ....Gen. xxxix. 1.
7. Moses ....Acts vii. 23, 30; Deut. viii. 2.
8. Aaron ....Lev. x. 9.
9. Baalam ....II Peter ii. 15.
10. Miriam ....Num. xii. 10.
11. Joshua (Joshua means "he shall save")....................Num. xiii. 8, 16.
12. Deborah ....Judges iv. 4.
13. Barak.......................Judges iv. 10.
14. Ehud (?)....................Judges iii. 15-30.
15. Eli ....I Sam. ii. 12.
16. Samuel ....I Sam. ix. 13.
17. Hannah.....................I Sam. i. 20.
18. Ahiah......................I Sam. xiv. 3.
19. David......................
20. Nathan ....II Sam. xii. 7.
21. Gad ....I Chron. xxi. 11-13.
22. Ahijah ....I Kings xi. 29, 30.
23. Solomon ....I Kings vi. 1.
24. Iddo ....II Chron. xii. 15.
25. Shemaiah..................I Kings xii. 23, 24.

26. The man of God from Judah.....I Kings xiii. 24, 27.
27. Oded ....II Chron. xxviii. 9.
28. Azariah ....II Chron. xv. 1-15.
29. Hanani ....II Chron. xiv. 7.
30. Jehu.........................II Chron. xix. 1, 2.
31. Elijah ....II Kings ii. 11.
32. Micaiah ....I Kings xxii. 27.
33. Elisha ....II Kings iv. 7.
34. Jahaziel ....II Chron. xx. 14, 15.
35. Zechariah (son of Jehoida)....... " xxiv. 20, 21.
36. Zechariah ....II Chron. xxvi. 5.
37. Urijah ....Jer. xxvi. 23.
38. John the Baptist...............

CHAPTER IX.

THE CANONICAL PROPHETS.

1. Jonah.......840–784..........Jonah i.
2. Joel ....810–795..........Joel i. 20.
3. Amos.......810–785..........Amos v. 25.
4. Hosea ......800–725..Hos. vi. 6 { Matt. ix, 13.
                                   { Matt. xii. 7.
5. Isaiah.......765–698..........
6. Micah ......758–699.......... { Micah i. 2.
                                 { I Kings xxii. 28.
7. Nahum .....720–698..........Nahum ii. 8, 13.
8. Zephaniah ...640–609..........Zeph. i. 1.
9. Jeremiah ....628–585..........Jer. i. 6.
10. Habakkuk...612–598..........Hab. ii. 15.
11. Daniel ......606–534..........Dan. viii. 27.
12. Ezekiel .....595–574..........Eze. viii. 3.
13. Obadiah.....588–583..........
14. Haggai......520–518..........Hag. ii. 9.
15. Zechariah....520–510..........Eze. vi. 14.
16. Malachi .....420–397..........

CHAPTER X.

THE HIGH-PRIESTS.

1. Aaron ....Lev. viii. 1–13.
2. Eleazor ....Num. xx. 28.
3. Phinehas ....Num. xxv. 7–14.
4. Abishua ....I Chron. vi. 4–5.
5. Eli ....I Sam. iii. 12, 13.
6. Ahiah ....I Sam. xiv. 3.
7. Zadok ....I Kings i. 34.
8. Abiathar ....I Kings ii. 26, 27; I Kings i. 7.
9. Azariah ....I Chron. vi. 10.
10. Johanan ....See Hervey's Genealogies, ch. x.
11. Azariah ....I Chron. vi. 10.
12. Amariah ....II Chron. xix. 11.
13. Jehoida ....II Kings xi.
14. Zechariah ....II Chron. xxiv. 20, 21.
15. Azariah ....II Chron. xxvi. 17, 18.
16. Azariah ....II Chron. xxxi. 10–13.
17. Urijah ....II Kings xvi. 10, 11.
18. Shallum ....Smith's Bible Dict., High-priest.
19. Hilkiah ....II Chron. xxxiv. 14.
20. Seraiah ....Jer. lii. 24–27.
21. Jehozadak ....I Chron. vi. 15.
22. Jeshua ....Ezra iii. 2.
23. Joiakim ....Neh. xii. 10, 11, 22.
    Eliashib ....   "   "
    Joiada ....   "   "

     Johanan....................Neh. xii. 10, 11, 22.
     Jaddua.....................   "   "
24. Annas ....Luke iii. 2.
25. Caiphas ....John xviii. 24.
26. Theophilus ....Josh. Ant. xix. 6.
27. Ananias ....Acts xxiii. 1, 2.

CHAPTER XI.

THE JUDGES OF ISRAEL.

	NAMES.	LENGTH OF REIGN.	REFERENCE.
1.	Othniel	40 yrs.	Judges iii. 9–11.
2.	Ehud	40 "	" iii. 15.
3.	Shamgar		" iii. 31.
4.	Deborah and Barak.	40 "	" iv. 4, 6.
5.	Gideon	40 "	" viii. 22, 23.
6.	Abimelech	3 "	" ix. 53, 54.
7.	Tola	23 "	" x. 1, 2.
8.	Jair	22 "	" x. 3, 4.
9.	Jephthah	6 "	" xi. 30.
10.	Ibzan	7 "	" xii. 8–10.
11.	Elon	10 "	" xii. 11, 12.
12.	Abdon	8 "	" xii. 13, 14.
13.	Samson	20 "	" xv. 4.
14.	Eli		I Sam. i. 9.
15.	Samuel	"All the days of his life."	{ I Sam. viii. 6, 7. { I Sam. vii. 15.

CHAPTER XII.

THE KINGS OF ISRAEL AND JUDAH.

KINGS OF ISRAEL BEFORE THE REVOLT.

NAMES.	LENGTH OF REIGN.	REFERENCE.
1. Saul	40 years	I Sam. x. 1.
2. David	40 "	II Sam. xxiii. 15. 17.
3. Solomon	40 "	I Kings x. 27.

THE KINGS OF ISRAEL AFTER THE REVOLT.

Ten Tribes.

1. Jeroboam	22 years	I Kings xii. 28.
2. Nadab	2 "	I " xv. 25–30.
3. Baasha	24 "	I " xvi. 4.
4. Elah	2 "	I " xvi. 8, 9.
5. Zimri	7 days	I " xvi. 15.
6. Omri	12 years	I " xvi. 24.
7. Ahab	22 "	I " xxii. 39.
8. Ahaziah	2 "	II Kings i. 2.
9. Joram or Jehoram	12 "	II " iii. 1, 2.
10. Jehu	28 "	II " ix. 30–33.
11. Jehoahaz	17 "	II " xiii. 7.
12. Joash or Jehoash	16 "	II " xiii. 14.
13. Jeroboam II	41 "	II " xiv. 25, 28.

INTERREGNUM.

14. Zachariah	6 months	II " xv. 8.
15. Shallum	1 "	II " xv. 13.
16. Menahem	10 "	II " xv. 19, 20.
17. Pekaiah	2 years	II " xv. 22.
18. Pekah	20 "	II " xv. 29.

ANARCHY.

19. Hoshea	9 years	II " xvii. 5, 6, 24.

The Kings of Judah after the Revolt.

Two Tribes.

NAMES.	LENGTH OF REIGN.	REFERENCE.
1. Rehoboam	17 years	I Kings xiv. 27.
2. Abijah or Abijam	3 "	I " xv. 4.
3. Asa	41 "	I " xv. 13.
4. Jehoshaphat	25 "	II Kings iii. 14–17.
5. Jehoram or Joram	8 "	II Chron. xxi. 19.
6. Ahaziah or Azariah	1 "	II " xxii. 2.
7. Athaliah	6 "	II Kings xi. 1.
8. Jehoash or Joash	40 "	II " xi. 21.
9. Amaziah	29 "	II Chron. xxv. 16.

INTERREGNUM 11 years

10. Uzziah or Azariah	52 "	II " xxvi. 18–21.
11. Jotham	16 "	II " xxvii. 6.
12. Hezekiah	29 "	Isa. xxxviii. 1–5.
13. Manasseh	55 "	II Chron. xxxiii. 7. Smith's Bible Dict.
14. Amon	2 "	II Chron. xxxiii. 18. II Kings xxii. 2.
15. Josiah	31 "	II " xxxiv. 14.
16. Jehoahas	3 months	II " xxiii. 34.
17. Jehoiakim	11 years	II " xxiv. 1.
18. Jehoiachin	3 m's & 10 d	II " xxiv. 15.
19. Zedekiah	11 years	II " xxiv. 17.

Governors of Jerusalem after the Captivity.

1. Zerubbabel ....Zech. iv. 9.
2. Ezra ....Neh. viii. 1, 2.
3. Nehemiah ....Neh. ii.

CHAPTER XIII.

THE HEATHEN MONARCHS OF THE BIBLE.

1. The Pharaoh of Abraham, king of Egypt....Gen. xii. 17.
2. Amraphel, ... " Shinar..Gen. xiv. 1, 2, 9,
   Arioch, ... " Ellasar.. " "
   Chedorlaomer, ... " Elam... " "
   Tidal, ... " Nations. " "
   Bera, ... " Sodom.. " "
   Birsha, ... " Gomorrah " "
   Shinab, ... " Admah.. " "
   Shemeber, ... " Zeboiim. " "
                  The " Bela(Zoar) " "
3. Melchizedek, ... " Salem... " xiv. 19.
4. Abimelech, ... " Gerar... " xx. 3.
5. The Pharaoh of Joseph, . " Egypt... " xl. 3-22.
6. Pharaoh of the Oppression " " ....Ex. i. 3.
7. Pharaoh of the Exodus.. " " .... " xiv. 23.
8. Pharaoh, father-in-law of Mered, king of Egypt, I Ch. iv. 18.
9. Sihon, king of the Amorites............Num. xxi. 23.
10. Barak, ...king of Moab.........Num. xxiii. 7.
11. Agag, ... " Amalek ...... " xxiv. 7.
12. Og, ... " Bashan.........Deut. iii. 11.
13. .... " Ai............Josh. viii. 29.
14. Adoni-zedec, ... " Jerusalem..Josh. x. 3, 16, 27.
    Hoham, ... " Hebron....Josh. x. 3, 16, 27.
    Piram, ... " Jarmuth...Josh. x. 3, 16, 27.
    Japhia, ... " Lachish ...Josh. x. 3, 16, 27.
    Debir, ... " Eglon.......Josh. x. 3, 16, 27.

15. Jabin, ... king of Hazor .... Josh. xi. 1-4.
    Jobab, ... " Madon ...... " "
16. One hundred and thirty rulers .... " xii.
17. Adoni-bezek, ... king of Bezek .... Judges i. 5.
18. Eglon, ... " Moab .... Judges iii. 14.
19. Cushan-rishathaim " Mesopotamia .. Judges iii. 8-10.
20. Jabin, ... " Canaan .... Judges iv. 7.
21. Agag, ... " Amalek .... I Sam. xv. 33.
22. Achish, ... " Gath .... I Sam. xxi. 13.
23. Hiram, ... " Tyre .... II Sam. v. 11.
24. Hadadezer, ... " Zobah .... II Sam. viii. 3.
25. Toi, ... " Hamath ...... " viii. 9, 10.
26. Rabbah, king of the Ammonites .... II Sam. xii. 26, 30.
27. Pharaoh, the father-in-law of Solomon, king of Egypt.
                                                I Kings iii. 1.
28. Shishak, ... king of Egypt .... I Kings xiv. 25.
29. Ethbaal, ... " Tyre .... " xvi. 31.
30. Ben-hadad I., ... " Damascus ...... " xx. 34.
31. Mesha, ... " Moab .... II Kings iii. 4.
32. Ben-hadad II., .. " Syria .... " viii. 8.
33. Hazael, ... " Assyria ...... " x. 32.
34. Ben-hadad III., .. " " .... Amos i. 4.
35. Pul, ... " " ...... II Kings xv. 19.
36. .... The " Moab .... " iii. 27.
37. Rezin, ... " Damascus ...... " xvi. 5.
38. Tiglath-pileser ... " Assyria .... " xvi. 10.
39. So, ... " Egypt .... " xvii. 4.
40. Shalmaneser, ... " Assyria .... "xviii. 9, 10.
41. Sargon, ... " " .... Isa. xx. 1.
42. Pharaoh, opponent of Sennacherib, king of Egypt.
                                                II Kings xviii. 21.
43. Sennacherib, ... king of Assyria ... II Kings xix. 36, 37.
44. Berodach-baladan, " " ...... II Kings xx. 12.

45. Esar-haddon .... king of Assyria........... Ezra iv. 2.
46. Ahasuerus (Cyaxares), king of Media ...... " " 6.
47. Pharaoh-nechoh, ...   " Egypt, II Kings xxiii. 29, 33.
48. Nebuchadnezzar, ... " Babylon.
49. Pharaoh-hophra, ... " Egypt....... Jer. xliv. 30.
50. Evil-merodach, ...   " Babylon. II Kings xxv. 27.
51. Belshazzar, ...   " Babylon.
52. Darius, the Mede, ... " Media........ Dan. vi. 9.
53. Cyrus, ...   " Persia........ Ezra i. 1–3.
54. Ahasuerus (son of Cyrus), "   "   .... Dan. ix. 1.
55. Artaxerxes (Pseudo-Smerdis), king of Persia.. Ezra iv. 7.
56. Darius, ... king of Persia........ Ezra vi. 12.
57. ....   " Nineveh........ Jonah iii.
58. Ahasuerus, ...   " Persia........ Ezra ii. 17.
59. Artaxerxes (Artaxerxes Longaminus), king of Persia.
    Neh. v. 14.
60. King of the south (Ptolemy Philadelphus), king of Egypt.
    Dan. xi. 6.
   King of the north (Antiochus II.), king of Syria.
    Dan. xi. 6.
   King of the north (Antiochus III.), king of Syria.
    Dan. xi. 15.
   King of the south (Ptolemy Philopater), king of Egypt.
    Dan. xi. 15.
61. Augustus Cæsar, emperor of Rome........ Luke ii. 1.
62. Herod the Great...................... Matt. ii. 16.
63. Tiberius Cæsar, emperor of Rome....... Luke iii. 1–3.
64. Archelaus, tetrarch of Idumea, Samaria, Judea.
    Matt. ii. 22.
65. Herod (Herod Antipas), tetrarch of Galilee.
    Luke ix. 9.
66. Philip (Herod Philip I.).............. Mark vi. 17.
67. Pilate, procurator of Judea............ John xix. 12.

68. Philip (Herod Philip II.), tetrarch of Iturea and Trachonitis.................Matt. xvi. 13, Luke iii. 1.
69. Claudius Cæsar, emperor of Rome.... ...Acts xi. 28.
70. Herod (Herod Agrippa), tetrarch of Iturea, Trachonitis, and Abilene........................Acts xii. 2.
71. Sergius Paulus, proconsul of Cyprus.......Acts xiii. 7.
72. Gallio, the Roman proconsul of Asia.....Acts xviii. 17.
73. Felix, procurator of Judea.............Acts xxv. 14.
74. Festus, procurator of Judea............Acts xxv. 23.
75. Agrippa (Herod Agrippa), procurator of Chalcis.
Acts xxvi. 28.
76. Nero, emperor of Rome..............II Tim. last ¶.

CHAPTER XIV.

THE APOSTLES.

1. Simon Peter (Cephas)....................John i. 42.
2. Andrew (Simon Peter's brother).........John vi. 8, 9.
3. James (the son of Zebedee)..............Acts xii. 1.
4. John (the son of Zebedee)....... ....
5. Philip..............................John xiv. 8.
6. Bartholomew (Nathanael), Asseman Bible..Or. iii. 2, 20.
7. Thomas (called Didymus)....John xi. 16, John xx. 25.
8. Matthew the Publican (Levi)..............Matt. x. 3.
9. James the Less (the Just), Clement of Alexandria.
10. Judas (Libbaeus Thaddaeus)............John xiv. 22.
11. Simon Zilotes (the Canaanite)............Luke vi. 15.
12. Judas Iscariot....................Matt. xxvi. 14–16.
13. Matthias............................Acts i. 26.
14. Paul..............................I Cor. xv. 9.

CHAPTER XV.

SOME OF THE UNTITLED MEN OF THE BIBLE.

1. Eliezer .... Gen. xv. 2.
2. Amram .... Ex. vi. 20.
3. Jethro Hohab-Jether, prince of Midian.... Ex. iv. 18.
4. Hur .... Ex. xvii. 10–12.
5. Nadab .... Lev. x. 1.
   Abihu .... Lev. x. 1.
6. Korah .... Num. xxvi. 9.
   Dathan .... Num. xxvi. 9.
   Abiram .... Num. xxvi. 9, 10.
7. On .... Num. xvi. 1.
8. Shammua, tribe of Reuben ...... Num. xiii. 4–16.
   Shaphat,   "   Simeon ......   "   "
   Caleb,   "   Judah ....   "   "
   Igal,   "   Issachar ..... "   "
   Oshea,   "   Ephraim .....   "   "
   Palti,   "   Benjamin ....   "   "
   Gaddiel,   "   Zebulun .....   "   "
   Gaddi,   "   Manasseh ....   "   "
   Ammiel,   "   Dan ....   "   "
   Sethur,   "   Asher ....   "   "
   Nahbi,   "   Naphtali ....   "   "
   Geuel,   "   Gad ....   "   "
9. Oshea (Joshua) ....   "   "
   Caleb .... Num. xiv. 6–9.
10. Achan .... Josh. vii. 4, 18.

11. Sisera	Judg. iv. 22.	
12. Elimelech	Ruth i. 1–3.	
13. Boaz	Ruth iv. 10.	
14. Obed	Ruth iv. 17.	
15. Jesse	Ruth iv. 17.	
16. Hophni	I Sam. ii. 12.	
Phinehas	I " ii. 12.	
17. Kish	I " ix. 1, 2.	
18. Jonathan	I " xviii. 1.	
19. Goliath of Gath	I " xvii. 4, 49.	
20. Eliab	I " xvii. 28.	
21. Doeg the Edomite	I " xxii. 18.	
	II Sam. iii. 33, 34.	
22. Abner	I Sam. xiv. 50.	
23. Nabal	I Sam. xxv. 3, 36.	
24. Mephibosheth	II Sam. ix. 6, 7.	
25. Ziba	II " ix. 2, 10.	
26. Uzzah	II " vi. 7.	
27. Obed-edom	II " vi. 11, 12.	
28. Urijah	II " xi. 15.	
29. Araunah	II " xxiv. 24.	
30. Nathan	II Sam. v. 14.	
	Luke iii. 31.	
31. Naaman	II Kings v. 1–14.	
32. Gehazi	II Kings v. 27.	
	Josh. vi. 26.	
33. Hiel	I Kings xvi. 34.	
34. Naboth	I Kings xxi. 15.	
35. Hananiah	Jer. xxviii. 15–17.	
36. Shephatiah	" xxxviii. 1.	
Gedaliah	" xxxviii. 1.	
Jucal	" xxxviii. 1.	
Pashur	" xxxviii. 1.	

37. Ebed-melech..................Jer. xxxviii. 7–10.
38. Nebuzar-adan ....II Kings xxv. 8.
39. Mordecai ....Esth. ii. 7.
40. Haman ....Esth. vii. 10.
41. Sanballat ....Neh. ii. 10–19.
    Tobiah.......................Neh. ii. 10–19.
42. Zacharias ....Luke i. 13.
43. Simeon ....Luke ii. 25–28.
44. Joseph ....Matt. ii. 14.
45. Nicodemus ....John iii. 1, 2.
46. Zaccheus ....Luke xix. 8.
47. Lazarus ....John xi. 43.
48. Barabbas ....John xviii. 40.
49. Joseph of Arimathea..........Luke xxiii. 50–53.
50. John ....Acts iv. 6–21.
    Alexander .... " iv. 6–21.
51. Ananias .... " v. 5.
52. Gamaliel .... " v. 34.
53. Theudas..................... " v. 36.
54. Judas of Galilee.............. " v. 37.
55. Stephen
56. Philip
57. Prochorus
58. Nicanor   } Seven Deacons....Acts vi. 5.
59. Timon
60. Parmenas
61. Nicolas
62. Simon Magus .... " viii. 9, 19.
63. Ananias, a Jewish disciple .... " iv. 36, ix. 27.
64. Barnabas (Joses) .... " ix. 27.
65. Cornelius .... " x.
66. Elymas (Bar-jesus) .... " xiii. 6–8.

67. John Mark .... Acts xv. 39.
68. Silas .... " xv. 40.
69. Timotheus (Timothy).......... I Cor. iv. 17.
70. Jason .... Acts xvii. 6-9.
71. Dionysius the Areopagite .... " xvii. 34.
72. Aquila .... " xviii. 3-11.
73. Justus...................... " xviii. 7-9.
74. Crispus............ Acts xviii. 8; I Cor. i. 14.
75. Demetrius .... Acts xix. 24-28.
76. Aristarchus........ Acts xix. 29; Col. iv. 10.
77. Theophilus.......... Luke i. 3; Acts i. 1.
78. Eutychus .... " xx. 10-12.
79. Claudius Lysias.............. " xxiii. 26-29.
80. Tertullus .... " xxiv. 1, 5.
81. Publius .... " xxviii. 7.
82. Apollos .... " xviii. 24, 25.
83. Onesimus.................... Phil. 16.
84. Onesiphorus .... II Tim. i. 15, 16.
85. Tertius .... Rom. xvi. 22.

CHAPTER XVI.

THE WOMEN OF THE OLD TESTAMENT.

1. Eve ....Gen. iv. 19–22.
   Adah .... "   "
   Zillah................... "   "
   Naamah.................. "   "
2. Noah's wife............. " vii. 13.
   Shem's wife............. "   "
   Ham's wife.............. "   "
   Japheth's wife........... "   "
3. Sarah .... " xxiii. 1.
   Iscah .... " xi. 29.
   Sarai .... " xvi. 1.
4. Milcah .... " xi. 29.
5. Reumah .... " xxii. 24.
6. Hagar .... " xxi. 14, 17.
7. Keturah ....I Chron. i. 32.
8. Lot's wife................Gen. xix. 26.
9. Lot's daughters.......... " xix. 26.
10. Rebekah ...Gen. xxvii. 46; Gen. xxiv. 59.
11. Deborah, Rebekah's nurse..Gen. xxxv. 8.
12. Judith, daughter of Elon, same as Adah, daughter of Elon ....Gen. xxvi. 34.
    Bashemath, daughter of Anah, same as Aholibamah, daughter of Beeri..Gen. xxvi. 34; Gen. xxxvi. 1, 2.
    Mahalath, daughter of Ishmael, same as Bashemath, daughter of Ishmael..Gen. xxvi. 34; xxxvi. 1, 2.
13. Leah ....Gen. xxix. 32.

14. Rachel.....Gen. xxix. 20; Gen. xxxi. 19.
15. Bilhah .... " xxxv. 25, 26.
    Zilpah .... " xxxv. 25, 26.
16. Dinah .... " xxxiv. 1.
17. Timna .... " xxxvi. 12.
18. Mehetabel .... " xxxvi. 39.
    Matred.................. " xxxvi. 39.
19. Tamar .... " xxxviii. 6.
20. Sarah ....Num. xxvi. 46.
21. Helah .... I Chron. iv. 5.
    Naarah.................. I Chron. iv. 5.
22. Potiphar's wife...........Gen. xxxix. 19.
23. Serah, Jacob's granddaughter Gen. xlvi. 17.
24. Maachah .... I Chron. vii. 16, 18.
    Hammoleketh............ " vii. 16, 18.
25. Sherah .... " viii. 24.
26. Hushim .... " viii. 8, 9, 29.
    Baara .... " viii. 8, 9, 29.
    Hodesh .... " viii. 8, 9, 29.
    Maachah .... " viii. 8, 9, 29.
27. Asenath ....Gen. xli. 45.
28. Job's wife...............Job ii. 9.
29. Jemima .... " xlii. 14.
    Kezia .... " xlii. 14.
    Keren-happuch .... " xlii. 14.
30. Shiphrah ....Ex. i. 15, 17.
    Puah .... " i. 15, 17.
31. Jochebed .... " vi. 20.
32. Pharaoh's daughter (Thermitis), Smith's Bible Dictionary......................Ex. ii. 9, 10.
33. Miriam ....Ex. xv. 20.
34. Zipporah .... " ii. 21.
35. Elisheba .... " vi. 23.

36. Mahlah .... Num. xxvii. 1–11.
    Noah .... "   xxvii. 1–11.
    Hoglah .... "   xxvii. 1–11.
    Milcah .... "   xxvii. 1–11.
    Tirzah .... "   xxvii. 1–11.
37. Cozbi .... Num. xxv. 15.
38. Rahab .... Josh. ii.
39. Azubah .... I Chron. ii. 18, 19, 48.
    Jerioth .... "   ii. 18, 19, 48.
    Ephrath .... "   ii. 18, 19, 48.
    Maachah .... "   ii. 18, 19, 48.
40. Achsah, Caleb's daughter... Josh. xv. 16–19.
41. Deborah .... Judg. iv. 4, 5.
42. Jael .... "   iv. 21.
43. The mother of Sisera ... "   v. 28.
44. A woman of Thebez ..... "   ix. 50, 54.
45. Jepthah's daughter .... "   xi. 34, 40.
46. Manoah's wife .... "   xiii. 2, 5.
47. Delilah .... "   xvi. 4–20.
48. Peninnah .... I Sam. i. 1–8.
49. Hannah .... "   ii. 18. 19.
50. Hannah's two daughters . "   ii. 21.
51. The mother of Milcah ... Judg. xvii. 2, 6.
52. The concubine of a certain Levite ...... Judg. xx. 6.
53. Naomi .... Ruth ii.
54. Ruth .... "   iv. 13.
55. Orpah .... "   i. iv.
56. Samuel's daughter-in-law, the wife of Phinehas.
                                       I Sam. iv. 19, 21.
57. Ahinoam .... I Sam. xiv. 50.
58. Witch of Endor .... "   xxviii. 7.
59. Merab .... "   xiv. 49.

AIDS TO BIBLICAL RESEARCH.   241

60. Michal,   David's wife....II Sam. vi. 20, 23.
61. Bathsheba,   "   " ....II " xi.
62. Abigail,   "   " I   " xxx. 5.
    Ahinoam,   "   " I   " xxx. 5.
63. Maacah,   "   " ....II " iii. 3.
64. Haggith,   "   " ....I Chron. iii. 2, 3.
    Abital,   "   " I   " iii. 2, 3.
    Eglah,   "   " I   " iii. 2, 3.
65. Zeruiah I   " ii. 16.
66. Abigail.................I   " ii. 17.
67. Tamar ....II Sam. xiii. 1.
68. A wise woman of Tekoah..II " xiv. 2.
69. Tamar ....II " xiv. 27.
70. David's ten concubines.....II " xx. 3.
71. The Wench..............II " xvii. 17.
72. A wise woman of Abel.....II " xx. 16.
73. Rizpah.................II " xxi. 10.
74. Abishag, a Shunamite ....I Kings i. 3, 4.
75. Pharaoh's daughter ....I " vii. 8.
76. Two women that were harlots. I " iii. 16.
77. Taphath ....I " iv. 11, 15.
    Basmath ....I " iv. 11, 15.
78. Taphenes................I " xi. 19.
79. The Queen of Sheba......II Chron. ix. 1.
80. Jeroboam's wife...........I Kings xiv. 1, 2.
81. Shelomith ....Lev. xxiv. 11–23.
82. Zeruah ....I Kings xi. 26.
83. Naamah ....I Kings xiv. 21.
84. Mahalath................II Chron. xi. 18.
85. Abihail ....II " xi. 18.
86. Michaiah ....II " xiii. 2.
87. Maachah, Absalom's daughter II " xi. 21.
88. Maachah, Asa's mother ....I Kings xv. 13.

89. Jehoshabeath............II Chron. xxii. 11.
90. Jezebel ....I Kings xxi. 25.
91. The widow of Zarephath....II Chron xvii. 9.
92. The widow whose oil Elisha increased. II Kings iv. 6, 7.
93. The Shunamite ....II Kings iv.
94. The captive maiden ....   "   v. 3.
95. Naaman's wife............   "   v. 2.
96. Athaliah.................II Chron. xxii. 10.
97. Zibiah ....II Kings xii. 1.
98. Jecholiah...............II Kings xv. 2.
99. Jehoaddan ....II Chron. xxv. 1.
100. Jerusha ....II Kings xv. 33.
101. Abi ....II Kings xviii. 2.
102. Gomer ....Hosea i. 3.
103. Lo-ruhamah ....Hosea i. 6.
104. Hephzibah ....II Kings xxi. 1.
105. Meshullemeth...........II   "   xxi. 19.
106. Jedidah II   "   xxii. 1.
107. Huldah II   "   xxii. 14, 15.
108. Zebudah II   "   xxiii. 36.
109. Nehushta II   "   xxiv. 8.
110. Hamutul...............II   "   xxiv. 18.
111. Bithiah................I Chron. iv. 18.
112. Ezekiel's wife ....Ezek. xxiv. 15, 18.
113. Vashti ....Esth. i.
114. Esther ....Esth. v. i.
115. Zeresh, Haman's wife.....Esth. v. 14.
116. Shallum's daughters ......Neh. iii. 12.
117. Noadiah ....Neh. vi. 14.
118. Shelomith ....I Chron. iii. 19.

CHAPTER XVII.

THE WOMEN OF THE NEW TESTAMENT.

1. Elisabeth ....Luke i. 5, 6.
2. Anna .... Luke ii. 36, 37.
3. The Virgin Mary .... Matt. ii. 14.
4. Peter's mother-in-law .... Matt. viii. 14, 15.
5. A woman of Samaria .... John iv. 6, 7, 26.
6. Jairus' daughter .... Mark v. 23–47.
7. Herodias .... Matt. xiv. 3.
8. The widow of Nain......... Luke vii. 11–15.
9. The Magdalene............ Luke vii. 37–50.
10. Salome...... Joseph. Ant. xviii. 4, 5; Matt. xiv. 8.
11. The Syrophenician woman.. Mark vii. 24.
12. Joanna.................. Luke viii. 3.
13. Susanna .... Luke viii. 3.
14. Salome... Matt. xx. 2; Matt. xxvii. 56; Mark xv. 40.
15. Martha.................. Luke x. 40.
16. Mary .... Luke x. 42.
17. The poor widow who cast in her mite... Luke xxi. 2.
18. Pilate's wife .... Matt. xxvii. 19.
19. Mary, wife of Cleophas...... John xix. 25.
20. Mary Magdalene .... John xx. 1.
21. Sapphira .... Acts v.
22. Candace .... " viii. 27.
23. Tabitha .... " ix. 40.
24. Mary, mother of Mark...... " xii. 12.
25. Rhoda .... " xii. 13.
26. Lydia .... " xvi. 14.

27. Damaris (wife of Dionysius the Areopagite), Acts xvii. 34.
28. Priscilla .... Rom. xvi. 3.
29. The daughter of Philip ...... Acts xxi. 9.
30. Drusilla .... Acts xxiv. 24.
31. Bernice .... Acts xxv. 13.
32. Mary .... Romans xvi. 6.
33. Tryphena ....   "   xvi. 12.
    Tryphosa ....   "   xvi. 12.
34. Persis ....   "   xvi. 12.
35. Phebe ....   "   (last clause.)
36. Lois .... II Tim. i. 5.
37. Eunice .... II Tim. i. 5.
38. Jezabel of Thyatira .... Rev. ii. 20.
39. Claudia .... II Tim. iv. 21.
40. Chloe .... I Cor. i. 11.

CHAPTER XVIII.

THE CHILDREN AND YOUTH OF THE BIBLE.

1. Ishmael ....Gen. xxi. 17.
2. Isaac .... " xxi. 8.
3. Joseph .... " xxxvii. 2-4.
4. Miriam ....Ex. ii. 4.
5. Moses .... " ii. 10.
6. Samuel ....I Sam. ii. 19.
7. David................... " xvii. 17-50.
8. The child of David and Bathsheba. II Sam. xii. 14, 15.
9. Hadad ....I Kings xi. 14-17.
10. The son of the widow of Zarephath. I Kings xvii. 9-24.
11. The Shunamite's son........II Kings iv. 36.
12. The little Syrian maid....... " v. 2.
13. Joash ....II Chron. xxiv. 1.
14. Manasseh ....II Kings xxi. 1.
15. Josiah .... " xxii. 1.
16. Jehoiachin ....II Chron. xxxvi. 9.
17. Jeremiah ....Jer. i. 6-10.
18. Daniel—Belteshazzar ......Dan. i. 12-21.
    Hananiah—Shadrach .... " i. 12-21.
    Mishael—Meshach .... " i. 12-21.
    Azariah—Abednego .... " i. 12-21.
19. John the Baptist ....Luke i. 59-66.
20. The holy child Jesus........
21. Jairus' daughter...........Mark v. 23-47.
22. Timothy ....II Tim. iii. 15.

CHAPTER XIX.

MOUNTAINS OF THE BIBLE.

ELEVATION: FEET.

1. Ararat ....17,260....Gen. viii. 4.
2. Lebanon or Libanus (west) 8,000....I Kings v. 6.
3. Lebanon (toward rising sun) 6,000....Josh. xiii. 6.
4. Hor ....Num. xxxiv. 7, 8.
5. Hermon ....10,000....Stanley.
6. Bashan................ ....Josh. xiii. 30.
7. Gilead ....Gen. xxxi. 25.
8. { Pisgah } ridge ....Deut. xxxiv. 1.
   { Nebo } peak ....Deut. xxxiv. 1.
9. Seir ....Gen. xiv. 6-12.
10. Hor .... 4,800....Num. xx. 27, 28.
11. Halak ....Josh. xi. 17.
12. Tabor .... 1,900....Hosea v. 1.
13. Moreh ....Judges vii. 1.
14. Gilboa .... 2,200....I Sam. xxxi. 1, 6.
15. Carmel............... 1,861....I Kings xviii. 20.
16. Samaria .... 1,674....Amos vi. 1.
17. Ebal.................. 3,375 ...Deut. xxvii. 13.
18. Gerizim .... 3,179....Judges ix. 7.
19. Mizpeh .... 2,649....I Sam. vii. 5, 6, 7.
20. Nob ....I Sam. xxii. 19.
21. Moriah ....II Chron. iii. 1.
22. Zion.................. ....Ps. cxxxvii. 1.
23. Sinai .... 8,000....Ex. xix. 1, 3.
24. Horeb ....Ex. iii. 1, 2.
25. Mount of Olives........ ....Matt. xxvi. 30.
    Olivet................. ....Acts i. 12.
26. Quarantania .... 1,068....

CHAPTER XX.

THE RIVERS OF THE BIBLE.

1. Pison, river of Paradise. .....Gen. ii. 11.
   Gihon, " " " ......Gen. ii. 13.
2. Hiddekel, " " " ......Dan. x. 4.
3. Euphrates, " " " ......Gen. xv. 18.
4. Nile ("The river of Egypt")......Gen. xv. 18.
5. Jabbok..............Gen. xxxii. 22-24.
6. Arnon ....Num. xxii. 36.
7. Eschol ....Num. xiii. 24.
8. Zered ....Deut. ii. 13, 14.
9. Kanah ....Josh. xvii. 9, 10.
10. Besor ....I Sam. xxx. 10.
11. Kidron (Cedron)............I Kings xv. 13.
12. Kishon..................... " xviii. 40.
13. Cherith .... " xvii. 3.
14. Abana ....II Kings v. 12.
    Pharpar .... " v. 12.
15. Habor ....I Chron. v. 26.
16. Chebar..................Ezek. i. 1.
17. Jordan ....

CHAPTER XXI.

SEAS OF THE BIBLE.

1. Red Sea........................Ex. xiv. 21, 23.
2. Waters of Merom..............Josh. xi. 5.
3. The Salt Sea ....Gen. xiv. 3.
   Sea of the Plain..;.............Deut. iv. 49.
   The East Sea...................Joel ii. 20.
4. Sea of Jazer ....Jer. xlviii. 32.
5.   " Chinnereth ....Num. xxxiv. 11.
      " Chinneroth ....Josh. xi. 2.
      " Galilee ....Matt. xv. 29.
      " Tiberias ....John vi. 1.
   Lake of Gennesaret ....Luke v. 1.
6. Agean Sea ....See Map.
7. Great Sea.......................Num. xxxiv. 6.
   Mediterranean Sea.....See Map...Acts xvi. 9, 10.

CHAPTER XXII.

THE PROMINENT CITIES OF THE BIBLE.

1. Damascus ....Gen. xv. 2.
2. Babylon..................Jer. l. 14, 15.
3. Nineveh.................Jonah iv. 5–11.
4. Sodom...................Deut. xxix. 23.
   Gomorrah .... "   xxix. 23.
   Admah .... "   xxix. 23.
   Zeboim .... "   xxix. 23.
5. Zoar....................Gen. xix. 22, 23, 30.
6. Hebron ....Gen. xxiii. 2–20.
7. Beer-sheba..............Judges xx. 1.
8. Shechem ....Josh. xxiv. 32.
9. Jericho................. "   vi. 26.
10. Gilgal .... "   iv. 19.
11. Shiloh ....See Bible Dictionary.
12. Bethel ....Judges xx. 18, 26, 31.
13. Bethlehem..............I Sam. xvi. 1–4.
14. Jerusalem ....II Chron. iii. 1.
15. Kedesh,   city of refuge...Josh. xx. 7.
    Shechem,   "   "   "   ... "   xx. 7.
    Kirjath-arba, "   "   "   ... "   xx. 7.
    Bezer,   "   "   "   ... "   xx. 8.
    Ramoth,   "   "   "   ... "   xx. 8.
    Golan,   "   "   "   ... "   xx. 8.
16. Ashdod, royal Philistine city..Josh. xv. 47; I Sam. v. 5.
17. Gaza,   "   "   "   ..Judges xvi. 3.
18. Askelon, "   "   "   ..Judges xiv. 19.

19. Gath, royal Philistine city....I Sam. xxi. 12, 13.
20. Ekron, " " " ... " v. 10.
21. Jabesh-gilead.............. " xxxi. 8–13.
22. Mizpeh .... " x. 17–25.
23. Samaria ....I Kings xiv. 24.
24. Dan....................Judges xx. 1.
25. Memphis...............Jer. ii. 16.
26. Rabbah ....II Sam. xii. 26.
27. Tarshish ....Jon. i. 3.
28. Bethany................Luke xxiv. 50.
29. Bethsaida...............John i. 44.
30. Chorazin ....Matt. xi. 21.
31. Capernaum ....Matt. xi. 23, 24.
32. Cæsarea-Philippi ....Mark viii. 27.
33. Nazareth ....Matt. ii. 23.
34. Antioch, in Syria.. ....Acts xi. 26.
35. Antioch, in Pisidia......... " xiii. 14–50.
36. Athens................. " xvii. 22–31.
37. Cæsarea .... " x. 1.
38. Corinth .... " xviii. 1, 2.
39. Ephesus............... " xix. 27.
40. Alexandria............ " xviii. 24.
41. Berea .... " xvii. 10, 11.
42. Iconium .... " xiii. 50.
43. Lystra .... " xiv. 19.
44. Joppa .... " ix. 36.
45. Tarsus .... " ix. 11.
46. Thessalonica .... " xvii. 5.
47. Tyre .... " xxi. 3–5.
48. Sidon................ " xxvii. 3.
49. Miletus .... " xx. 17–26.
50. Troas................ " xx. 6–9.
51. Rome .... " xxviii. 30.

CHAPTER XXIII.

THE PLANTS NAMED IN THE SCRIPTURES.

1. Almond, (translated "hazel" in Gen. xxx. 37); Jer. i. 11.
2. Almug .... I Kings x. 12.
3. Aloe.................... John xix. 39.
4. Anise .... Matt. xxiii. 23.
5. Apple.................... Prov. xxv. 11.
6. Barley .... Ruth. ii. 17.
7. Balm, (Balsam).......... Smith's Bible Dictionary.
8. Beans................... II Sam. xvii.
9. Box..................... Isa. ix. 13.
10. Bramble .... Judges ix. 15.
11. Brier .... Micah vii. 4.
12. Bulrush .... Ex. ii. 3.
13. Bush, (perhaps the blackberry). Ex. iii. 2, 3, 4.
14. Calamas, (sweet) .... Ezek. xxvii. 19.
15. Cane, (sweet) .... Isa. xliii. 24.
16. Cassia .... Psalm xlv. 8.
17. Cedar................... II Sam. vii. 2.
18. Champhire, (probably cypress). Songs of Solomon i. 14.
19. Chestnut .... Gen. xxx. 37.
20. Cinnamon .... Rev. xviii. 13.
21. Corn .... Ruth ii. 14.
22. Coriander .... Ex. xvi. 31.
23. Cucumber............... Num. xi. 5.
24. Cummin.. Isa. xxviii. 25, 27; Matt xxiii. 23.
25. Dates .... Margin of II Chron. xxxi. 5.
26. Ebony .... Ez. xxvii. 15.

27. Fig......................II Kings xx. 7.
28. Fir.......................II Sam. vi. 5.
29. Fitches, (Fennel)..........Isa. xxviii. 25, 27.
30. Flag......................Job viii. 11.
31. Flax ....Ex. ix. 31.
32. Garlic ....Num. xi. 5.
33. Gopher ....Gen. vi. 14.
34. Gourd, (Castor-oil plant)....Jonah iv. 6.
35. Grape ....Lev. xix. 10.
36. Grass ....Psa. xxxvii. 2; Isa. xl. 6, 7.
37. Hemlock ....Hos. x. 4.
38. Husks, (carob-tree ....Luke xv. 16.
39. Hyssop ....Ex. xii. 22.
40. Juniper ....I Kings xix. 5.
41. Leeks.....................Num. xi. 5.
42. Lentiles..................Gen. xxv. 34.
43. Lily ....I Kings vii. 26.
44. Mandrakes ....Gen. xxx. 14.
45. Mallow ....Job xxx. 4.
46. Melon ....Num. xi. 5.
47. Millet ....Ezek. iv. 9.
48. Mint ....Luke xi. 42.
49. Mustard...................Matt. xiii. 31.
50. Mulberry..................I Chron. xiv. 15.
51. Myrrh ....Matt. ii. 11.
52. Myrtle ....Neh. viii. 15.
53. Nard, or Spikenard ....Mark xiv. 3.
54. Nettle ....Job xxx. 7.
55. Nuts, (Pistachio) ....Gen. xliii. 11.
56. Oak, (elah, teil tree, elms)..Ez. xxvii. 6.
57. Olive ....Psa. cxxviii. 3.
58. Onions ....Num. xi. 5.
59. Palm ....John xii. 13.

60. Pine, (the wild olive).......Neh. viii. 15.
61. Pomegranate..............Ex. xxviii. 33, 34.
62. Poplar ....Gen. xxx. 37.
63. Reed ....II Kings xviii. 21.
64. Rose ....Isa. xxxv. 1.
65. Rue ....Luke xi. 42.
66. Saffron, (Saffron crocus)....Song of Solomon iv. 14.
67. Shittim, (Acacia) ....Ex. xxxvi. 20.
68. Sycamore ....Psa. lxxviii. 47.
69. Tares....................Matt. xiii. 38.
70. Thorn ....Isa. xxxiii. 12.
71. Tree of Knowledge.........Gen. ii. 17.
72. Tree of Life..............Gen. iii. 22.
73. Wheat ....Gen. xxx. 14.
74. Willow ....Psa. cxxxvii. 2.
75. Wormwood ....Jer. ix. 15.

CHAPTER XXIV.

THE MINERALS OF THE BIBLE.

1. Sardius .... Ex. xxviii. 17.
2. Topaz (chrysolite) .... Ezek. xxviii. 13.
3. Carbuncle .... Isa. liv. 12.
4. Emerald .... Rev. iv. 3.
5. Sapphire .... Ex. xxiv. 10.
6. Diamond .... Ex. xxviii. 18; Ezek. xxviii. 13.
7. Ligure .... Ex. xxviii. 19.
8. Agate .... Ex. xxviii. 19.
9. Amethyst .... Rev. xxi. 20.
10. Beryl .... Dan. x. 6.
11. Onyx .... Gen. ii. 12.
12. Jasper .... Rev. iv. 3.
13. Pearl .... I Tim. ii. 9.
14. Chalcedony .... Rev. xxi. 19.
15. Sardonyx .... " xxi. 20.
16. Chrysoprasus .... " xxi. 20.
17. Jacinth (hyacinthus) .... " xxi. 20.
18. Ruby .... Prov. iii. 15.
19. Coral .... Ezek. xxvii. 16.
20. Crystal .... Rev. xxii. 1.
21. Adamant .... Ezek. iii. 9.
22. Iron .... Gen. iv. 22.
23. Gold .... Job xxiii. 10.
24. Clay .... Job xxxviii. 14.
25. Copper .... Ezra viii. 27.

26. Salt ....Lev. ii. 13.
27. Silver ....Gen. xliv. 2.
28. Flint ....Isa. l. 7.
29. Alabaster ....Mark xiv. 3.
30. Tin, (see margin) ....Zech. iv. 10.
31. Lead ....Smith's Bible Dictionary
32. Lime ....Isa. xxxiii. 12.

CHAPTER XXV.

BEASTS, REPTILES, BIRDS, INSECTS, FISHES.

BEASTS.

1. Ape, the .... I Kings x. 22.
2. Ass, an .... II Kings vi. 25.
3. Badger, the, (Seal)............ Ex. xxv. 5.
4. Bat, the .... Deut. xiv. 18.
5. Bear, the .... II Kings ii. 24.
6. Behemoth, (Hippopotamus) ..... Job xl. 15.
7. Boar, the wild .... Psa. lxxx. 13.
8. Bull, the .... Jer. l. 11.
9. Bullock, the .... I Kings xviii. 33.
10. Calf, the..................... Gen. xviii. 7.
11. Camel, a .... Gen. xxv. 61.
12. Chamois, the...... .... Deut. xiv. 5.
13. Colt, the .... Zech. ix. 9.
14. Conies .... Prov. xxx. 26.
15. Cow, the .... Isa. xi. 7.
16. Deer, the .... I Kings iv. 22, 23; xxi. 19.
17. Dog, the .... I Kings xxii. 38.
18. Dromedary, the............... Esth. viii. 10.
19. Elephant, the .... I Kings x. 22.
20. Ewe, the .... Gen. xxxii. 14.
21. Fox, the .... Judges xv. 4.
22. Goat, to the................... Matt. xxv. 33.
23. Hare, the .... Lev. xi. 6.
24. Hart, the..................... Isa. xxxv. 6.

25. Heifer, to the ....Jer. xlvi. 20.
26. Hind, the ....Gen. xlix. 21.
27. Horse, a ....I Kings xx. 20.
28. Kid, a ....Gen. xxxvii. 31.
29. Kine ....Gen. xli. 18, 19.
30. Lamb, the ....II Sam. xii. 3, 4.
31. Leopard, the ....Jer. xiii. 23.
32. Lion, the....................Judges xiv. 18.
33. Mice........................I Sam. vi. 5.
34. Mule, a.....................II Sam. xviii. 9.
35. Oxen ....I Kings vii. 25.
36. Ram, the....................Dan. viii. 3–7.
37. Roe, the, (Roebuck) ....II Sam. ii. 18.
38. Sheep, the ....Isa. liii. 7.
39. Swine ....Luke viii. 33.
40. Unicorn, the ....Psa. xxii. 21.
41. Weasel, the ....Lev. xi. 29.
42. Wolf, the....................Gen. xlix. 27.

REPTILES.

1. Adder, the, (cockatrice) ....Prov. xxiii. 32.
2. Asp, the.....................Isa. xi. 8.
3. Chameleon, the ....Lev. xi. 30.
4. Dragon, the..................Rev. xii. 3, 4.
5. Frogs ....Ex. viii. 2, 3, 4.
6. Serpent, the ....Gen. iii. 1.
7. Tortoise, the ....Lev. xi. 29.
8. Turtle, the ....Song of Sol. ii. 12.

BIRDS.

1. Dove, the....................Gen. viii. 8–11.
2. Sparrow, the.................Psa. cii. 7.
3. Swallow, the ....Smith's Bible Dict.

4. Peacocks ....I Kings x. 22.
5. Ostrich, the...................Job xxxix. 13-15.
6. Cock, the.....................Mark xiv. 66-72.
7. Hen, the.....................Matt. xxiii. 37.
8. Partridge, the.................Jer. xvii. 11.
9. Quail, the....................Num. xi. 31.
10. Eagle, the ....Deut. xiv. 12-18.
    Hawk, the..................... "   "
    Osprey, the................... "   "
    Ossifrage, the .... "   "
    Vulture, the .... "   "
    Raven, the.................... "   "
    Cuckoo, the................... "   "
    Owl, the .... "   "
    Swan, the.................... "   "
    Glede, the .... "   "
    Kite, the .... "   "
    Pelican, the................... "   "
    Gier-eagle, the .... "   "
    Night-hawk, the .... "   "
    Cormorant, the................ "   "
    Stork, the .... "   "
    Heron, the .... "   "
    Lapwing, the .... "   "
11. Crane, the ....Jer. viii. 7.
12. Pigeons ....Lev. v. 7.
13. Bittern, the ....Isa. xiv. 23.

Insects.

1. Locust, the ....Lev. xi. 22.
    Bald-locust, the............... "   xi. 22.
    Beetle, the .... "   xi. 22.
    Grass-hopper, the .... "   xi. 22.

2. Bees ....Judges xiv. 18.
3. Hornets......................Josh. xxiv. 12.
4. Lice.........................Ex. viii. 16.
5. Flies........................Ex. viii. 24.
6. Spider, the..................Job viii. 14.
7. Scorpion, the ....I Kings xii. 11.
8. Ant, the.....................Prov. vi. 6.
9. Caterpillar, the ....Joel i. 4.
   Canker-worm, the............. " i. 4.
   Palmer-worm, the............. " i. 4.
10. Moth, the ....Job xxvii. 18.
11. Snail, the...................Psa. lviii. 8.

Fishes.

1. Fishes ....Gen. ix. 2.
2. Whale, (shark) ....Matt. xii. 40.

CHAPTER XXVI.

OFFICES AND SECTS.

1. Apostles.
2. Bishop.
3. Centurion.
4. Deacons.
5. Elders.
6. Epicurians.
7. Herodians.
8. Judges.
9. Libertines.
10. Nethenims.
11. Nicolaitanes.
12. Patriarchs.
13. Pharisees.
14. Priests.
15. Procurator.
16. Proconsul.
17. Prophets.
18. Proselytes of the Gate.
19. Proselytes of Justice.
20. Publicans.
21. The Rabbi.
22. Sadducees, (followers of Sadoc).
23. Samaritans.
24. Scribes.

25. Secretaries, (scribes).
26. Commissaries, (scribes).
27. Stoics.
28. Tetrach.
29. Tirshatha.

CHAPTER XXVII.

THE OLD TESTAMENT MIRACLES.

1. The creation..........................Gen. i.
2. The flaming sword..................Gen. iii. 24.
3. The mark on Cain..................Gen. iv. 15.
4. The translation of Enoch........ ....Gen. v. 24.
5. The flood......................Gen. vii., viii.
6. The rainbow the token of God's covenant with Noah. Gen. ix. 11, 13.
7. The confusion of tongues...........Gen. xi. 7, 9.
8. The smoking furnace and burning lamp which Abraham saw.......................Gen. xv. 17.
9. The appearance of the angel to Hagar. Gen. xvi. 7, 8.
10. The appearance of the three men to Abraham. Gen. xviii.
11. The warning of the angels to Lot......Gen. xix. 1.
12. The men of Sodom smitten with blindness. Gen. xix. 11.
13. Sodom, Gomorrah, Admah, and Zeboim, destroyed. Gen. xiv. 2, 3, 8; xix. 24, 25.
14. Lot's wife.........................Gen. xix. 26.
15. The gift of Isaac....................Gen. xxi. 2.
16. Water sent Hagar for Ishmael........Gen. xxi. 19.
17. The ram provided as a substitute for Isaac. Gen. xxii. 11–13.
18. The test by which Rebekah was identified as God's choice for the wife of Isaac........Gen. xxiv. 14.
19. Jacob's miraculous dream.........Gen. xxviii. 12.
20. The presence of a host of angels to Jacob. Gen. xxxii. 1, 2.
21. The angel wrestling with Jacob..Gen. xxxii. 24, 25.

22. Joseph's dreams.................Gen. xxxviii. 5.
23. The dreams of the butler and baker, and Joseph's interpretation ....Gen. xl.
24. Joseph's interpretation of Pharaoh's miraculous dreams. Gen. xli. 1–36.
25. Jacob's miraculous prevision when dying..Gen. xlix.
26. The burning bush not consumed........Ex. iii. 2
27. Moses' rod changed to a serpent.......Ex. iv. 2–4.
28. Moses' hand made leprous and healed. Ex. iv. 6, 7, 8.
29. Aaron's rod changed to a serpent.......Ex. vii. 10.
30. Aaron's rod swallows the magician's rods. Ex. vii. 12.
31. Water turned to blood...............Ex. viii. 19.
    Frogs ....Ex. viii.
    Lice ....Ex. viii.
    Flies................................Ex. viii.
    Murrain..............................Ex. ix.
    Boils ....Ex. ix.
    Thunder ....Ex. ix.
    Locusts ....Ex. x.
    Darkness.............................Ex. x.
    The first-born slain.................Ex. xi. 29.
32. The pillar of cloud by day and fire by night. Ex. xiii. 21.
33. The parting of the Red Sea...........Ex. xiv. 21.
34. Marah's waters sweetened...........Ex. xv. 23–25.
35. Quails sent.........................Ex. xvi. 13.
36. Manna sent daily—the Sabbath excepted. Ex. xvi. 14–35.
37. Water provided at Rephidim..........Ex. xvii. 6.
38. The miraculous correspondence between the rising and falling of Moses' hands, and the victory or defeat of the Israelites...............Ex. xvii. 11.
39. The phenomena of Sinai...............Ex. xix.
40. Three thousand fall on one day for setting up the golden calf.................. ...Ex. xxxii. 28.

41. Moses preserved without food on Mount Sinai.
    Ex. xxxiv. 28.
42. The glory of the Lord in the Tabernacle. Ex. xl. 35.
43. Fire from heaven.....................Lev. ix. 24.
44. Nadab and Abihu consumed............Lev. x. 2.
45. The congregation at Taberah burned. Num. xi. 1–3.
46. Quails sent..........................Num. xi. 31.
47. Plague at Kibroth-hattaarah..........Num. xi. 33.
48. Miriam smitten with, and healed of, leprosy.
    Num. xii. 10–13.
49. The ten spies destroyed by a plague..Num. xiv. 37.
50. The earth opened and swallowed Korah, Dathan, and Abiram................Num. xvi. 25–33.
51. Two hundred and fifty consumed by fire for offering incense....................Num. xvi. 35.
52. The plague which destroyed fourteen thousand seven hundred......................Num. xvi. 49.
53. Aaron's rod budded, blossomed, and bore fruit.
    Num. xvii. 8.
54. Water, miraculously supplied, at the desert of Sin.
    Num. xx. 7–11.
55. Fiery serpents.....................Num. xxi. 6.
56. The brazen serpent ....Num. xxi. 8, 9.
57. Balaam's ass reproved him.........Num. xxii. 28.
58. Twenty-four thousand destroyed by a plague.
    Num. xxv. 9.
59. Clothing preserved forty years.......Deut. xxix. 5.
60. The stoppage of the Jordan.......Josh. iii. 14–17.
61. The walls of Jericho fall down......Josh. vi. 6–20.
62. Achan's sin detected by lot.............Josh. vii.
63. Hailstorm in aid of Israel.............Josh. x. 11.
64. The sun and moon stand still......Josh. x. 13, 14.
65. Shamgar slays six hundred Philistines. Judges iii. 31.

66. Fire from out a rock consumes Gideon's sacrifice.
    Judges vi. 21.
67. Gideon's fleece of wool.......Judges vi. 37, 38, 39.
68. The test of the men who should go with Gideon.
    Judges vii. 5.
69. The dream of the barley cake........Judges vii. 13.
70. Trumpets and pitchers and lamps defeat the Midianites......................Judges vii. 15–22.
71. The appearance of the angel to Manoah and his wife.
    Judges xiii.
72. The gift of Samson...................Judges xiii.
73. The miraculous strength of Samson. Judges xiv–xvii.
74. Samson rends a lion...............Judges xiv. 6.
    Thirty men slain by Samson........Judges xiv. 19.
    Three hundred foxes tied tail to tail with firebrands between them....................Judges xv. 4.
    Samson breaks the cords which bind him.
    Judg. xv. 11–14
    He slays one thousand men with a jawbone.
    Judg. xv. 15.
    He carries the gates of Gaza thirty miles.
    Judg. xvi. 1–3.
    He breaks the seven green withs........Judg. xvi. 9.
    He breaks the new ropes............Judg. xvi. 12.
    He escapes with "the pin of the beam and the web.'
    Judg. xvi. 14.
    Destruction of Dagon's temple... Judg. xvi. 29, 30.
75. Water sent to quench Samson's thirst.. Judg. xv. 19.
76. The gift of Samuel.....................I Sam. i.
77. God's call to Samuel.......... ....I Sam. iii.
78. Falling of Dagon................I Sam. v. 3, 4.
79. Destruction of many Philistines, at Ashdod, Gath, and Ekron...................I Sam. v. 9–12.

80. Emerods afflict the Philistines......I Sam. v. 10–12.
81. 50,070 men of Bethshemesh smitten for looking into the Ark......................I Sam. vi. 19.
82. Thunder storm frightens the Philistines.
I Sam. vii. 10–12.
83. Thunder and rain in harvest........I Sam. xii. 18.
84. The miraculous appearance of Samuel. I Sam. xxviii.
85. The sound in the mulberry trees.. II Sam. v. 23–25.
86. Uzzah struck dead for steadying the Ark.
II Sam. vi. 6, 7.
87. Seventy thousand destroyed by a pestilence.
II Sam. xxiv. 15, 25.
88. Solomon's miraculous dream........I Kings iii. 5.
89. Fire from heaven consumes Solomon's sacrifice.
I Kings viii. 2.
90. Jereboam's hand withered..........I Kings xiii. 4.
91. A disobedient prophet slain by a lion.
I Kings xiii. 24–26.
92. Jehoram smitten with an incurable disease.
II Chron. xxi. 18.
93. Uzziah stricken with leprosy....II Chron. xxvi. 19.
94. Rain withheld three years and six months.
I Kings xvii. 1.
95. Elijah fed by the ravens...........I Kings xvii. 6.
96. The widow's meal and oil increased. I Kings xvii. 16.
97. The widow's son raised...........I Kings xvii. 23.
98. The sacrifice on Mount Carmel consumed.
I Kings xviii. 38.
99. Elijah's prayer brings rain.....I Kings xviii. 41–45.
100. Elijah miraculously fed by an angel..I Kings xix. 7.
101. Elijah sustained forty days and nights. I Kings xix. 8.
102. Miracles before the presence of the Lord when he reproved Elijah..............I Kings xix. 11. 12.

103. Ahaziah's captains and company consumed.
            II Kings i. 10–12.
104. Dividing of the Jordan............II Kings ii. 8.
105. Elijah's translation...............II Kings ii. 11.
106. Parting the river Jordan..........II Kings ii. 14.
107. Elisha heals the waters of Jericho with salt.
            II Kings ii. 20.
108. Two bears destroy forty-two mockers. II Kings ii. 24.
109. The ditches in the valley of Moab filled.
            II Kings iii. 16, 20.
110. The widow's oil multiplied....II Kings iv. 2, 7.
111. The Shunamite's son given.....II Kings iv. 16, 17.
112. The Shunamite's son raised from the dead.
            II Kings iv. 34, 35.
113. The deadly pottage cured with meal. II Kings iv. 41.
114. A hundred men fed with twenty loaves.
            II Kings iv. 42, 44.
115. Naaman cured of leprosy.......II Kings v. 10–14.
116. Gehazi stricken with leprosy.....II Kings v. 20–27.
117. An iron axe swims at Elisha's command.
            II Kings vi. 5–7.
118. Benhadad's plans discerned by Elisha.
            II Kings vi. 12.
119. Spiritual perception supernaturally imparted to Elisha and his servant.................II Kings vi. 17.
120. The Syrian army smitten with blindness.
            II Kings vi. 18, 20.
121. Elisha's bones revive the dead....II Kings xiii. 21.
122. Jonah saved by a whale...........Jonah ii. 1–10.
123. The withered gourd..............Jonah iv. 6–10.
124. An angel smote the Assyrian camp. II Kings xix. 35.
125. Hezekiah's life prolonged fifteen years.
            II Kings xx. 6, 7.

126. The return of the sun's shadow on the dial.
II Kings xx. 11.
127. The Lord hides Jeremiah and Baruch.Jer. xxxvi. 26.
128. Shadrach, Meshach, and Abed-nego delivered.
Dan. iii. 19–21.
129. Nebuchadnezzar smitten with insanity..Dan. iv. 33.
130. Belshazzar's feast interrupted............Dan. v. 5.
131. Daniel saved from the lions...........Dan. vi. 23.

CHAPTER XXVIII

THE NEW TESTAMENT MIRACLES.

1. The appearance of the angel to Zacharias. Luke i. 13.
2. Zacharias stricken dumb............... Luke i. 20.
3. The gift of John the Baptist............ Luke i. 63.
4. The miraculous conception............ Matt. i. 18.
5. The wise men guided to the Saviour by the star in the east .... Matt. ii. 9.
6. The wise men warned of God not to return to Herod. Matt. ii. 12.
7. The appearance of the angels to the shepherds. Luke ii. 9.
8. An angel warns Joseph to flee into Egypt. Matt. ii. 13.
9. An angel informs Joseph of Herod's death. Matt. ii. 19.
10. The manifestation at Christ's baptism. Matt. iii. 16, 17.
11. Christ fasted forty days and nights....... Matt. iv. 2.
12. Water changed to wine.............. John ii. 1–11.
13. Driving the money changers out of the temple. John ii. 13–17.
14. The nobleman's son cured.......... John iv. 46–54.
15. A demoniac cured................ Mark i. 21–28.
16. Christ passed unseen through the multitude. Luke iv. 29, 30.
17. Peter's mother-in-law healed.. ..... Mark i. 30, 31.
18. Many sick and diseased healed.......... Mark i. 32.
19. Miraculous draught of fishes......... Luke v. 1–11.
20. A leper Christ healed............... Luke v. 12–14.

21. Christ forgives a palsied man's sins, and heals him.
Mark i. 45.
22. Miracle at Bethesda..................John, v. 2, 8.
23. Man healed of a withered hand........Matt. xii. 10.
24. A centurion's servant healed.......Matt. viii. 5, 13.
25. Healing the widow's son...........Luke vii. 11-17.
26. Healing the demoniac............Matt. xii. 22-24.
27. The tempest calmed...... ....Matt. viii. 23, 27.
28. Christ casts out a devil and suffers it to enter the swine.
Matt. viii. 28, 34.
29. Woman diseased twelve years cured..Mark v. 25-29.
30. Jairus' daughter restored to life......Mark v. 41-42.
31. Two blind men healed............Matt. ix. 27-31.
32. Dumb spirit cast out.............Matt. ix. 32, 33.
33. Feeding the five thousand. Luke ix. 12; Matt. xiv. 13; John vi. 1; Mark vi. 30.
34. Christ walking on the water..........Matt. xiv. 25.
35. Many healed in Gennesaret....Matt. xiv. 34, 35, 36.
36. The Syrophenician's daughter healed....Mark vii. 26.
37. Healing the deaf and dumb man.......Mark vii. 34.
38. Lame, blind, dumb and maimed healed.
Matt. xv. 29-31.
39. Four thousand fed..................Matt. xv. 38.
40. Restoring a blind man at Bethsaida. Mark viii. 22, 26.
41. The Transfiguration..............Matt. xvii. 1, 2.
42. Christ healed a demoniac child....Matt. xvii. 14-18.
43. The stater in the mouth of the fish....Matt. xvii. 27.
44. Jesus hid Himself..................John viii. 59.
45. A blind man healed at Siloam...........John ix. 7.
46. Jesus escapes........................John x. 39.
47. Lazarus raised from the grave............John xi.
48. The dumb devil cast out.............Luke xi. 14.
49. A woman healed of an infirmity....Luke xiii. 11-17.

50. A man healed of dropsy............Luke xiv. 1-4.
51. The ten healed of leprosy.........Luke xvii. 11-14.
52. Blind Bartimeus healed..............Mark x. 46.
53. Two blind men restored to sight.......Matt. xx. 30.
54. Cursing the barren fig-tree............Mark xi. 14.
55. Healing the ear of Malchus..........Luke xxii. 51.
56. The vail of the temple rent.........Matt. xxvii. 52.
57. The resurrection of the saints.......Matt. xxvii. 52.
58. The Resurrection of Christ...........Luke xxiv. 6.
59. Christ's appearance to the ten......John xx. 10-19.
60. The miraculous draught of fishes......John xxi. 14.
61. Christ's appearance to the eleven..Luke xxiv. 36, 37.
62. The ascension.....................Luke xxiv. 51.
63. The gift of the Holy Ghost............Acts ii. 1-8.
64. Peter healed the impotent man........Acts iii. 1-10.
65. Ananias and Sapphira struck dead.....Acts v. 1-11.
66. The shadow of Peter heals the sick at Jerusalem.
                Acts v. 15.
67. Peter and John rescued from prison by an angel.
                Acts v. 19.
68. Miracles wrought by Stephen............Acts vi. 8.
69. Philip translated to Azotus............Acts viii. 40.
70. The phenomena attending Saul's conversion.
                Acts ix. 1-19.
71. Eneas healed of the palsy at Lydda..Acts ix. 33, 34.
72. Tabitha restored to life.............Acts ix. 36-41.
73. Peter liberated from prison..........Acts xii. 5-12.
74. Herod smitten with disease and death.Acts xii. 20-23.
75. Elymas the sorcerer smitten with blindness.
                Acts xiii. 8-11.
76. Paul cured a cripple at Lystra.......Acts xiv. 8-11.
77. Paul exorcised an evil spirit............Acts xvi. 18.
78. Prison doors opened by an earthquake..Acts xvi. 26.

79. At Ephesus Paul communicates the Holy Ghost to twelve ....Acts xix. 6, 7.
80. The sick cured by Paul's clothing brought to them. Acts xix. 11, 12.
81. Eutychus restored to life............Acts xx. 9–12.
82. Paul unharmed by the sting of a viper. Acts xxviii. 4–6.
83. The father of Publius cured............Acts xviii. 7.
84. Paul heals the people of Melita........Acts xviii. 9.

CHAPTER XXIX.

THE PARABLES OF CHRIST.

1. The sower....................Matt. xiii. 1–23.
2. The tares ....Matt. xiii. 24–43.
3. The seed springing up ....Mark iv. 26–29.
4. The mustard-seed ....Matt. xiii. 31, 32.
5. The leaven ....Matt. xiii. 33.
6. The hid treasure ....Matt. xiii. 44.
    The goodly pearl ....Matt. xiii. 45, 46.
7. The draw net ....Matt. xiii. 47–50.
8. The two debtors ....Luke vii. 36–50.
9. The unmerciful servant.........Matt. xviii. 33–35.
10. The Good Samaritan ....Luke x. 25–27.
11. The rich fool.................Luke xii. 16–21.
12. The servants who waited for the Lord. Luke xii. 35–48.
13. The barren fig-tree ....Luke xiii. 6–9.
14. The lost sheep...............   " xv. 3–7.
15. The lost piece of money........   " xv. 8–10.
16. The prodigal son.............   " xv. 11–32.
17. The unjust steward ....   " xvi. 1–12.
18. The rich man and Lazarus.......   " xvi. 19–31.
19. The unjust judge ....   " xviii. 1–8.
    The midnight friend.........   " xi. 5.
20. The Pharisee and the Publican... " xviii. 9–14.
21. The laborer in the vineyard .....Matt. xx. 1–16.
22. The pounds of money ....Luke xix. 12–27.
23. The two sons.................Matt. xxi. 28–32.

24. The wicked husbandman ....Matt. xxi. 33-46.
25. The marriage feast ....Matt. xxii. 1-14.
26. The ten virgins ....Matt. xxv. 1-13.
27. The house-holder in a far country. Mark xiii. 34.
28. The ten talents ....Matt. xxv. 14-30.
29. The sheep and the goats........Matt. xxv. 31-46.
30. The wedding feast..............Luke xiv. 7-11.
    The great supper ....Luke xiv. 15-25.
31. The unprofitable servants........Luke xvii. 7-10.

CHAPTER XXX.

THE PROPHECIES CONCERNING CHRIST.

		PROPHECY.	FULFILMENT.
1.	The first promise of Christ's coming	Gen. iii. 15.	Heb. ii. 14.
2.	The promise to Abraham	Gen. xii. 3.	Acts iii. 25.
3.	Isaac	Gen. xxvi. 4.	Gal. iv. 28.
4.	Jacob	Gen. xxviii.	Rom. ix. 13.
5.	The tribe of Judah	Gen. xlix. 10.	Heb. vii. 14.
6.	Jesse	Isa. xi. 1.	Acts xiii. 23.
7.	David	II Sam. vii. 16.	Rom. i. 3.
8.	That He should be born of a virgin	Isa. vii. 14.	Matt. i. 23.
9.	The time when He should appear	Dan. ix. 25.	Luke ii.
10.	He should be born in Bethlehem	Micah v. 2.	Luke ii. 11, 15.
11.	A messenger should go before Him	Mal. iii. 1.	Matt. iii. 3.
12.	The wise men	Isa. lx. 3, 6.	Matt. ii. 2.
13.	His different names	Isa. ix. 6.	
14.	His divinity	Jer. xxiii. 6.	I Cor. i. 30.
15.	His poverty	Isa. liii. 2.	Luke ix. 58.
16.	His power	Num. xxiv. 19.	Luke xxiii. 43.
17.	His piety	Isa. xi. 5.	Heb. vii. 26.
18.	His integrity	Psa. xlv. 7.	Heb. vii. 26.
19.	The massacre at Bethlehem	Jer. xxxi. 15.	Matt. ii. 13.
20.	That He should be carried to Egypt	Hos. xi. 1.	Matt. ii. 15.
21.	The spirit of the Lord upon Him	Isa. xi. 2.	Matt. iii. 17.
22.	He should be a prophet	Deut. xviii. 15.	Luke xxiv. 19.
23.	He should be a priest	Psa. cx. 4.	Heb. iv. 14.
24.	His riding triumphantly into Jerusalem	Zech. ix. 9.	Luke xix. 35.
25.	His meekness and patience	Isa. liii. 7.	Matt. xxvi. 63.

		PROPHECY.	FULFILMENT.
26.	The blind should see	Isa. xxxv. 5, 6	Matt. xi. 5.
	The deaf should hear	Isa. xxxv. 5, 6	Matt. xi. 5.
	The lame leap	Isa. xxxv. 5, 6	Matt. xi. 5.
	The dumb speak	Isa. xxxv. 5, 6	Matt. xi. 5.
27.	That He should pardon sin	Zech. xiii. 1	Matt. ix. 2.
28.	That He should be a Nazarene	Psa. lxix. 9	Matt. ii. 23.
29.	He should cast the buyers and sellers out of the temple	Psa. lxix. 9	John ii. 17.
30.	Jews and Gentiles should conspire to destroy Him	Psa. ii. 2	Acts iv. 27.
31.	That kings should be subject to Him	Isa. lx. 3, 10, 16	
32.	Should be despised and rejected	Isa. liii. 3	John i. 10; Heb. iv. 15.
33.	His ministry should commence in Galilee	Isa. ix. 1, 2	Matt. iv. 15.
34.	The Gentiles should be converted	Isa. xi. 10; xlii. 1	Matt. xv. 28.
35.	He should be sold for thirty pieces of silver	Zech. xi. 12	Matt. xxiv. 15.
36.	The potter's field bought	Zech. ii. 13	Matt. xxvii. 9.
37.	Be betrayed by His familiar friends	Psa. xli. 9	John xiii. 18.
38.	His betrayer should die suddenly and miserably	Psa. lv. 15, 23; cix. 17	Matt. xxvii. 5.
39.	Forsaken by His disciples	Zech. xiii. 7	Mark xiv. 27.
40.	Accused by false witnesses	Psa. xxxv. 11; cix. 2	Matt. xxvi. 59.
41.	Should not answer His accusers	Isa. liii. 7	Luke xxiii. 9.
42.	That He should be scourged, and spit upon	Isa. l. 6	Matt. xxvii. 26.
43.	Should be insulted, buffeted, and spit upon	Psa. xxxv. 15-21	Matt. xxvi. 67.
44.	That He should be crucified	Psa. xxii. 14, 17	Matt. xxvii. 26.
45.	That He should endure taunts	Psa. xxii. 8	Matt. xxvii. 29.
46.	Offered gall and vinegar	Psa. lxix. 21	Matt. xxvii. 34.
47.	His garments parted and lots cast for His vesture	Psa. xxii. 18	Matt. xxvii. 35.
48.	He should be pierced	Zech. xii. 10	John xix. 34.
49.	Should be smitten on the cheek	Micah v. 1	Matt. xxvii. 30.
50.	He should suffer for others	Dan. ix. 26; Isa. liii. 4	Matt. viii. 17.
51.	Patient under suffering	Isa. liii. 7	Matt. xxvii.
52.	Should pray for His enemies	Psa. cix. 4	Luke xxiii. 34.
53.	His innocence	Isa. liii. 9	1 Pet. ii. 22.

	PROPHECY.	FULFILMENT.
54. Crucified with malefactors	Isa. liii. 12	Mark xv. 28.
55. His bones should remain unbroken	Psa. xxxiv. 20	John xix. 36.
56. Should be cut off in the midst of His days	Psa. lxxxix. 45	Matt.
57. The earthquake	Zech. xiv. 4	Matt. xxvii. 51.
58. Great darkness	Amos v. 20, Zech. xiv. 6	Matt. xxvii. 45.
59. Buried with the rich	Isa. liii. 6	Matt. xxvii. 57.
60. Christ's resurrection	Psa. xvi. 10; Hos. vi. 2	Matt. xxviii.
61. His ascension	Psa. xvi. 11	Acts i. 9.
62. The descent of the Holy Ghost	Joel ii. 28, 29	Acts ii. 4.
63. His dominion should be universal	Psa. lxxii. 8	
64. His kingdom should be everlasting	Isa. ix. 7	

CHAPTER XXXI.

THE APPEARANCES OF CHRIST AFTER HIS RESURRECTION.

1. Mary Magdalene.....................Mark xvi. 9.
2. The women returning from the sepulchre. Matt. xviii. 9.
3. Peter.............................I Cor. xv. 5.
4. The two going to Emmaus.......Luke xxiv. 13, 31.
5. The apostles at Jerusalem, Thomas being absent.
                                                John xx. 19.
6. Thomas and the other disciples at Jerusalem.
                                            John xx. 26, 29.
7. The seven disciples at the sea of Tiberias. John xxi. 1–3.
8. The eleven disciples on a mountain in Galilee.
                                              Matt. xxviii. 16.
9. Above five hundred brethren at once....I Cor. xv. 6.
10. James..............................I Cor. xv. 7.
11. The eleven disciples on Mount Olivet...Acts i. 1–11.

CHAPTER XXXII.

CHRONOLOGICAL ITINERARY OF PAUL'S LIFE.

1. Of the tribe of Benjamin............Acts xiii. 21.
2. At Tarsus ....Acts xii. 3.
3. Taught the trade of tentmaking ....Acts xviii. 3.
4. Educated at Jerusalem by Gamaliel .....Acts xii. 3.
5. Started for Damascus ....Acts ix. 2.
6. His miraculous conversion...............Acts ix.
7. His journeys to Arabia...............Gal. i. 17.
8. Three years in Arabia................ " i. 18.
9. To Jerusalem .... " i. 18.
10. Peter .... " i. 18.
11. To Cæsarea ....Acts ix. 30.
12. To Tarsus ....Acts ix. 30.
13. Barnabas ....Acts xi. 25, 26.
14. A year at Antioch ....Acts xi. 26.
15. To Jerusalem....................Acts xi. 27-30.
16. Accompanied to Antioch by John Mark.Acts xii. 25.

First Missionary Journey.

17. From Antioch in Syria.......See Bible Dictionary.
18. Accompanied by Mark and Barnabas...Acts xii. 25.
19. To Selucia.... ....Acts xiii. 4.
20. Salamis, on the isle of Cyprus ....Acts xiii. 5.
21. Paphos......................Acts xiii. 6.
22. Sergius Paulus converted.........Acts xiii. 7-12.
23. Name changed from Saul to Paul....Acts xiii. 7-12.

24. Elymas, the sorcerer, smitten with blindness.
   Acts xiii. 7–12.
25. From Cyprus to Perga in Pamphilia...Acts xiii. 13.
26. John Mark returned to Jerusalem.....Acts xiii. 13.
27. Paul and Barnabas journey to Antioch in Pisidia.
   Acts xiii. 13.
28. The Gentiles accepted the Gospel..Acts xiii. 46, 48.
29. To Iconium..................... .....Acts xiii. 51.
30. Lystra ....Acts xiv.
31. To Derbe........................Acts xiv. 20.
32. Return through Lystra, Iconium, Antioch in Pisidia, Perga, Attalia, to Antioch in Syria.
   Acts xiv. 20–28.
33. To Jerusalem, by way of Phenice and Samaria.
   Acts xv. 3.
34. Return to Antioch bringing the apostolic letter, containing the amicable decision of the council of the churches with reference to the circumcision and keeping of the law ....Acts xv. 23–30.

Second Missionary Journey.

35. From Antioch with Silas.............Acts xv. 40.
36. To Derbe, through Syria and Cilicia....Acts xvi. 1.
37. At Lystra ....Acts xvi. 1–4.
38. Phrygia, Galatia....................Acts xvi. 6.
39. Troas ....Acts xvi. 11.
40. Macedonia ....Acts xvi. 9.
41. Samothracia ....Acts xvi. 11.
42. Neapolis.......................Acts xvi. 11.
43. At Philippi....................Acts xvi. 14.
44. The damsel possessed of a spirit, healed. Acts xvi. 18.
45. Paul and Silas imprisoned..........Acts xvi. 24.

46. The prison-doors opened by an earthquake.
Acts xvi. 27.
47. The conversion of the jailor..........Acts xvi. 33.
48. A public vindication...............Acts xvi. 37.
49. Amphipolis, Appolonia..............Acts xvii. 1.
50. Persecuted and sent by night to Berea..Acts xvii. 10.
51. Athens.........................Acts xvii. 15.
52. Encountered the Epicureans and Stoics.Acts xvii. 18.
53. Mars' Hill.....................Acts xvii. 22.
54. Dionysius, the Areopagite and Damaris his wife, converted........................Acts xvii. 34.
55. At Corinth ....See Bible Dictionary.
56. A year and six months............Acts xviii. 11.
57. Aquila and Priscilla ....Acts xviii. 2.
58. Occupation, tentmaking. He wrote First and Second Thessalonians....................Acts xviii. 3.
59. Reasoned in the Synagogue every Sabbath. Acts xviii. 4.
60. Preached in the house of Justus.......Acts xviii. 7.
61. Crispus, the ruler of the synagogue....Acts xviii. 8.
62. Encouraged by a vision.............Acts xviii. 9.
63. Performs a vow at Cenchrea.........Acts xviii. 18.
64. Ephesus ....Acts xviii. 21.
65. Cæsarea.......................Acts xviii. 22.
66. Feast of Pentecost at Jerusalem and returns to Cæsarea.
Acts xviii. 21.
67. Antioch, in Syria.................Gal. ii. 11, 12.

THIRD MISSIONARY JOURNEY.

68. From Antioch, through Galatia and Phyrgia, visiting the churches ....Acts xix. 1.
69. Ephesus ....Acts xix. 1.
70. For the space of two years...........Acts xix. 10.

71. Clothing brought from Paul, to the sick, healing them..................................Acts xix. 12.
72. First Corinthians written in Ephesus. See Bible Dict.
73. Fought with wild beasts........II Cor. i. 8, 9, 10.
74. Macedonia and Greece...............Acts xix. 22.
75. II Corinthians, in Macedonia, Galatians and Romans at Corinth..............See Bible Dictionary.
76. Abode seven days in Troas in company with Sopater, Aristarchus, Secundus, Gaius, Timothy, Tychicus, Trophimus, and Luke...............Acts xx. 4–6.
77. Eutychus restored to life...........Acts xx. 9, 12.
78. Assos...............................Acts xx. 13.
79. Mitylene, Chios, Samos, Trogyllium, Miletus.
Acts xx. 14, 15.
80. For the elders of the church at Ephesus.
Acts xx. 17.
81. His address to the elders..........Acts xx. 18–35.
82. His sad parting with the elders.....Acts xx. 36, 38.
83. Coos........................ ......Acts xxi. 1.
84. Patara ....   " xxi. 1.
85. Tyre.............................. " xxi. 3.
86. Seven days .... " xxi. 4.
87. Cæsarea .... " xxi. 8.
88. Philip, the Evangelist............. " xxi. 8.
89. Agabas, the prophet, with others, besought Paul not to go to Jerusalem..................Acts xx. 13.
90. To Jerusalem......................Acts xxi. 15.
91. James............................Acts xxi. 18.
92. Persecuted, beaten, and a prisoner for two years.
Acts xxi. 32.
93. His defence before the people.........Acts xxi. 1.
94. His address to the council..........Acts xxiii. 3.
95. Forty men conspire to slay him......Acts xxiii. 13.

96. Paul's nephew informs the Roman captain of the conspiracy ....Acts xxiii. 16.
97. To Cæsarea, under a Roman guard...Acts xxiii. 23.
98. Before Felix....................Acts xxiv. 10-21.
99. Festus ....Acts xxv. 1-10.
100. Agrippa ....Acts xxvi. 2, 3.
101. Several years.............. See Bible Dictionary.
102. Appealed to Cæsar..... ....Acts xxvi. 32.

Voyage to Rome.

103. Cæsarea ....
104. In charge of Julius, a centurion........Acts xxvi. 1.
105. Luke and Aristarchus.... ....Acts xxvii. 2.
106. At Sidon .... " xxvii. 3.
107. Allowed to visit his friends.......... " xxvii. 3.
108. Myra in Lycia .... " xxvii. 5.
109. Cnidus......................... " xxvii. 7.
    Crete .... " xxvii. 7.
    Salome .... " xxvii. 7.
    Fair Havens............. ..... " xxvii. 8.
    Lasea.......................... " xxvii. 8.
110. Shipwreck.... ....Acts xxvii. 44.
111. Melita (Malta)...................Acts xxviii. 1.
112. Paul unharmed by the viper......Acts xxviii. 5, 6.
    The father of Publius cured.........Acts xxviii. 8.
    Many healed of disease............. " xxviii. 9.
113. Three months in Melita..........Acts xxviii. 11.
114. Syracuse..... .... " xxviii. 12.
115. Rhegium .... " xxviii. 13.
116. Puteoli .... " xxviii. 13.
117. Appii Forum, Three Taverns....... " xxviii. 15.
118. Rome...................... ... " xxviii. 16.
119. Preaching and teaching .. .. " xxviii. 31.

120. Philemon, Colossians, Ephesians and Philippians, written at Rome..........See Bible Dictionary.
121. Macedonia .... " " "
122. I Timothy................. " " "
123. In Ephesus................. " " "
124. II Timothy................. " " "
125. Rome..................... " " "
126. Martyred, June 29th, A. D., 66. " " "
127. Under Nero................ " " "
128. Buried in the Catacombs of Rome...See Bible Dict.

PAUL'S JOURNEYS.

FIRST JOURNEY.

1. Antioch,　　　　　　Derbe,
   Selucia,　　　　　　 Lystra,
   Salamis,　　　　　　 Iconium,
   Paphos,　　　　　　 Antioch in Pisidia,
   Perga,　　　　　　 Perga,
   Antioch in Pisidia,　Attalia,
   Iconium,　　　　　　 Antioch in Syria.
   Lystra,

SECOND JOURNEY.

2. Antioch,　　　　　　Neapolis,
   Syria,　　　　　　　Philippi,
   Cilicia,　　　　　　 Amphipolis,
   Derbe,　　　　　　 Appolonia,
   Lystra,　　　　　　 Thessalonica,
   Phrygia,　　　　　　 Berea,
   Galatia,　　　　　　 Athens,
   Mysia,　　　　　　　Corinth,
   Troas,　　　　　　 Cenchrea,
   Samothracia,　　　　 Ephesus.

THIRD JOURNEY.

3. Antioch,
Galatia,
Phyrgia,
Ephesus,
Macedonia,
Greece,
Philippi,
Troas,
Assos,
Mitylene,
Chios,

Trogyllium,
Samos,
Miletus,
Coos,
Rhodes,
Patara,
Tyre,
Ptolemais,
Cæsarea,
Jerusalem,
Cæsarea.

JOURNEY TO ROME.

4. Cæsarea,
Sidon,
Myra,
Lasea,
Melita,

Syracuse,
Phegium,
Puteoli,
Rome.

THE EPISTLES OF PAUL IN CHRONOLOGICAL ORDER.

1. —I Thessalonians, from Corinth, ... A. D. 52.
2. —II Thessalonians, " Corinth, ... " 53.
3. —I Corinthians, " Ephesus, ... " 57.
4. —II Corinthians, " Macedonia, ... " 57.
5. —Galatians, " Corinth, ... " 57.
6. —Romans, " Corinth, ... " 58.
7. —Philemon, " Rome, ... " 62.
8. —Colossians, " Rome, ... " 62.
9. —Ephesians, " Rome, ... " 62.
10. —Philippians, " Rome, ... " 62.
11. —I Timothy, " Macedonia, ... " 67.
12. —Titus, " Ephesus, ... " 67.
13. —II Timothy, " Rome, ... " 68.

CHAPTER XXXIII.

THE JEWISH CALENDAR.

DAYS.

1. Abib, or Nisan (Mar., Apr.)...30..Deut. xvi. 1.
2. Zif, or Jyar (April, May).....29..I Kings vi. 1.
3. Sivan (May, June)...........30..Esther viii. 9.
4. Tamus, or Thamuz (June, July) 29..
5. Ab (July, Aug.).............30..Ezra vii. 9.
6. Elul (Aug., Sept.)..........29..Neh. vi. 15.
7. Tisri (Sept., Oct.).........30..Lev. xxiii. 34.
8. Bul, or Marchesvan (Oct., Nov.) 29..I Kings vi. 38.
9. Chisleu (Nov., Dec.).......30..Neh. i. 1.
10. Tebeth (Dec., Jan.)........29..Esther ii. 16.
11. Shebat (Jan., Feb.)........30..I Ch. xxvii. 14.
12. Adar (Feb., Mar.)..........29..Esther ix. 19-26.
13. Veadar (the additional Adar).
14. The *Natural Day* was from sunrise to sunset.
15. The *Natural Night* was from sunset to sunrise.
16. The *Civil Day* was from sunset one evening to sunset the next..........................Gen. i. 5.

THE ANCIENT DAY AND NIGHT.

17. Morning, from 6 A. M. to 10 A. M......Judges vi. 31.
18. Heat of the day, from 10 A. M. to 2 P. M. Gen. xviii. 1.
19. Cool of the day, from 2 P. M. to 6 P. M....Gen. iii. 8.
20. First watch, from 6 P. M. till midnight....Lam. ii. 19.
21. Second watch, from midnight to 3 A. M. Judges vii. 19.
22. Morning watch, from 3 A. M. to 6 A. M...Ex. xiv. 24.

THE NEW TESTAMENT DAY AND NIGHT.

23. Third hour, from 6 to 9 A. M ....Mark xv. 25.
24. Sixth hour, from 9 to 12 midday..........Acts x. 9.
25. Ninth hour, from 12 to 3 P. M............Acts iii. 1.
26. Twelfth hour, from 3 to 6 P. M...........
27. First watch, evening, from 6 to 9 P. M...John xx. 19.
28. Second watch, midnight, from 9 to 12 P. M. Acts xx. 7.
29. Third watch, cock crow, from 12 to 3 A. M. Matt. xxvi. 34.
30. Fourth watch, morning, from 3 to 6 A. M. Matt. xiv. 25.

CHAPTER XXXIV.

QUESTIONS FOR LITTLE PEOPLE.

1. Methuselah ....Gen. v. 27.
2. Solomon ....I Kings iv. 30, 31.
3. Moses ....Num. xii. 3.
4. Samson ....Judges xv., xvi.
5. Og, king of Bashan.......Deut. iii. 11.
6. Job ....Book of Job.
7. Abraham ....Gen. xxii. 2–12.
8. Absalom ....II Sam. xiv. 25.
9. Elijah..................II Kings ii. 11.
10. Daniel ....Dan. vi. 16.
11. Shadrach, Meshach, Abed-nego....Dan. iii. 20, 21
12. Moses ....Deut. xxxiv. 5, 6.
13. Lot's wife..............Gen. xix. 26.
14. Ananias and Sapphira.....Acts v. 5, 10.
15. Jesus Christ ....Luke ii. 7.
16. Jonah ....Jonah i. 17.
17. Cain...................Gen. iv. 8.
18. Solomon ....I Kings vi. 1.
19. Joseph ....Gen. xxxvii. 27.
20. John ....John xix. 26.
21. Peter ....Mark xiv. 67, 68.
22. Judas ....Mark xiv. 43–45.
23. David.................I Sam. xvii. 49.
24. Lazarus ....John xi. 43.
25. Peter ....Matt. xiv. 28, 29.
26. Stephen ....Acts vii. 60.

27. Moses .... Deut. xxix. 5.
28. Noah .... Gen. vi. 14–22.
29. Jerusalem .... Rev. iii. 12.
30. Elisha .... II Kings vi. 6.
31. Abraham .... Gen. xxii.
32. Moses .... Ex. xxiv. 18.
    Elijah .... I Kings xix. 8.
    Christ .... Matt. iv. 2.
33. James .... Acts xii. 1, 2.
34. Mary .... John xii. 3.
35. Saul .... Acts ix. 9.
36. Paul .... Acts xiii. 9.
37. David .... Bible Dictionary.
38. Queen of Sheba .... II Chron. ix. 1.
39. Joshua .... Josh. i. 1, 2.
40. Jacob .... Gen. xxxii. 2–4.
41. Hezekiah .... II Kings xx. 6.
42. Balaam .... Num. xxiii. 10.
43. Obadiah .... I Kings xviii. 4.
44. Deborah .... Gen. xxxv. 8.
45. Daniel .... Dan. vi. 10.
46. A man of Gath .... II Sam. xxi. 20.
47. The bones of Elisha restore the Moabite. II Kings xiii. 2.
48. Og, king of Bashan ..... Deut. iii. 11.
49. Job .... Job i. 19.
50. Abraham .... Gen. xvii. 1.
51. Sycamore .... Luke xix. 4.
52. Jonah .... Jonah iv. 5–11.
53. Daniel .... Dan. v. 29.
54. Isaac .... Gen. xviii. 10.
    Samson .... Judg. xiii. 13.
    John the Baptist .... Luke i. 13.
    Jesus .... Luke i. 28.

55. Lazarus ....Luke xvi. 22.
56. Peter ....Acts xii. 8.
57. Moses ....Ex. iii. 5.
    Joshua ....Josh. v. 13–15.
58. Joseph ....Matt. ii. 13.
59. Just before they entered the Mt. of Olives.
                                     Matt. xxvi. 30.
60. Samson ....Judges xiii. 14; xvi. 17.
61. Timothy ....II Tim. iii. 15.
62. Joshua ....Josh. v. 13.
63. Gabriel ....Dan. ix. 21.
    Michael ....Rev. xii. 7.
64. Lot ....Gen. xix.
65. A coat of many colors...Gen. xxxvii. 3.
66. Jesus Christ............John xix. 23.
67. His mantle ....II Kings ii. 13.
68. Hagar ....Gen. xxi. 17.
69. Balaam's ass ....Num. xxii. 27.
70. Gideon..................Judg. vi. 19, 20.
71. Micah ....Judg. xvii. 1–4.
72. Peter ....Acts x. 9.
73. Three times.............Ps. lv. 17; Dan. vi. 10.
74. Seventeen ....Gen. xxxvii. 2.
75. Elijah ....II Kings iii. 15, 17, 20.
76. The widow's two mites...Mark xii. 42.
77. Mount Ararat ....Gen. viii. 4.
78. Hadassah, (Esther)......Esther ii. 7.
79. Not waiting for the arrival of Samuel. I Sam. xiii. 8–14.
80. Wisdom..................I Kings iii. 9.
81. Absalom's ....II Sam. xviii. 9–15.
82. Jacob ....Gen. xxvii. 16.
83. John the Baptist ....Mark i. 6.
84. Ezekiel ....Eze. viii. 3.

85. By dedicating the last chapter of Proverbs to her.
Prov. xxxi. 1.
86. Ahab and Jezebel . . . . .I Kings xxi. 7–15.
87. Joshua . . . . .Josh. iv. 14.
88. Gideon . . . . .Judg. vi. 14.
89. Chenaniah . . . . .I Chron. xv. 22.
90. These men were bound in their coats, their hozen, and their hats . . . . .Dan. iii. 21.
91. The Lord God . . . . .Gen. iii. 21.
92. Junia . . . . .Rom. xvi. 7.
93. Solomon . . . . .Ecc. ii. 5.
Abraham . . . . .Gen. xxi. 33.
94. See .II Kings xxii. 14.
95. Quartus . . . . .Rom. xvi. 23.
96. Isaiah . . . . .Isa. iii. 18–23.
97. Felix . . . . .Acts xxiii. 24.
Festus . . . . .Acts xxiv. 27.
Fortunatus . . . . .I Cor. xvi. 17.
98. Vashti, queen of Ahasuerus. Es. i. 9.
Vajezatha, a son of Haman. Es. ix. 9.
Vashni, Samuel's eldest son. I Chron. vi. 28.
Vophsi, father of the spy chosen from Naphtali.
Num. xii. 14.
99. Forty days . . . . .Jonah iii. 4.
100. Enoch . . . . .Gen. v. 24.
101. Absalom's . . . . .II Sam. xiv. 26.

CHAPTER XXXV.

MISCELLANEOUS QUESTIONS.

1. When Solomon made the descendants of Canaan pay tribute to the Israelites....... II Chron. viii. 7, 8.
2. Jonathan..................... I Sam. xiv. 1–14.
3. Saul .... I Sam. xxviii. 17.
   Ahab......................... I Kings xxii.
4. Hananiah, son of Azur......... Jer. xxviii. 16, 17.
5. Not one Israelite was slain........ Num. xxxi. 49.
6. See........................ Isa. lviii. 13, 14.
7. Obadiah .... I Kings xviii. 4.
8. The brazen serpent............. II Kings xviii. 4.
9. A part of Lamentations........... Jer. xxxvii. 32.
10. Amaziah .... II Chron. xxv. 14.
11. Deborah .... Judges iv.
    Esther .... Esther viii.
    Jael .... Judges v. 24–31.
12. Isaiah .... Isa. xliv. 28.
13. Four times .... Isa. xlv. 1.
    By the Egyptians in the reign of Rehoboam.
               I Kings xiv. 26.
    By the Arabians in the reign of Joram. II Ch. xxi. 17.
    By the Syrians in the reign of Joash. II Ch. xxiv. 23.
    By the Israelites in the reign of Amaziah.
               II Ch. xxv. 23, 24.
14. The Moabites.................. II Kings iii. 27.

15. The tribe of Levi...............Deut. xvii. 8–13.
16. Idolatry.................See Ezra and Nehemiah.
17. Daniel ....Ezek. xiv. 14.
    Job.......................Ezek. xiv. 14.
    Noah ....Ezek. xiv. 14.
18. Fifty........................II Kings ii. 17.
19. Only those which bore no fruit....Deut. xx. 19–26.
20. Manasseh, king of Judah.....See Bible Dictionary.
21. Jerubbaal, by his father, after he had destroyed Baal's altar ....Judges vi. 27–32.
22. The newly married..................Deut. xx. 7.
    Those who had planted a vineyard and not yet eaten the fruit......................Deut. xx. 6.
    Those who had built a house and not dedicated it. Deut. xx. 5.
23. Jezebel ....I Kings xviii. 4.
24. Her cousin and adopted father........Esther ii. 7.
25. Judah ....Dan. i. 6.
26. Saul..........................I Sam. xiv.
27. Epaphroditus ....Phil. iv. 18.
28. See ....Col. iv. 16.
29. Straight....................Life of St. Paul.
30. Joshua's anticipated death..........Josh. xxiv. 15.
    The trial of Baal's prophet........I Kings xviii. 21.
31. The lord of a king of Israel....II Kings vii. 19, 20
32. Samuel......................I Sam. xii. 2, 3
33. See ....Lev. xix. 18.
34. Telegraphy ....Job xxxviii. 35.
35. Pleiades........................Job ix. 9.
    Orion ....Job ix. 9.
    Arcturus ....Job ix. 9.
36. The walls of Babylon................Jer. li. 58.
    The temple of Diana at Ephesus......Acts xix. 27.

37. The rebellion of Absalom............II Sam. xv.
    The rebellion of Sheba...............II Sam. xx.
    The rebellion of Adonijah.............I Kings i.
38. Jehoida ....II Chron. xxiv. 16.
39. The island of Rhodes...............Acts xxi. 1.
40. No, destroyed by an earthquake, B. C. 227.
                                   See Cyclopædia.
41. "The sun rises," "the sun sets".. ...Josh. x. 12.
42. "Seed-time and harvest, cold and heat, summer and winter, day and night, shall not cease." Gen. viii. 22.
43. Jeremiah......................Jer. xxxiii. 20.
44. The revolution of the earth on its axis.
    If there was the least variation, the calculations of astronomers would be at fault.
45. Persons were appointed to watch on the mountain for the first appearance of the new moon. Notice was immediately given to the Sanhedrim, the president of which shouted, "It is consecrated." This was twice repeated by the people and then trumpets were blown.
46. The month began with the change of the moon and they had no astronomical knowledge to determine the time................See Bible Dictionary.
47. Not one of them was slain in battle........Judges.
48. Daniel.........................Dan. xii. 2.
49. See..........................Num. xi. 29.
50. Five months into one hundred and fifty days, make thirty days to a month............Gen. vii. 11.
    See..........................Gen. viii. 3.
    See..........................Gen. viii. 4.
51. The flood came in the six hundredth year of Noah's life. He uncovered the ark on the first day of the six hundredth and first year. Add the different peri-

AIDS TO BIBLICAL RESEARCH. 295

ods, ten months, forty days, seven days, and seven days, and the result is three hundred and sixty-five days, one year..................Gen. vii. 11.
See......................Gen. vii. 5, 6, 10, 12.
See.............................Gen. viii. 13.
52. Hushai.............. ....II Sam. xvii. 14.
53. Barzillai, the Gileadite and others. II Sam. xvii. 27, 29.
54. The Passover........................Ex. xii.
55. "Thou shalt rise before the hoary man.". Lev. xix. 32.
56. From the Lord...............I Chron. xxviii. 11.
57. In the reign of Saul.............I Sam. xxviii. 6.
58. Joab betrayed Amasa...........II Sam. xx. 9, 10.
Judas betrayed Jesus...............Luke xxii. 47.
59. Ant........................Prov. xxx. 24, 28.
Coney......................Prov. xxx. 24, 28.
Locust......................Prov. xxx. 24, 28.
Spider......................Prov. xxx. 24, 28.
60. Caleb.......... ....Jos. xiv. 10. 11.
61. The five kings, who fought against Gideon. Josh. x. 27.
62. Amos...........................Amos vii. 14.
63. Solomon to Hiram........ ...I Kings ix. 11, 13.
64. Judah......................Num. i. 26, 27.
65. Judah........................ Num. x. 14.
66. The sixth year............. ....Lev. xxv. 27.
67. A man breaking the Sabbath.....Num. xv. 32, 36.
The widow who fed Elijah ...I Kings xvii. 10, 16.
Paul........................Acts xxviii. 3–5.
68. The chief-butler..............Gen. xl. 9, 13, 23.
69. Jehoshaphat...............II Chron. xx. 18–21.
70. King Herod's birth-day feast......Mark vi. 21, 27.
71. Sinim, (Sin).....................Isa. xlix. 12.
72. $3,500,000......................I Kings x. 10.
73. Mount Ebal...................... Deut. xxvii. 4.

74. Ploughing with twelve yoke of oxen.
    I Kings xix. 19.
75. Jotham.
76. See.........................Ex. xxxiii. 4.
77. Absalom........................II Sam. xv.
78. Forty..........................Deut. xxv. 3.
79. Eliphaz.........................Job iv. 15.
80. Aaron.........................Num. xvi. 48.
81. The workmen on Solomon's temple.
    II Kings xxii. 7.
82. Esau's.......................Gen. xxxvi. 15.
83. All...Matt. xxvi. 51; Mark xiv. 47; Luke xxii. 50; John xviii. 10.
84. John..........................John xviii. 10.
85. Mark..........................Mark xiv. 47.
86. Nehemiah......................Neh. vi. 10–13.
87. Nebuchadnezzar................II Kings xxv. 7.
88. Rehoboam.....................II Chron. xi. 21.
89. The widow's...................Deut. xxv. 17.
90. A potter......................Jer. xviii. 1, 2.
91. Malachi.........................Mal. iv. 3.
92. Elijah........................I Kings xix. 13.
93. Jonathan......................II Sam. xvii. 17.
    Ahimaaz......................II Sam. xvii. 17.
94. Agur............................Prov. xxx. 8.
95. Abraham................Gen. xii. 13; xx. 1–12.
    David..........................I Sam. xxi. 13.
96. See................Lev. xxvi. 22; Judges v. 6.
97. His robe and implements of war....I Sam. xviii. 4.
98. King Saul......................I Sam. xx. 33.
99. Adoram........................I Kings xii. 18.
100. Pashur..........................Jer. xx. 4.
101. Miriam..........................Ex. xv. 20.

Deborah . . . . Judges vi. 4.
Huldah . . . . II Kings xxii. 14.
Anna . . . . Luke ii. 36.
Philip's four daughters . . . . Acts xxi. 9.
102. Moses . . . . Num. xi. 15.
Elijah . . . . I Kings xix. 4.
Jonah . . . . Jonah iv. 3; v. 8.
103. See . . . . Dan. ii. 46.
104. The fall of Adam . . . . Gen. iii. 6.
The agony of Christ . . . . Luke xxii. 39, 44.
The burial of Christ . . . . John xix. 41, 42.
105. The coming of John the Baptist . . . . Mal. iv. 5.
The manifestation of Christ . . . . Mal. iv. 2.
The destruction of Jerusalem . . . . Mal. iv. 1.
106. To watch the flocks . . . . Job xxx. 1.
107. Benaiah . . . . I Chron. xi. 23.
108. Jacob and his brethren . . . . Gen. xxxi. 46.
109. Absalom . . . . II Sam. xviii. 18.
110. Saul . . . . I Sam. xxxi. 4.
Saul's armor-bearer . . . . I Sam. xxxi. 4.
Ahithophel . . . . II Sam. xvii. 23.
Samson . . . . Judges xvi. 35.
Zimri . . . . I Kings xvi. 18.
Judas . . . . Matt. xvii. 5.
111. Sin, nor repent, nor deny himself . . . . II Tim. ii. 13.
112. Fifty thousand pieces of silver . . . . Acts xix. 19.
113. Adam . . . . Gen. ii. 21.
Abraham . . . . Gen. xv. 12.
Saul and his army . . . . I Sam. xxvi. 12.
114. Samson . . . . Judges xiv. 5.
David . . . . I Sam. xvii. 34.
Benaiah . . . . II Sam. xxiii. 20.
115. Gideon . . . . Judges viii. 24.

116. David ....II Sam. xxiv. 13.
117. A three day's pestilence................
118. Friday, man's creation..................Gen. i. 31.
    Friday, man's redemption..........Luke xxiii. 54.
119. To a broken tooth and a foot out of joint. Prov. xxv. 19.
120. Their clothing waxed not old.........Deut. viii. 4.
121. Six hundred........................Ex. xiv. 7.
122. When Adam named the animals.......Gen. ii. 19.
123. Elisha's.............. ....II Kings vi. 13, 14.
124. "A man drew a bow at a venture and smote."
    II Chron. xviii. 33.
    "By chance there came down a priest and passed by on the other side."................Luke x. 31.
125. Three thousand....................Judges xv. 27.
126. Four thousand..................II Chron. ix. 25.
127. At the grave of Lazarus...............John xi. 33.
    Over Jerusalem.....................Luke xix. 41.
    In Gethsemane.... ....Heb. v. 7.
128. His coming by night to Jesus..........John iii. 1.
    His defence of Christ................John vii. 50.
    His anointing Christ's body for burial. John xix. 39.
129. After His temptation.................Matt. iv. 11.
    In the garden......................Luke xxii. 43.
130. Descendants of Heth, the second son of Canaan.
    Gen. x. 15.
131. Descendants of Elam, son of Shem.....Gen. x. 22.
132. Descendants of Amelek, grandson of Esau.
    Gen. xxxvi. 12.
133. Descendants of Ben-Ammi, the son of Lot. Gen. xix. 38.
134. The progenitor of the tribe is not known, they were citizens of Jebus (Jerusalem) ....Josh. xv. 8.
135. Descendants of Sidon, the eldest son of Canaan. Gen. x.
136. Inhabitants of the land of Palestine....Gen. xiii. 7.

137. Descendants of Midian, son of Abram and Keturah.
　　　　　　　　　　　　　　　　　　　　　Gen. xxv. 2.
138. Descendants of Esau or Edom......Gen. xxxvi. 1.
139. Descendants of Mizraim...........Gen. x. 13, 14.
140. Descendants of Mizraim...........Gen. x. 6–13.
141. Descendants of Abram and Keturah....Gen. xxv. 4.
142. Natives of Syria...... ....Gen. xxv. 20.
143. Descendants of Shem..............I Chron. i. 4.
144. Descendants of Canaan, son of Ham.I Chron. i. 15.
145. Samuel...........................I Sam. i. 4.
　　　Ahijah......................I Kings xiv. 1–13.
　　　Josiah........ ....II Kings xxii. 1–2.
　　　Obadiah ....I Kings xviii. 12.
　　　Solomon......................
　　　David........................
　　　Shadrach ....Dan. i. 17.
　　　Meshach.......................... " i. 17.
　　　Abed-nego .... " i. 17.
　　　Daniel .... " i. 17.
　　　Timothy ....II Tim. iii. 15.
146. Chemosh,　the god of the Moabites....I Kings xi. 7.
　　　Molech,　　　"　　"　Ammonites..I Kings xi. 7.
　　　Milcom,　　 "　　"　Ammonites.I Kings xi. 33.
　　　Bel,　　　　"　　"　Babylonians...Isa. xlvi. 1.
　　　Nebo,　　　"　　"　Babylonians...Isa. xlvi. 1.
　　　Baal,　　　 "　　"　Babylonians.I K. xvi. 31,32.
　　　Merodach,　"　　"　Babylonians......Jer. l. i.
　　　Baal-Berith,"　　"　Shechemites.Judg. viii. 33.
　　　Dagon,　　 "　　"　Philistines...Judg. xvi. 23.
　　　Baal-peor,　"　　"　Moabites.Num. xxv. 3, 5,18.
　　　Baal-zebub,"　　"　Syrians......II Kings i. 2.
　　　Jupiter,　　"　　"　Greeks.......Acts xiv. 12.
　　　Mercurius,　"　　"　Greeks.......Acts xiv. 12.

147. Ashteroth, goddess of the Zidonians...I Kings xi. 7.
     Diana, goddess of the Ephesians......Acts xix. 28.
148. Menander..........................I Cor. xv. 33.
     Epimenides ....Titus i. 12.
149. Temple of Dagon.................I Chron. x. 10.
       "   " Belus..............II Chron. xxxvi. 7.
       "   " Diana...................Acts xix. 27.

CHAPTER XXXVI.

CHRISTIAN EVIDENCE.

1. The reasons for receiving the Bible as a divine book.
2. External evidences,
   Internal evidences,
   Collateral evidences.
3. Arguments establishing the authenticity and genuineness of the Scriptures, and the proofs of the Bible arising from miracles and the fulfilment of prophecy.
4. A book is authentic when it is written by the person whose name it bears; it is genuine when the incidents it contains are true and not fictitious.
5. The question of authenticity refers to the author of the book, the genuineness to the truth of the narrative. The "Innocents Abroad" is an authentic book because written by Mark Twain to whom it is ascribed, but not a genuine book because not a record of facts. The "Travels of Anacharsis the Younger" is a genuine book, being a true description of the manners, customs, and ceremonies of the ancient Greeks, but not an authentic book because not written by the Scythian philosopher, but in the eighteenth century by Barthelemy. Irving's "History of Columbus" is both authentic and genuine being a true history and worthily honored with the name of the distinguished author by whose pen it professes to have been written.

6. From the quotations of the Scriptures which are found in the writings of the early fathers.
From the ancient versions of the Bible.
From the decisions of early and learned counsels.
In early controversies between Christians and their opponents the genuineness of the books was unquestioned.
The reverent and scrupulous care of copyists in all ages.
7. 1,364.
8. Josephus.
9. More than two hundred.
10. From quotations in ancient manuscripts.
11. "It is ordained that nothing beside the canonical Scriptures be read in the church under the name of divine Scriptures." Then follows the enumeration of our New Testament books.
12. The Jews as a people, for long ages before Christ came, believed the statements of the Old Testament.
13. Multitudes of people, beginning at Jerusalem and extending far in all directions, accepted the Scriptures as the rule of their lives.
14. By suffering untold tortures and sacrificing their lives rather than deny Christ. Some perished by fire, some by drowning, some by crucifixion, some by the sword, some by starvation, some by cold, some by stoning; they were stabbed with forks of iron, torn by wild beasts, had their limbs torn asunder, their tongues cut out, their skins plucked off, and were tortured in every horrible way which the ingenuity of men could devise.
15. Jerome,
Augustine,
Philastrius,
Gregory Nazeanzen,
Epphanius, bishop of Constantia,
Athanasius,

Cyril, bishop of Jerusalem,
Eusebius, bishop of Cæsarea.
16. Origen,
Victorinus, a bishop in Germany,
Cyprian, bishop of Carthage,
Gregory of Neo-Cæsarea,
Dionysius of Alexandria.
17. Tertullián of Carthage,
Irenæus of Alexandria,
Clement of Alexandria,
Melito, bishop of Sardis,
Hegesippus, a converted Jew,
Tatian,
Justin Martyr,
Papias, bishop of Hieropolis, in Asia.
18. Barnabas,
Clement,
Hermas.
19. Polycarp,
Ignatius.
20. The testimony of the enemies of Christianity.
21. Celsus,
Porphyry,
Hierocles, president of Bithynia,
Emperor Julian.

22. Every word and letter and yohd was sacred. Not the smallest part of a letter was allowed to be written from memory. The copyist entered into a sacred engagement, and was required before commencing his task to bathe his whole body in holy water and array himself in Jewish costume. He must not write the name of God with a pen which had been used before, and if a king addressed him while writing that holy name he must not answer him.

23. The fact that it was made public in the midst of the generation who were familiar with the incidents narrated therein and not one denial of the truth of the narrative can be found.

24. The Christian religion.

25. They were performed in public.
    They were addressed to the senses.
    They were numerous.
    They were of every conceivable variety.
    They extended over a period of hundreds of years.
    They were performed in many and remote countries.
    They were wrought before citizens of the most enlightened ages.

26. A coin struck at Apamea in the reign of Philip. On this is represented a square chest floating on the waters, which a man and woman are leaving. Above flutters a dove with an olive branch. A raven is on the roof. In one of the panels on the chest is the word Noe in Greek letters.

27. A rock in Horeb. It is an isolated mass of granite about twenty feet square. In the face of the rock are horizontal fissures produced by flowing water. No natural fountain would flow at the height of a dozen feet from the face of a rock. We are compelled to believe that this is the rock from which water was miraculously brought as Moses affirms.

28. The fulfilment of prophecy.

29. More than sixty-four.

30. "And thou shalt become an astonishment, a proverb and a by-word among all nations."

31. Tyre,
    Sidon,
    Babylon,
    Nineveh.

32. Zedekiah was delivered to the king of Babylon and

alked with him at Riblah. There his eyes were put out by command of Nebuchadnezzar. Blind, he went a captive to Babylon and died there, having never seen the city.

33. Chaldean, Persian, Macedonian, Roman.
34. The total destruction of Jerusalem.
35. That not one stone should be left upon another.
36. That the gospel should be preached in all nations.
37. The famine in the days of Claudius Cæsar.
38. The proofs of the divine origin of the gospel.
39. Its incomparable system of morality.
40. The elevated and holy character of its Founder.
    Its adaptation to the wants and condition of all mankind.
    The accuracy, consistency and inspiration which are inherent in the gospel.
41. The history of Christianity itself.
42. Its marvellous propagation.
    Its social and personal benefits.
    Its effects upon the progress of society.
    The self-convincing power of religion in personal experience.

CHAPTER XXXVII.

THE PROMINENT COUNTRIES OF THE BIBLE.

1. Achaia .... Acts xviii. 12.
2. Arabia .... Gal. iv. 25.
3. Aram in Mesopotamia ...... Num. xxiii. 7.
4. Armenia .... II Kings xix. 37.
5. Asia .... I Cor. xvi. 19.
6. Assyria .... II Kings xv. 29.
7. Bashan .... Deut. i. 4.
8. Bithynia .... Acts xvi. 7.
9. Canaan, Land of .... Gen. xvi. 3.
10. Cappadocia ...... Acts ii. 9; I Pet. i. 1.
11. Chaldea .... Gen. xi. 28.
12. Cilicia .... Acts ix. 11.
13. Dalmatia .... II Tim. iv. 10.
14. Edom .... Gen. xxv. 30.
15. Egypt, the land of Ham, Rahab. Gen. xlv. 9.
16. Ethiopia .... Acts viii. 27.
17. Galatia .... II Tim. iv. 10.
18. Galilee .... See map.
19. Gilead, Mt. Gilead, land of Gilead ... I Kings xvii. 1.
20. Goshen, Rameses .... Ex. ix. 26.
21. Greece, Javan .... Ezek. xxvii. 13.
22. Illyricum .... Rom. xv. 9.
23. India .... Es. i. 1.
24. Italy .... Acts xviii. 2.

25.	Judea................	...See map.
26.	Lycaonia	Acts xiv.
27.	Macedonia	Acts xvi. 9.
28.	Mamre................	Gen. xviii. 1.
29.	Media	Dan. ix. 1.
30.	Mesopotamia..........	Judges iii. 8.
31.	Midian	Ex. xviii. 1.
32.	Moab.................	Gen. xix. 37.
33.	Moriah	Gen. xxii. 2.
34.	Mysia................	Acts xvi. 8.
35.	Padan Aram	Gen. xxv. 20.
36.	Palestine	Joel iii. 4.
	Palestina	...Ex. xv. 14.
	Philistia	Psa. lx. 8.
	Canaan	Zeph. ii. 5.
	Land of the Hebrews.......	Gen. xl. 15.
	Land of the Hittites........	Josh. i. 4.
	Land of Israel............	I Sam. xiii. 19.
	Land of Jehovah..........	Hos. ix. 3.
	The Holy Land...........	Zech. ii. 12.
	The Glorious Land........	Dan. xi. 41.
	The Land of the Amorite....	Amos ii. 10.
	The Land..............	Ruth i. 1.
	Judea................	Mark x. 1.
	The Land of Promise.......	Heb. xi. 9.
	The Land of Canaan.......	Josh. xxi. 2.
37.	Parthia................	Acts ii. 9.
38.	Pathros	Ezek. xxx. 14.
39.	Persia................	Dan. xi. 2.
40.	Phœnicia	See map.
41.	Phrygia	See map.
42.	Pisidia	See Bible Dictionary.
43.	Pontus................	Acts xviii. 2.

44. Rameses ....Gen. xlvii. 11.
45. Samaria ....John iv. 4.
46. Sheba....................I Kings x. 10.
47. Shinar ....Gen. xi. 2.
48. Sinim, China.............Isa. xlix. 12.
49. Spain ....Rom. xv. 24.
50. Syria ....See map.

CHAPTER XXXVIII.

CHRONOLOGY.

1. Seven days and nights.
2. 140 years.
3. From Adam to Christ 4004 years.
4. The book of Genesis covers 2309 years.
5. From Adam to the deluge 1656 years.
6. From the deluge to Abram's call 427 years.
7. From Abram's call to the birth of Christ 1921 years.
8. From Abram's call to the removal to Egypt 215 years.
9. The children of Israel in Egypt 215 years.
10. The wandering in the wilderness 40 years.
11. The period of the judges 356 years.
12. The kingdom of Israel 120 years.
13. The kingdom of Israel divided 387 years.
14. The Babylonish captivity 70 years.
15. From the return to the birth of Christ 518 years.
16. Methuselah, 969 years,
    Jared, 962 years,
    Noah, 950 years,
    Adam, 930 years,
    Seth, 912 years,
    Canain, 910 years,
    Enos, 905 years.
17. Mahalaleel 895 years.
18. Lamech 770 years.
19. Enoch 365 years.
20. Methuselah cotemporary with Adam 243 years.
21. Methuselah,   "   "   Noah 600 years.

22. Methuselah, cotemporary with Shem 98 years.
23. Shem, " " Isaac 50 years.
24. Isaac, " " Levi 53 years.
25. Levi, " " Amram 14 years.
26. Amram, " " Moses 58 years.
27. In the year 2348.
28. 120 years.
29. 600 years.
30. One year.
31. 350 years.
32. Eber, 464 years.
33. 2083 years.
34. The Exodus, Solomon's Temple, Babylonish captivity.
    From the call of Abram to *the Exodus* 450 years.
    From the Exodus to the dedication of *Solomon's Temple* 451 years.
    From Solomon's Temple to the end of *Babylonish Captivity* 526 years.
    From the end of Babylonish Captivity to the *Birth of Christ* 518 years.
35. 340 years.
36. In the year 2017.
37. 15 years.
38. 100 years.
39. 17 years.
40. 13 years.
41. 7 years.
42. 80 years.
43. Joseph 110 years.
44. Levi 137 years.
45. 144 years.
46. Three months.
47. Three days.

48. Seven days.
49. Fifty days.
50. Forty days and nights.
51. One year.
52. Forty days.
53. Three periods of 40 years each.
    In Egypt 40 years.
    In Midian 40 years.
    In the wilderness 40 years.
54. Thirty years.
55. Aaron 120 years.
56. 141 years.
57. Nine months.
58. 3 years.
59. 300 years.
60. 40 years.
61. Seven months.
62. Three months.
63. 7 years.
64. 18 years.
65. 18 years.
66. B. C. 1095.
67. Seven years and six months.
68. Saul reigned 40 years.
    David   "   40   "
    Solomon "   40   "
69. 70 years.
70. 440 years.
71. 13 years.
72. 7 years.
73. Seven days.
74. 410 years from its commencement.
75. B. C. 599.

76. 79 years.
77. 19 years.
78. B. C. 520.
79. 46 years.
80. A. D. 70.
81. Jeroboam II. reigned 41 years.
82. Manasseh 55 years.
83. Zimri seven days.
84. Jehoahas three months.
85. 3 years.
86. B. C. 975.
87. 5 years.
88. Fourteenth day of the month.
89. Eli, 98 years of age.
90. At 25 years of age.
91. For 25 years.
92. 100 years.
93. 20 years.
    7 years for Rachel.
    7 years for Leah.
    6 years for cattle.
94. 15 years.
95. 8 years.
96. 40 years.
97. 40 years.
98. Every fiftieth year.
99. Three years and six months.
100. Forty days.
101. 25 years.
102. Every 3 years.
103. About 400 years.
104. 216 years after.
105. Every sixth year.

106. 3 years.
107. Until the high-priest's death.
108. 40 years.
109. B. C. 445.
110. B. C. 335.
111. B. C. 277.
112. B. C. 170.
113. B. C. 63.
114. B. C. 18.
115. B. C. 4.
116. B. C. 4.
117. Four hundred and fifty.
118. A. D. 22.
119. 33 years.
120. 3 years.
121. Forty days.
122. A. D. 29.
123. 40 days.
124. 7 days.
125. A. D. 36.
126. Three days.
127. A. D. 44.
128. A. D. 62.
129. 2 years.
130. A. D. 52.
131. A. D. 68.
132. A. D. 68.
133. A. D. 68.
134. A. D. 95.
135. A. D. 97.
136. A. D. 97.
137. A. D. 100.
138. 1600 years.

CHAPTER XXXIX.

PUZZLES.

1.

BIBLICAL ENIGMA.

"For this cause shall a man leave father and mother, and shall cleave to his wife: and they twain shall be one flesh."—Matt. xix. 5.

2.

ACROSTIC.

Initials, Reuben.   Finals, Simeon.

R-echabite-*s* ....Jer. xxxv. 2–9.
E-l-*i* ....I Sam. ii. 11.
U-ri-*m* ....Cruden's Concordance.
B-ernic-*e* ....Acts xxv. 13.
E-ch-*o* ....Webster.
N-aama-*n* ....II Kings v. 1.

3.

ACROSTIC.

Initials, Issachar.   Finals, Naphtali.

1. I-mr-*i*.
2. S-amue-*l*.
3. S-yri-*a*.
4. A-rara-*t*.
5. C-us-*h*.
6. H-ar-*p*.
7. A-rban-*a*.
8. R-oma-*n*.

4.
Enigma.
"In every thing give thanks.".............I Thess. v. 18.

5.
A Double Acrostic.
Initials, Ramoth-Gilead. Finals, Bethlehemite.

1. R-aha-*b*................Josh. ii. 1; Psa. lxxxvii. 4.
2. A-ppl-*e*....................Joel i. 12.
3. M-erchan-*t*...............Ez. xxvii. 20.
4. O-badia-*h*..................See Bible.
5. T-eke-*l*.....................Dan. v. 25.
6. H-eg-*e*....................Est. ii. 3.
7. G-emaria-*h*................Jer. xxxvi. 25.
8. I-mmutabl-*e*...............Heb. vi. 18.
9. L-udi-*m*...................I Chron. i. 11.
10. E-l-*i*......................I Sam.
11. A-rara-*t*...................Gen. viii. 4.
12. D-erb-*e*....................Acts xvi. 1.

6.
An Acrostic
Initials, The Immaculate Conception.

1. T-iglath-pileser..............II Chron. xxviii. 20.
2. H-erod.....................Acts xii. 23.
3. E-lim......................Ex. xv. 27.
4. I-scariot....................John xiii. 26.
5. M-ark......................See Bible.
6. M-ephibosheth ....II Sam. iv 4.
7. A-bner.....................II Sam. iii. 32.
8. C-yrus ....II Chron. xxxvi. 22.
9. U-zziah ....II Chron. xxvi. 1.
10. L-eviathan ....Job xli. 1.

11. A-barim .... Deut. xxxii. 49.
12. T-etrarch .... Matt. xiv. 1.
13. E-unice .... II Tim. i. 5.
14. C-leopatra .... Luke xxiv. 18.
15. O-thniel...................... Josh xv. 17.
16. N-isan ....
17. C-ain .... Gen. iv. 8.
18. E-lias .... Luke iv. 25.
19. P-urim........................ Esth. ix. 26.
20. T-erah .... I Chron. i. 26.
21. I-chabod .... I Sam. iv. 21.
22. O-bed-edom .... I Chron. xiii. 14.
23. N-azareth..................... Matt. ii. 23.

7.

Acrostic.

Initials, Mediterranean Sea.

1. M-emucan...................... Est. i. 15.
2. E-lhanan .... II Sam. xxi. 19.
3. D-aniel .... Book of Daniel.
4. I-saiah....................... Bible Dictionary.
5. T-homas .... John xx. 25.
6. E-r........................... Gen. xxxviii. 3.
7. R-achel .... Gen. xxix. 18.
8. R-euben .... Gen. xxix. 32.
9. A-bigail .... I Sam. xxvii. 3.
10. N-athan .... II Sam. xii. 7.
11. E-noch........................ Gen. v. 21.
12. A-dmah....... Gen. xix. 28, 29; Gen. xiv. 2.
13. N-ahshon...................... Num. ii. 3.
14. S-imon, the sorcerer .... Acts viii. 20.
15. E-phraim...................... Gen. xli. 52.
16. A-maziah .... II Kings xxii. 19–31.

8.
Hidden Bible Characters.
1. Seth.   2. Pilate, Ruth.   3. Mark.   4. Ham, On.

9.
Hidden Acrostic.
Leviathan.

10.
Rhomboid.

```
H  A  I  L
   I  D  O  L
      A  V  E  S
         E  D  O  M
```

11.
Biblical Arithmetical Puzzle.

```
  7   The months the ark of God was with the Philistines.
120   The years Noah was building the ark.
───
127

 40   The years David reigned over Israel.
───
 87

  4   The number of days Lazarus was in the grave.
6)348   The number of years Jacob served Laban for his cattle.
───
 58

 49   The number of years between the jubilee.
  9   The number of cubits in Og's bedstead.
```

12.
Bible Animals Hidden in Bible Texts.
1. Ram.   2. Lamb, horse.   3. Ewe.

13.
Enigma.
"Neither as being lords over God's heritage, but being ensamples to the flock."—I Peter v. 3.

14.

Hidden Kings.

So .... II Kings xvii. 4.
Og .... Deut. xxxi. 4.
Herod .... Matt. ii. 12.
Asa .... II Chron. xv. 19.
Pul .... II Kings xv. 19.

15.

Perspective Cross.

```
            A B R A M
            M       O G
            R       S U
            A       E R
    H I R A M       S A I N T
    E                       I S
    R                       T   A
    O                       U   C
    D I A N A       T R O A S   H
      A     H       H           A
        E L I       E   A A R O N
            T       O   L
            H       P   E
            O       H   X
            P       I   A
            H       L   N
            E       U   D
            L I M E S   R
              T       O I
                K E S I A
```

Across: Abram, Og, us, er, Hiram, Saint, is, Diana, Troas, ah, Eli, Aaron, Limes, Toi, Kesia.

Down: Amram, Moses, Uri, Herod, Titus, Achan, Ahithophel, Theophilus, Alexandria.

16.

Perspective Cube.

```
            N A T H A N A E L
          O E             M A
        M   T               I   O
      A     H             M     D
    A R I M A T H E A           I
    R       N         R         C
    C       E         I         E
    H       E         M         A
    E       L E V I A T H A N
    A     A           T     O
    L     U           H     D
    U     H           E     M
    S A H A D U T H A
```

Across: Nathanael, Arimathea, Leviathan, Sahadutha.
Down: Archealus, Nethaneel, Arimathea, Laodicean.
Diagonals: Aaron, Ariel, Shual, Abdon.

17.

Puzzles.

Asa—Anna—Nun—Eve—Hannah.

18.

Word Square.

```
I D D O
D E A R
D A T E
O R E B
```

19.

Star Diamond.

```
          I
        A S P
      A S H E R
    I S H M A E L
      P E A C E
        R E E
          L
```

20.

An Acrostic.

S-hishak .... I Kings xiv. 25.
H-innon .... Josh. xv. 8.
A-bdon .... Judges xii. 13.
L-ysias .... Acts xxiii. 26.
M-anoah .... Judges.
A-rphaxad .... Gen. x. 22.
N-eapolis .... Acts xvi. 11.
E-liam .... II Sam. xi. 3.
Z-oan .... Num. xiii. 22.
E-zel .... I Sam. xx. 19.
R-ephan .... Acts vii. 43.
Shalmanezer.

21.

SCRIPTURE ANAGRAM.

"The Lord our righteousness." ...... Jer. xxxiii. 6.
1. T-ongue .... James iii. 8.
2. H-erod .... Acts xii. 1.
3. E-li .... I Sam. i. 25.
4. L-ois .... II Tim. i. 5.
5. O-rion .... Job ix. 9.
6. R-eu .... I Chron. i. 25.
7. D-en .... Dan.
8. O-g .... Deut. xxxi. 4.
9. U-ri .... Ezra x. 24.
10. R-oe .... Prov. vi. 5.
11. R-uth .... Ruth i. 14.
12. I-rons .... Job xli. 7.
13. G-ihon...................... Gen. ii. 13.
14. H-en .... Zech. vi. 14.
15. T-hree .... Ex. ii. 2.
16. E-glon .... Judges iii. 17.
17. O-n .... Num. xvi. 1.
18. U-r......................... Gen. xv. 7.
19. S-o......................... II Kings xvii. 4
20. N-o .... Jer. xlvi. 25.
21. E-d .... Josh. xxii. 34.
22. S-eth .... Gen. v. 3.
23. S-eir....................... Gen. xiv. 6.

22.

REVERSALS.

1. Laban—Nabal.   5. Ire—Eri.
2. Oren—Nero.   6. Mate—Etam.
3. Leal—Lael.   7. Mane—Enam.
4. Mode—Edom.   8. Harcs—Serah.

23.
Transpositions.

1. Hurt—Ruth.
2. Robe—Oreb.
3. Myra—Mary.
4. Lie—Eli.
5. Mesh—Shem.
6. Share—Rhesa.
7. Bale—Abel.
8. Bare—Reba.
9. Beast—Sebat.
10. Lone—Elon.

24.
Hollow Square.

```
R O M E
U     S
T     L
H E L I
```

25.
Star Diamond.

```
        D
      B E H
    B A B E L
  D E B O R A H
    H E R O D
      L A D
        H
```

26.

Hollow Square.

```
E T H I O P I A
P               D
E               O
N               N
A               I
T               J
U               A
S H A M M A U H
```

27.

Star Diamond.

```
        P
      N E R
    P E T E R
      R E D
        R
```

28.

Numerical Cities.

Bethlehem—Judah.
Bethel.
Bethlehem.
Mysia.
Jerusalem.
Timnath.

29.

Drop Letter Puzzle.

"The Lord is my shepherd, I shall not want."

30.
Word Square.

```
T E M A
E L O N
M O A N
A N N A
```

31.
Double Acrostic.
Elijah—Elisha.
E-zr-*a*.
L-achis-*h*.
I-shmaelite-*s*.
J-ehovah-niss-*i*.
A-hithophe-*l*.
H-eg-*e*.

32.
Scripture Enigma.
1. On.   2. Hor.   3. Peor.   4. Sin.   5. Sun.
Onesiphorus.

33.
Double Diagonals.

```
T h e u d a S ................. Acts v. 36.
J A h a z A h ................. Josh. xxi. 36.
D e B o R a h ................. Gen. xxxv. 8.
A r t E m a s ................. Titus iii. 12.
A p P a R e l ................. I Tim. ii. 9.
I T h a m A r ................. Ex. vi. 2, 3.
A h a z i a H ................. I Kings xxii. 40.
       Sarepta ......... Luke iv. 26.
       Taberah ......... Deut. ix. 22.
```

34.
MESOSTICH.

```
A d r a m M e l e c h
  A s h t A r o t h
      A s H e r
    A t t A l i a
      E g L o n
        p l A i n
      S h a L l u m
          o m E g a
        A r m E n i a
S h i h o r L i b n a t h
```
Mahalaleel.

35.
AN ACROSTIC.

C-andace .... Acts viii. 27.
A-baddon .... Rev. ix. 11.
I-taly .... Acts xviii. 2.
P-aari .... II Sam. xxiii. 35.
H-arod .... Judges vii. 1.
A-bib .. .. Ex. xiii. 4.
S-harezer....................... II K. xxx. 37.

Caiphas.

36.
NUMERICAL CITIES.

Helkath Hazzurim .... II Sam. ii. 16.
Zelzah .... I Sam. x. 2.
Nineveh .... Gen. x. 11.
Azekah .... Jer. xxxiv. 7.
Ashkelon .... Judges xiv. 19.
Hamath .... II Sam. viii. 9.

37.

Numerical Enigma.

"Charity never faileth."—I Cor. xiii. 8.

38.

Scripture Enigma.

"Wealth maketh many friends, but the poor is separated from his neighbors."—Prov. xix. 4.

39.

Riddles.

1. What is sweeter than honey, what is stronger than a lion?
2. Moses.
3. Peter—he slept on his watch.
4. Nehemiah—Knee high Miah.
5. His father did not die at all.
6. Preserved pears (pairs).
7. When the dove brought the green back to Noah.
8. Chap I.
9. Jenny Sis (Genesis).
10. Joshua the son of Nun (none)
11. Noah—he went forth (fourth) from the ark.

40.

Acrostical Central Deletions.

R a H a b	..............Josh. ii.
E l E p h	..............Josh. xviii. 28.
I m M e r	..............Neh. vii. 61.
e n A d a d	..............Neh. x. 9.
I m N a h	..............I Chron. vii. 35.
Heman..........I Kings iv. 31.	

41.

A Scripture Alphabet.

Adam .... Gen.
Babel .... Gen. xi. 9.
Carmel .... I Kings xviii. 42.
Damascus .... Bible Dictionary.
Elijah .... I Kings xviii. 40.
Felix .... Acts xxiv. 27.
Goat .... Lev. ix. 15.
Holiness .... I John iii. 12.
Iscariot .... Matt. x. 4.
Jehu .... II Chron. xix. 2.
Kezia........................... Job xlii. 14.
Lebanon .... Deut. i. 7.
Miphkad .... Neh. iii. 31.
Naaman .... II Kings v. 1.
Obed........................... Ruth iv. 17.
Peter .... Matt. xxv. 70.
Quartus......................... Rom. xvi. 13.
Rachel .... Gen. xxix. 18.
Samson .... Judges xiv. 5, 6.
Thomas .... John xx. 27.
Uzzah .... I Chron. xiii. 9.
Vophsi .... Num. xiii. 14.
Women.......................... I Tim. ii. 19.
Xerxes.......................... Dan. xi. 2.
Yellow .... Lev. xiii. 30.
Zaccheus........................ Luke xix. 2, 3.

42.

Hour Glass Puzzle.

```
W o o d o f E p h r a i m
    t r e s s P a s s e d
        Z e c h A r i a h
            h a r P e r s
                A s H e r
                  U R i
                  R O E
                I n D i a
            P e l I c a n
        R a m a T h i t e
    M e r c U r i u s
S o o t h S a y e r s
```
Epaphroditus.

43.

Scripture Enigma.

1. L-ydia ....Acts xvi. 14.
2. O-phir ....I Kings ix. 28.
3. V-ashti ....Es. i. 12.
4. E-unice ....II Tim. i. 5.
5. Y-oke ....Lam. iii. 27.
6. O-shea ....Num. xiii. 8.
7. U-pharsin.....................Dan. v. 25.
8. R-est ....Heb. iv. 10.
9. E-sau ....Gen. xxv. 34.
10. N-oah ....Gen. viii. 1.
11. E-ngedi ....I Sam. xxiii. 29.
12. M-oses ....Ex. xxxii. 11.
13. I-saiah ....Isa. lix. 1.
14. E-leazar ....Num. xvi. 39.
15. S-heba ....I Kings x. 1.

Love your enemies.—Mat. v. 44

44.
ARITHMOREMS.
Bible Cities.

Damascus	Gen. xv. 2.
Cabul	I Kings ix. 13.
Adoraim	II Chron. ix. 9.
Iconium	Acts xiii. 51.
Mitylene	Acts xx. 14.
Salem	Gen. xiv. 18.

45.
BIBLE CITIES HIDDEN IN BIBLE VERSE.

1. On................Gen. xli. 45.
2. Ai.................Gen. xiii. 3.
3. Ur.................Gen. xi. 28.
4. Rome..............Acts xix. 21.
5. No.................Nahum iii. 8.
6. Gath...............I Sam. v. 8.
7. Nob................I Sam. xxi. 1.
8. Dan................Judg. xx. 1.
9. Cana, Nazareth....John ii. 1; Matt. ii. 23.

46.
ACROSTIC CENTRAL DELETIONS.

J a C o b	Gen. l. 13.
A c H a n	Josh. vii. 18.
E n E a s	Acts xix. 34.
C y p R e s s	Isa. xlii. 14.
E r E c h	Gen. x. 10.
G a T a m	Gen. xxvi. 11.
E p H a h	Ex. xvi. 36.
C o r I n t h	Acts xviii. 1.
C i s T e r n	Jer. xxxviii. 6.
P h E b e	Rom. xvi. 1.
C r i S p u s	I Cor. i. 14.
Cherethites	II Sam. viii. 18.

47.

ARITHMOREMS.

Bible Islands.

Arrad..................Ezek. xxvii. 8, 11.
Clauda ....Acts xxvii. 16.
Crete .... " xxvii. 13.
Melita.................. " xxviii. 1.
Rhodes .... " xxi. 1.
Chios .... " xx. 15.
Coos .... " xxi. 1.

48.

BIBLE CHARACTERS HIDDEN IN BIBLE VERSE.

1. Elon.......... ....Gen. xxxvi. 2.
2. Eli ....Psa. xciii. 3.
3. On ....Num. xvi. 1.
4. Uri..........................Ex. xxxi. 2.
5. Tola.........................Gen. xlvi. 13.
6. Er...........................Gen. xxxviii. 3.
7. Gad ....Gen. xxx. 11.
8. Dan ....Gen. xxx. 6.

49.

LETTER RIDDLE.

The Seven Churches of Asia.

1. Ephesus.   u
2. Smyrna.   s
3. Pergamos.   e
4. Thyatyra.   h
5. Sardis.   s
6. Philadelphia. P
7. Laodicea.   e

AIDS TO BIBLICAL RESEARCH. 331

50.

ANAGRAMS.

Prominent Bible Countries.

1. Achaia.
2. Arabia.
3. Bithynia.
4. Armenia.
5. Chaldea.
6. Assyria.
7. Cilicia.
8. Mesopotamia.

51.

BIBLICAL ARITHMETICAL PUZZLE.

525 feet, length of Noah's ark.
87 feet, breadth of Noah's ark.
52 feet, height of Noah's ark.
2)664 years Absalom dwelt in Jerusalem.
332
205 years, the age of Terah.
127
3 years Isaiah walked barefoot.
130
7 years, the famine in Joseph's time.
137 years, the age of Amram.

CHAPTER XL.

THINGS WORTH KNOWING.

1. The Pyramids of Egypt.
    The Colossus of Rhodes.
    The Temple of Diana at Ephesus.
    The Walls and Hanging Gardens of Babylon.
    The Statue of Jupiter Olympius.
    The Mausoleum of Artemisia.
    The Pharos of Alexandria.

2. | | B. C. |
   |---|---|
   | Marathon | 490 |
   | Syracuse | 413 |
   | Arbela | 331 |
   | Metaurus | 207 |
   | | A. D. |
   | Teutoberg | 9 |
   | Chalons | 451 |
   | Touro | 732 |
   | Hastings | 1066 |
   | Orleans | 1429 |
   | Spanish Armada | 1588 |
   | Blenheim | 1704 |
   | Pultowa | 1709 |
   | Saratoga | 1777 |
   | Valmy | 1792 |
   | Waterloo | 1815 |

3. The Fall.
    The Flood.
    The Dispersion.

The Giving of the Law on Sinai.
The Building of Solomon's Temple.
The End of the Babylonish Captivity.
The Coming of Christ.
The Descent of the Holy Ghost.
4. The Fall of the Roman Empire.
The Translation of the Bible into English.
The Invention of Printing.
The Discovery of America.
The Reformation.
The Declaration of Independence.
The Emancipation Proclamation.
5. Moses, the Leader of Israel.
David, the Sweet Singer of Israel.
Isaiah, the Evangelical Prophet.
Ezra, the Scribe.
Luke, the Physician.
Paul, the Apostle to the Gentiles.
John, the Beloved Disciple.
6. Constantinople.
Theodosius.
Charlemagne.
Alfred the Great.
Cromwell.
Washington.
Victoria.
7. Bias.
Chilo.
Cleobulus.
Pittacus.
Periander.
Solon.
Thales.

8. *Three Gentiles—*
    Hector, son of Priam,
    Alexander the Great,
    Julius Cæsar.
   Three Jews—
    Joshua, conqueror of Caanan,
    David, king of Israel,
    Judas Maccabeus.
   Three Christians—
    Arthur, king of Britain,
    Charlemagne,
    Godfrey of Bouillon.

9. Calliope . . . . Muse of Eloquence.
   Clio . . . . " History.
   Polymnia . . . . . . " Rhetoric.
   Erato . . . . " Love.
   Euterpe . . . . . . " Music.
   Melpomene . . . . . " Tragedy.
   Thalia . . . . , . . " Comedy.
   Terpsichore . . . . . " Dancing.
   Urania . . . . " Astronomy.

10. *The Furies—*
    Tisiphone,
    Megaera,
    Alecto.

11. *The Gorgons—*
    Stheno,
    Euryale,
    Medusa.

12. *The Fates—*
    Clotho, with distaff in hand,
    Lachesis, the spinner,
    Atropos, with scissors.

13. *The Graces—*
    Aglia,
    Thalia,
    Euphrasyne.
14. Hercules.
15. The slaughter of the Nemean lion.
    The conquest of the Lernæan hydra.
    The capture of the golden-horned stag of Ceryneia.
    The combat with the Erymanthian boar.
    The cleaning of the stables of Augeas.
    The destruction of the Stymphalian birds.
    The capture of the Cretan bull.
    The capture of the carniverous mares of Diomede.
    The successful theft of the girdle of Hippolyte.
    The slaughter of Geryon, and capture of the oxen.
    The finding of the golden apples of the Hesperides.
    The fetching Cerbeus up from the lower world.
16. Aœlus . . . . . .God of the Winds.
17. Apollo . . . . . . " the Light.
18. Bacchus, Dionysus . . " Wine.
19. Comus . . . . . . " Revelry.
20. Cupid, Eros . . . . " Love.
21. Esculapius . . . . . " Medicine.
22. Jupiter, Zeus . . . . " Heaven.
23. Mars, Ares . . . . . " War.
24. Mercury, Hermes . . . " Eloquence.
25. Momus . . . . . . " Folly.
26. Neptune, Poseidon . . " Water.
27. Pan . . . . " Hunting.
28. Pluto, Hades . . . . " the Lower Regions.
29. Plutus . . . . . . " Riches.
30. Saturn, Cronos . . . " Chronology.
31. Somnus . . . . . . " Sleep.

32. Sylvanus . . . . . God of Groves.
33. Terminus . . . . . " Boundaries.
34. Vulcan, Hephætos . . " Fire
35. Astrea . . . . . . Goddess of Justice.
36. Aurora . . . . . . " the Morning.
37. Ceres, Demeter . . . " Tillage.
38. Cybele, Rhea . . . . " Chronology.
39. Diana, Artemis . . . " Hunting.
40. Flora . . . . . . " Flowers.
41. Feronia . . . . . . " Woods.
42. Hebe . . . . . . " Youth.
43. Hygia . . . . . . " Health.
44. Iris . . . . " the Rainbow.
45. Juno, Hera . . . . " Heaven.
46. Lactura . . . . . . " Corn.
47. Minerva, Athena . . . " Wisdom.
48. Meltona . . . . . " Honey.
49. Nemesis . . . . . " Vengeance.
50. Nox . . . . " Night.
51. Pomona . . . . . " Fruit.
52. Proserpine, Persephone . " Lower Regions.
53. Themis . . . . . . " Law.
54. Thetis . . . . . . " Discord.
55. Venus, Aphrodite . . . " Beauty.
56. Vesta . . . . . . " the Hearth.
57. People half man, half horse.
58. Beautiful sea nymphs, half fish, half woman.
59. The guards of the golden apples.
60. The nymphs of the woods.
61. The nymphs of the fountains.
62. The nymphs of the sea.
63. Sea-gods, half fish, half man.
64. Gods of the household.

65. Giants who warred with the gods.
66. Monsters who turned the beholders to stone.
67. One-eyed giants.
68. Monsters with women's faces, vultures' bodies, and dragons' claws.
69. Infernal deities who presided over sepulchral monuments.
70. Minos.
    Rhadamanthus.
    Acanthus.
71. Elysium.
    Tartarus.
72. Sisyphus.
    Ixion.
    Tantalus.
73. Theseus.
    Orpheus.
    Perseus.
    Hercules.
    Minos.
    Jason.
74. Olympic, in honor of Jupiter, held at Elis, every fifth year.
    Pythian, in honor of Apollo, held at Delphi, third year of each Olympiad.
    Isthmean, in honor of Neptune, held at Corinthian Isthmus, biannually.
    Nemean, in honor of Jupiter, held at Nemea, biannually.
75. Socrates. . . . . . . B. C., 470–399.
    Plato. . . . .   "   429–348.
    Demosthenes . . . . . "   385–322.
    Aristotle. . . . . . . "   384–322.

76. Alexander the Great.
    Miltrades.
    Themistocles.
    Aristides.
    Leonidas.
77. Homer.
78. Lycurgus.
79. Demosthenes.
80. Cicero.
81. Xerxes.
82. Shakespeare.
83. Acquaviva, A. M.
84. St. Alban.

APPENDIX.

TABLES

of

BIBLE WEIGHTS, MEASURES, AND MONEYS.

No. 1.

JEWISH WEIGHTS, REDUCED TO ENGLISH TROY WEIGHT.

	LBS.	OZ.	PEN.	GR.
The Gerah, one-twentieth of a shekel	0	0	0	12
The Bekah, half a shekel	0	0	5	0
The Shekel	0	0	10	0
The Maneh, 60 shekels	2	6	0	0
The Talent, 50 manehs, or 3,000 shekels	125	0	0	0

No. 2.

BIBLE MEASURES OF LENGTH, REDUCED TO ENGLISH MEASURE.

							ENG. FEET.	INCHES.
A Digit							0	0.912
4 = A Palm							0	3.648
12 =	3 = A Span						0	10.944
24 =	6 =	3 = A Cubit					1	9.888
96 =	24 =	6 =	2 = A Fathom				7	3.552
144 =	36 =	12 =	6 =	1.5 = Ezekiel's reed			10	11.328
192 =	48 =	16 =	8 =	2 =	1.3 = An Arabian pole		14	7.104
1920 =	480 =	160 =	80 =	20 =	13.3 =	10 = A Measuring Line	145	11.04

No. 3.

THE LONG BIBLE MEASURES.

						ENG. MILES.	PACES.	FEET.
A Cubit						0	0	1.824
400 = A Stadium or Furlong						0	145	4.6
2000 =	5 = A Sabbath-day's Journey					0	729	3.
4000 =	10 =	2 = An Eastern Mile				1	403	1.
12000 =	30 =	6 =	3 = A Parasang			4	153	3.
96000 =	240 =	48 =	24 =	8 = A Day's Journey or stage		33	172	4.

No. 4.

BIBLE LIQUID MEASURES REDUCED TO ENGLISH WINE MEASURE.

		GAL.	PINTS.
A Caph		0	0.625
1.3 = A Log		0	0.833
5.3 = 4 = A Cab		0	3.333
16 = 12 = 3 = A Hin		1	2.
32 = 24 = 6 = 2 = A Seah		2	4.
96 = 72 = 18 = 6 = 3 = A Bath, Ephah, or Firkin		7	4.50
960 = 720 = 180 = 60 = 20 = 10 = A Kor, Choros, or Homer		75	5.25

No. 5.

BIBLE DRY MEASURES REDUCED TO ENGLISH CORN MEASURE.

	BUSH.	PKS.	GAL.	PINTS
A Gachal	0	0	0	0.14
20 = A Cab	0	0	0	2.833
36 = 1.8 = An Omer or Gomer	0	0	0	5.1
120 = 6 = 3.3 = A Seah	0	1	0	1.
360 = 18 = 10 = 3 = An Ephah	0	3	0	3.
1800 = 90 = 50 = 15 = 5 = A Letech	4	0	0	0.
3600 = 180 = 100 = 30 = 10 = A Homer or Kor	8	0	0	1.

No. 6.

JEWISH MONEY, REDUCED TO ENGLISH AND AMERICAN STANDARDS.

	£.	s.	d.	$	cts.
A Gerah	0	0	1.3687	0	02.5
10 = A Bekah	0	1	1.6875	0	25.00
20 = 2 = A Shekel	0	2	3.375	0	50.187
1200 = 120 = 50 = A Maneh, or Mina Hebr.	5	14	0.75	25	09.35
60000 = 6000 = 3000 = 60 = A Talent	342	3	9.	1505	62.5
A Solidus Aureus, or Sextula	0	12	0.5	2	64.09
A Siclus Aureus, or Gold Shekel	1	16	6.	8	03.
A Talent of Gold	5475	0	0.	24309	00.

No. 7.

ROMAN MONEY, REDUCED TO ENGLISH AND AMERICAN STANDARD.

	£.	s.	d.	far.	$	cts.
A Mite	0	0	0	0.75	0	00.343
A Farthing	0	0	0	1.50	0	00.687
A Penny, or Denarius	0	0	7	2.	0	13.75
A Pound, or Mina	3	2	6	0.	13	75.

CHRONOLOGICAL SCRIPTURE INDEX.

PERIOD I.

THE CREATION TO THE DELUGE, 1,656 YEARS.

A.M.	B. C.		
1	4004	The creation..	Genesis i. 2.
"	"	Fall of our first parents. Promise of a Saviour......	" iii. 3.
2	4002	Cain born	" iv. 1.
3	4001	Abel born	" iv. 2.
129	3875	Abel murdered by Cain.............................	" iv. 8.
130	3874	Seth born, Adam being 130 years old...............	" v. 3.
622	3382	Enoch born...	" v. 18, 19.
687	3317	Methuselah born....................................	" v. 21.
930	3074	Adam dies, aged 930 years..........................	" v. 5.
987	3017	Enoch translated, aged 365 years...................	" v. 24.
1042	2962	Seth dies, aged 912 years...........................	" v. 8.
1056	2948	Noah born	" v. 28, 29.
			" vi. 3–22.
1536	2468	The Deluge	I Pet. iii. 20.
			II Pet. ii. 5.
1656	2348	Methuselah dies, aged 969 years...................	Genesis v. 27.
		Noah enters the ark, being 600 years old...........	" vii. 6, 7.

PERIOD II.

THE DELUGE TO THE CALL OF ABRAHAM, 427 YEARS.

A.M.	B. C.		
1657	2347	Noah, with his family, leaves the ark after the deluge, offers sacrifices, receives the covenant of safety, of which the rainbow was the token.........	Gen viii. 18, 20.
			" ix. 8, 17.
1770	2234	Babel built	" xi.
1770	2234	The Dispersion	" xi.
1771	2233	Nimrod lays the foundation of the Babylonian monarchy	" x. 8–11.
1816	2188	Mizraim lays the foundation of the Egyptian monarchy	" x. 13.
2006	1998	Noah dies, aged 950 years..........................	" ix. 29.
2008	1996	Abram born	" xi. 26.

PERIOD III.
THE CALL OF ABRAHAM TO THE EXODUS, 430 YEARS.

A.M.	B. C.		
2068	1936	The call of Abram	Genesis xi. 31.
2091	1913	Abram's victory over the kings, and rescue of Lot	" xiv. 1-24.
2094	1910	Ishmael born, Abram being 86 years old	" xvi.
2107	1997	God's covenant with Abram, changing his name to *Abraham;* circumcision instituted—Lot delivered, Sodom, Gomorrah, Admah, and Zeboiim destroyed by fire	" xvii. 19.
2108	1896	Isaac born, Abraham being 100 years old	" xxi.
			" xxii.
2133	1871	Abraham offers Isaac as a sacrifice to God	Heb. xi. 17-19. Jas. ii. 21.
2145	1859	Sarah dies, aged 127 years	Genesis xxiii. 1.
2148	1856	Isaac marries Rebecca	" xxiv.
2168	1836	Jacob and Esau born, Isaac being 60 years old	" xxv. 26.
2183	1821	Abraham dies, aged 175 years	" xxv. 7, 8.
2245	1759	Jacob goes to his uncle Laban in Syria, and marries his cousins, Leah and Rachel	" xxviii.
2258	1746	Joseph born, Jacob being 90 years old	" xxx. 23, 24.
2265	1739	Jacob returns to Canaan	" xxxi. 32.
2275	1729	Joseph sold by his brethren	" xxxvii.
2288	1716	Joseph explains Pharaoh's dreams, and is made governor of Egypt	" xli.
2298	1706	Joseph's brethren settle in Egypt	" xliii. 44.
2315	1689	Jacob foretells the advent of Messiah, and dies in Egypt, aged 147 years	" xlix.
2368	1636	Joseph dies, aged 110 years	" l. 26.
2430	1574	Aaron born	Ex. vi. 20; vii. 7.
2433	1571	Moses born	" ii. 1-10.
2473	1531	Moses flees to Midian	" ii. 11-13.
2513	1491	Moses commissioned to deliver Israel	" iii. 2.

PERIOD IV.
THE EXODUS TO THE BUILDING OF SOLOMON'S TEMPLE, 487 YEARS.

A.M.	B. C.		
2513	1491	Passage of the Red Sea by the Israelites	Exod. xiv. 15.
2514	1490	The law delivered on Sinai	" xix. 40.
2552	1452	Miriam, sister of Moses, dies	Num. xx. 1.
"	"	Aaron dies, aged 123 years	" xx. 28, 29
2553	1451	Moses dies, aged 120 years, Joshua his successor	Deut. xxxiv.
"	"	The Israelites pass the Jordan, the manna ceases, Jericho taken	Josh. 1-6.
2561	1443	Joshua dies, aged 110 years	" xxiv.
2849	1155	Samuel born	I Sam. i. 19.
2888	1116	Eli, the high-priest, dies. Ark of God taken by the Philistines	" iv. 1.
2909	1095	Saul anointed king	" x. 11, 12.
2919	1085	David born	
2941	1063	David anointed king, and slays Goliath	{ " xvi. 13. { " xvii. 4, 9.
2949	1055	Saul defeated in battle, in despair kills himself. David acknowledged king by Judah	" xxxi.
2956	1048	Ishbosheth, king of Israel, assassinated, and the kingdom united under David	II " i.

PERIOD IV.—Continued.

A.M.	B. C.			
2957	1047	Jerusalem taken by David from the Jebusites and made a royal city............................	II Sam.	v.
2969	1035	David contrives the death of Uriah................	II "	xi.
2970	1034	David repents of his sin through the influence of Nathan the prophet............................	II "	xii.
2971	1033	Solomon born.....................................	II "	xii. 24.
2981	1023	Absalom is slain by Joab in his rebellion against his father..	II "	xv. 18.
2989	1015	Solomon proclaimed king..........................	I Kings	i.
2990	1014	David dies at 70 years of age.....................	I "	ii.
3000	1004	Solomon's temple completed.......................	II "	vi; vii.

PERIOD V.

FROM THE BUILDING OF SOLOMON'S TEMPLE TO THE CAPTIVITY OF THE ISRAELITES IN BABYLON, 412 YEARS.

PROPHETS of JUDAH.	Years of Reign.	KINGS of JUDAH.	Judah.	Israel.	KINGS of ISRAEL.	Years of Reign.	PROPHETS of ISRAEL.
Shemaiah ..	17	Rehoboam	975	975	Jeroboam	22	Man of God from Judah.
	3	Abijah, or Abijam.	958	—			
Oded	41	Asa	955	—			Ahijah.
Azariah			—	954	Nadab	2	
Hanani....			—	953	Baasha	24	
Jehu, son of			—	930	Elah	2	
Hanani...			—	929	Zimri	7 d.	
			—	929	Omri...........	12	Elijah.
			—	918	Ahab	22	Micaiah.
	25	Jehosaphat	914	—			
			—	898	Ahaziah	2	Elisha.
Eliezer			—	896	Joram, or Jehoram	12	
Jahaziel	8	Jehoram, or Joram	892	—			
	1	Ahaziah, or Azariah	885	—			
	6	Athaliah	884	884	Jehu	28	
	40	Jehoash, or Joash.	878	—			
Zechariah,			—	856	Jehoahaz........	17	Jonah.
son of Je-			—	841	Joash, or Jehoash.	16	
hoida	29	Amaziah	839	—			
		Interregnum, 11 years, according to Hales..		—	825	Jeroboam II......	41	Hosea. Amos.
Zechariah, (who had under- standing in the vis- sions of God, 2 Ch. xxvi. 5.)	52	Uzziah, or Azariah	810	—			
			—	784	*Interregnum, 22 years, according to Hales..*	11	
			—	773	Zechariah	6 m.	
			—	772	Shallum	1 m.	
			—	772	Menahem	10	
			—	761	Pekaiah	2	
			—	759	Pekah...........	20	
Isaiah	16	Jotham	758	—			
Micah......	16	Ahaz............	742	—			
			—	739	Anarchy	9	Oded.
			—	730	Hoshea	9	
Nahum	29	Hezekiah........	726	—			
			—	724	Shalmanezer car- ried Israel cap- tive to Assyria in 724 B. C......		
Joel	55	Manasseh	698	—			
	2	Amon	643	—			
Jeremiah...	31	Josiah...........	641	—			
Habakkuk..	3 m.	Jehoahaz........	610	—			
Zephaniah..	11	Jehoiakim	610	—			
Ezekiel.....	3 m. 10 d.	Jehoiachin, or Je- coniah..........	599	—			
Daniel		Zedekiah	599	—			
Obadiah....	11	Jerusalem destroy- ed and Judah carried captive..	588	—			

CHRONOLOGICAL SCRIPTURE INDEX. 347

PERIOD VI.

THE DESTRUCTION OF JERUSALEM BY NEBUCHADNEZ-ZAR, TO THE BIRTH OF CHRIST, 588 YEARS.

B. C.	HISTORICAL EVENTS.	PROPHETS.
588	Destruction of Jerusalem, and captivity of the Jews.	Ezekiel.
538	Babylon taken by Cyrus........................	
536	Proclamation of Cyrus; Zerubbabel and Joshua.	
534	Foundation of the temple.	
529	Artaxerxes (Cambyses) forbids the work.	
520	Favorable decree of Ahasuerus (Darius Hystaspes.)..	Haggai.
518	Esther made queen............................	Zechariah.
515	The second temple finished.	
510	Haman's plot frustrated.	
484	Xerxes, king of Persia.	
464	Artaxerxes Longimanus.	
457	Ezra sent to govern Jerusalem.	
445	Nehemiah sent as governor.	
397	Malachi	Malachi.
335	Alexander the Great invades Persia, and establishes the Macedonian empire.	
323	Alexander dies.	
320	Ptolemæus Lagus surprises Jerusalem.	
277	Septuagint version made by order of Ptolemæus Philadelphus.	
170	Antiochus Epiphanes takes Jerusalem.	
167	His persecution.	
166	Judas Maccabæus governor.	
161	Jonathan governor.	
152	He becomes high-priest.	
143	Simon: treaty with the Romans and Lacedemonians.	
107	Judas (Aristobulus) high-priest and king.	
88	Anna the prophetess born.	
63	Jerusalem taken by Pompey, and Judea made a Roman province.	
40	Herod made king.	
28	Augustus Cæsar emperor of Rome.	
19	The poet Virgil dies.	
18	Herod begins to rebuild the temple.	
4	John the Baptist born.	
4	Christ born, 4 years before the era known as A. D.	

PERIOD VII.

THE BIRTH OF JESUS CHRIST TO THE CLOSE OF THE FIRST CENTURY.

A. D.		
	Nativity of Jesus Christ, 4 years before A. D. 1........	Luke ii. 1-16.
8	Jesus visits Jerusalem............................	" 41-52.
22	Pilate sent from Rome as governor of Judea.........	" iii. 1.
25	John Baptist begins his ministry...................	Matt. iii. 1.
26	Jesus baptized by John...........................	" iii. 1.
29	Jesus Christ crucified, and rose from the dead.......	" xxvii; xxviii.

PERIOD VII.—CONTINUED.

A.D.		
36	Conversion of Saul	Acts ix. 13, 9.
38	Conversion of the Gentiles	" x.
44	James beheaded	" xii. 1–19.
	Peter liberated from prison by an angel.	
62	Paul sent a prisoner to Rome	" xxvi. 28.
65	The commencement of the Jewish war.	
68	Paul suffers martyrdom at Rome under Nero.	
68	The Roman general raises the siege of Jerusalem.	
68	Death of Nero.	
70	Jerusalem taken by Titus.	
71	Jerusalem and the temple destroyed.	
95	John banished to the isle of Patmos.	
96	John, the last of the apostles, dies at the age of 100 years.	

CHRONOLOGICAL TABLES.

No. 1.

The years of the birth and decease of the patriarchs, the comparative length of their lives, and who of them were cotemporary. From Adam to Moses was 2500 years.

YEARS FROM THE CREATION.	100	200	300	400	500	600	700	800	900	1000	1100	1200	1300	1400	1500	1600	1700	1800	1900	2000	2100	2200	2300	2400	2500
Adam	1								930																
Seth	130									1042															
Enos		235									1140														
Cainan			325									1235													
Mahalaleel			395									1290													
Jared				460										1422											
Enoch						622			987																
Methuselah						687										1656									
Lamech								874		1056						1651									
Noah																1658				2006					
Shem															1558	1693				2006 2158					
Arphaxad																				2126 2187					
Salah																	1723			2026					
Eber																	1757		1996	2049					
Peleg																	1787								
Reu																		1819		2083					
Serug																		1849 1997		2008 2183					
Nahor																		1878		2108 2168					
Terah																					2183				
Abraham																					2255	2289			
Isaac																					2288		2315		
Jacob																							2371		
Levi																							2367	2421	
Kohath																								2433	2504
Amram																									2553
Moses																									
YEARS B. C.	4000	3900	3800	3700	3600	3500	3400	3300	3200	3100	3000	2900	2800	2700	2600	2500	2400	2300	2200	2100	2000	1900	1800	1700	1600 1500

Deluge A. M. 1656.

Deluge B. C. 2348.

No. 2.

THE STORY OF THE CREATION WAS CONVEYED TO MOSES THROUGH ONLY FIVE INDIVIDUALS.

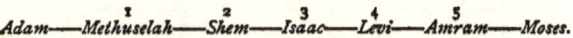

Adam——Methuselah——Shem——Isaac——Levi——Amram——Moses.

Methuselah was cotemporary with Adam 243 years.
Shem   "   "   " Methuselah 98 years.
Isaac   "   "   " Shem 50 years.
Levi   "   "   " Isaac 53 years.
Amram   "   "   " Levi 14 years and Moses 58 years.

No. 3

THE DESCENDANTS OF ADAM, SHEM AND ABRAHAM.

FROM ADAM TO SHEM NINE GENERATIONS.

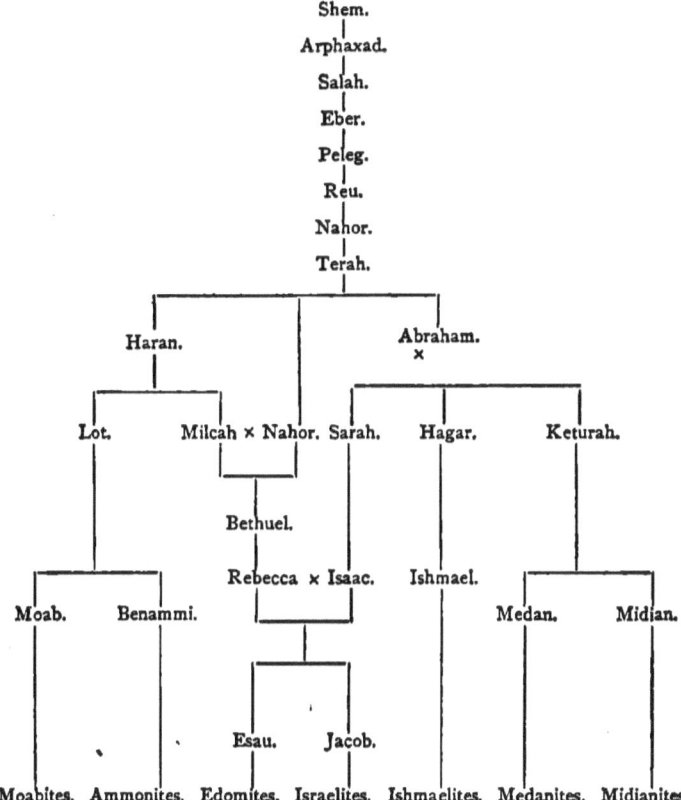

No. 4.

THE DESCENT OF DAVID AND SOLOMON FROM THE TRIBE OF JUDAH.

Judah.	Aminadab.	Obed.
Pharez.	Nahshon.	Jesse.
Hezron.	Salmon × Rahab.	David.
Ram.	Boaz × Ruth.	Solomon.

No. 5.

THE GENEALOGY OF CHRIST.

Adam.	Serug.	Nathan
Seth.	Nahor.	Mattaths
Enos.	Terah.	Menan.
Cainan.	Abraham.	Melea.
Mahalaleel.	Isaac.	Eliakim.
Jared.	Jacob.	Jonan.
Enoch.	Judah.	Joseph.
Methuselah.	Pharez.	Judah.
Lamech.	Hezron.	Simeon.
Noah.	Ram.	Levi.
Shem.	Aminadab.	Matthat.
Arphaxad.	Nahshon.	Jorim.
Cainan	Salmon.	Eliezer.
Salah.	Boaz.	Jose.
Eber.	Obed.	Er.
Peleg.	Jesse.	Elmodam
Reu.	David.	Cosam.

Addi.	Joseph.	Mattathias.
Melchi.	Semei.	Joseph.
Neri.	Mattathias.	Janna.
Salathiel.	Maath.	Melchi.
Zorobabel.	Nagge.	Levi.
Rhesa.	Esli.	Malthat.
Joanna.	Naum.	Heli.
Judah.	Amos.	Joseph.
		JESUS.

www.ingramcontent.com/pod-product-compliance
Lightning Source LLC
Chambersburg PA
CBHW030405230426
43664CB00007BB/764